Identity and Belonging

Identity and Belonging

Edited by Kate Huppatz, Mary Hawkins and Amie Matthews

 palgrave

First published 2016 by
PALGRAVE

Palgrave in the UK is an imprint of Macmillan Publishers Limited,
registered in England, company number 785998, of 4 Crinan Street,
London, N1 9XW.

Palgrave Macmillan in the US is a division of St Martin's Press LLC,
175 Fifth Avenue, New York, NY 10010.

Palgrave is a global imprint of the above companies and is represented
throughout the world.

Palgrave® and Macmillan® are registered trademarks in the United States,
the United Kingdom, Europe and other countries.

ISBN 978–1–137–33492–3 hardback
ISBN 978–1–137–33489–3 paperback

This book is printed on paper suitable for recycling and made from fully
managed and sustained forest sources. Logging, pulping and manufacturing
processes are expected to conform to the environmental regulations of the
country of origin.

A catalogue record for this book is available from the British Library.

A catalog record for this book is available from the Library of Congress.

Printed in China

Contents

Chapter 5: Sexuality   57
Scott McKinnon and Andrew Gorman-Murray

Chapter 6: Youth   71
Amie Matthews

Chapter 7: Households and neighbourhoods   86
Emma Power

Chapter 8: Nation   99
Tim Rowse

Chapter 9: Religion
Alphia Possamai-Inesedy

Chapter 10: Migration
Mary Hawkins

Chapter 11: Work
Kate Huppatz

Chapter 12: Leisure
Amie Matthews

List of contributors

Philippa Collin is a research fellow at the Institute for Culture and Society at the University of Western Sydney.

Joanne Finkelstein is an honorary professor in the Faculty of Education and Social Work at the University of Sydney.

Andrew Gorman-Murray is a senior lecturer at the Urban Research Centre in the School of Social Sciences and Psychology at the University of Western Sydney.

Mary Hawkins is an associate professor in the School of Social Sciences and Psychology at the University of Western Sydney.

Kate Huppatz is a senior lecturer in the School of Social Sciences and Psychology at the University of Western Sydney.

Tracey Jensen is a senior lecturer in the School of Law and Social Sciences at the University of East London.

Melissa Johnson Morgan is an associate professor in the School of Management and Enterprise at the University of Southern Queensland.

Amie Matthews is a lecturer in the School of Social Sciences and Psychology at the University of Western Sydney.

Scott McKinnon is a post-doctoral research fellow at the Urban Research Centre in the School of Social Sciences and Psychology at the University of Western Sydney.

Alphia Possamai-Inesedy is a senior lecturer in the School of Social Sciences and Psychology at the University of Western Sydney.

Emma Power is a senior lecturer in the School of Social Sciences and Psychology at the University of Western Sydney.

Tim Rowse is a professorial fellow in the School of Humanities and Communication Arts and the Institute for Culture and Society at the University of Western Sydney.

CHAPTER 1

Introduction

Mary Hawkins, Kate Huppatz and Amie Matthews

In one of Shakespeare's best-known plays, *Romeo and Juliet*, Juliet opines, 'What's in a name? that which we call a rose/By any other name would smell as sweet'. While this phrase is most often quoted in order to demonstrate the arbitrariness of names – a rose may be called 'dog' but its scent would still be alluring; Romeo may be named something other than Montague and he would still be attractive to Juliet – in sociological terms it is a problematic statement. Names may indeed be arbitrary, but they do matter. Around a name a person builds his or her sense of self, of attachment to others and of his or her place in the world. Names and titles – personal, professional and kin based – are the stuff on which we construct identity, and through which we experience belonging – belonging to family, place and cultural groups.

The primary concerns of this collection are to firstly explore the varied meanings and values that are attached to names, titles and other categories and markers of identity today. Secondly, the collection explores how such categories and markers shape, influence and/or mediate our experiences of belonging in everyday life. As demonstrated by many of the chapters in this volume, our understandings of identity and belonging have shifted over time, and they continue to shift and evolve in response to some of the rapid social changes that are being witnessed today under globalisation. That said, identity and belonging have been a preoccupation for theorists for longer than you may think.

Those social theorists that we associate with the founding of the social sciences in general, and sociology in particular – Comte, Saint Simon, Spencer, Durkheim, Weber and Marx – are not usually thought of as 'identity theorists', primarily because all these men, with perhaps the exception of Weber, focused on groups, institutions and social laws – in a word, structure. Saint Simon, for example, was concerned with social order and how it could be achieved and maintained. His student Comte developed an approach which he first called 'social physics', and only later 'sociology', and Spencer, defined by Marvin Harris as 'the most effective scientific spokesman of early industrial capitalism' (1983, p. 125), was somewhat obsessed with social evolution.

For Spencer, society was like an organism, and like all organisms it was in the process of evolving from the simple to the complex. The task of social science was to map out the stages of evolution, to find 'the law of organic process (which is) the law of all progress' (Bottomore and Nisbet, 1979, p. 63).

A focus on groups and laws, however, did not prevent Durkheim from theorising about identity and belonging (even if he did not refer to it in these terms). In *The Division of Labour in Society* (1984 [1893]) Durkheim documented the shift from an agrarian-based society, where the division of labour was founded on age and gender, to an industrial economy characterised by a more complex division of labour. In so doing, he explored the transformation of what he termed 'social solidarity'. According to Durkheim, agrarian societies have segmental structures; that is, they are made up of similar units, such as lineages or tribes. Each individual within the unit has only a limited number of roles they may play – for example, mother or brother, hunter or gatherer – and it is their common roles, practices, expectations and beliefs that bind them in mechanical, as Durkheim put it, solidarity. In such societies, belonging is also produced in a mechanical manner. By Durkheim's formulation though, as the economic base of the society diversifies, and the number of roles available expands, the uniformity of beliefs and moral ideas decreases, and mechanical solidarity is replaced by organic solidarity, informed by recognition of interdependence. In such circumstances, our sense of identity and belonging shifts from one based on the idea that 'all others are like me', to the notion that 'we are different but interdependent'. Our social solidarity, our sense of belonging, is founded then on generalised notions such as the value of work, our duty towards others and our social relationships (Hawkins, 2014, pp. 20–21) (for further discussion of Durkheim see Chapter 11).

Durkheim's notion of social solidarity is clearly also an outline of group identity and attachment or filiation to that identity – in a word, belonging. At much the same time as Durkheim was writing, Max Weber developed accounts of ethnic and racial identity (see Chapter 2), which were provoked by his fascination with the cultural diversity evident in North America. Social anthropologists of the early twentieth century – Boas, Mead, Benedict and Bateson – challenged the notion of racial 'identity' and offered interpretations of non-Western group identity and cohesion, based on group subjectivity. Studies of individual subjectivity, however, did not often stray outside of the field of psychology; sociologists and anthropologists remained focused on groups.

Several factors forced a change in this division of labour within the social sciences. Importantly, social movements of the late nineteenth and twentieth centuries, from the anti-slavery movement to women's rights, gay rights and indigenous rights, all called into question easy assumptions about identity and belonging. By the beginning of the twenty-first century only the most chauvinistic would assert that 'a woman's place is in the home' or 'homosexuality is a disease'. At the same time, the process of globalisation has brought increasing numbers of people into contact, virtual and face-to-face, with other peoples, who hold different values and live different lives.

Indeed, globalisation or 'glocalisation' (Robertson, 1995), referring to a process, or more rightly processes of simultaneous compression and expansion, by which the local and global are brought together, leads ultimately to increased interconnectedness between different individuals, societies and cultures. Spurred by developments in technology and increased mobility, as well as changes to socio-political organisations and various socio-cultural structures, globalisation also increases our awareness of *others* and their ways of life. These processes have made a significant contribution to the proliferation of choices or opportunities for decision-making in contemporary society. Though it is tempting to think of globalisation simply as the 'interpenetration of geographically distinct "civilizations"' (Robertson, 1995, p. 27) and thus a means by which remote cultures or less powerful nations come to be ruled by a dominant Western culture, globalisation is by no means a one-way or singularly homogenising process. Certain aspects of 'Western' popular culture (food, music, media and fashion) have spread throughout the globe. Take, for example, the inevitability of finding Coca-Cola, Starbucks or McDonalds in various parts of the world or the global reach of CNN, the BBC, 'pop' music and Hollywood films. However, these products are not consumed or given the same meanings everywhere (see for example, the discussion of the global reach of 'punk' in Chapter 6). They are frequently interpreted according to local cultural norms and positioned alongside local repertoires of food, music, media and fashion (which are also circulated, globally). Thus, Indian curry becomes a mainstay meal for many British people, fashion trends are influenced by traditional costumes and dress and Bollywood films and manga comics have cult following in the 'west'. While the political and power dimensions of globalisation should not be overlooked (the International Monetary Fund and World Bank for instance continue to wield significant influence over many developing countries), these examples from popular culture (and many of the examples that feature in this collection) demonstrate how globalisation contributes to the increased heterogeneity and pluralism witnessed in contemporary society.

As a result, in many of our social interactions today we are increasingly left with the sense that there is no singular authority to be obeyed or at least no singular claims-maker to agree with (Giddens, 1994). Subsequently, choice or at the very least, decision-making, becomes the norm. As Zygmunt Bauman (2000, p. 7) argues:

> These days patterns and configurations are no longer 'given', let alone 'self-evident'; there are just too many of them, clashing with one another and contradicting one another's commandments, so that each one has been stripped of a good deal of compelling, coercively constraining powers.

In such a context, diversity has become commonplace, and the questions 'who am I, and to what do I belong' may now have multiple answers. But whether those answers are *correct* or not is something that the individual is often left to decide (Bauman, 2000). Without binding authority figures and with an increased distrust, or at the very least, neutralising of expert knowledge (Giddens, 1994), it is the individual who must weigh her or his choices and the risks associated with them (Beck, 1992). This has significant repercussions for both identity and belonging; not only do they become choices, they become also *responsibilities*.

The question plaguing many today then is 'not so much how to obtain the identities of their choice ... but *which* identity to choose', that is, how to ensure the right choice is made and failing that 'how to keep alert and vigilant so that *another* choice can be made in case the previously chosen identity is withdrawn from the market or stripped of its seductive powers' (Bauman, 2001, p. 147, original emphasis). This same vigilance and concern with 'keeping one's options open' also infiltrates interpersonal relationships, which according to Bauman (2003, p. viii) become 'mixed blessings', providing a sense of connection and belonging on the one hand but also curtailing individual freedom on the other. Caught between a desire for the security of tradition and being fixed in place and the freedom but risks of fluidity, pluralism and decision-making, a number of social theorists have come to argue that for many people today (especially in Western societies) identity is a project: something to be worked at, built, fostered, dismantled and rebuilt again. Belonging, by extension, also becomes somewhat precarious and subject to a series of active positionings, navigations and compromises. Probyn (1996, p. 19), for example, argues that identity and belonging are always in transition: 'Individuals and groups are caught within wanting to belong, wanting to become, a process that is fuelled by yearning rather than positing of identity as a stable state'.

It should be pointed out though, lest choice be assumed to mean absolute freedom and disembeddedness, that none of this takes place in a vacuum. As already indicated, thanks to globalisation, individual and group identities are formed in contexts of diversity and plurality (so much so that some, like Bauman (1996, 2001) and Hall (1996), argue we should in fact speak of *identities* in plural, rather than *identity* in singular). Importantly, the choices individuals make with respect to who they want to be and where they see themselves as belonging are also enacted within, alongside and in response to various intersecting social structures (like social class, gender and ethnicity), which may curtail, limit or encourage certain options. Ultimately then, identity and belonging become negotiated projects in late modernity, and it is these negotiations and the hybridised results that follow, that the chapters in this collection address.

About this book

This book consists of fourteen chapters of student-orientated sociological engagement with the complexities of identity and belonging in a global society. As this is an edited collection, each chapter speaks with its own voice (indeed, some are written in the first person while others are not, some have more case studies and others less and some are more influenced than others by the authors' own geographic positioning). Together, the chapters present contrasting but also complementary accounts of identity and belonging. Chapters 2 to 14 focus on key modes or sites of local, global and/or transnational identity formation and group membership. The topics covered have been chosen to align with the authors' research strengths and so are not exhaustive; however, they are intended to give students a broad overview of identity and belonging as they are understood and experienced. For the most part, each chapter unpacks key sociological understandings of their mode or site of analysis, and in doing so, a number of chapters necessarily not only engage with contemporary theory but also identify the legacies of the classical theorists we described above. Each chapter discusses how experiences of identity and belonging may have changed in late modernity, how they have been impacted by processes of globalisation and how they intersect with other modes of identity and belonging.

The first part of the book is concerned with the most commonly identified 'modes' of identity making – ethnicity, social class, gender, sexuality and age (addressed here with a selective focus on the life stage of 'youth'). These markers of identity are perhaps the best recognised because they have been actively mobilised within identity politics and because they are most likely to structure, and be shaped by, the remaining nine sites of identity making and belonging discussed within this book. Although we do not wish to create a hierarchy of identities, the first five modes occupy a central space in our personal and public lives; they inform our practices, relationships, world views and life chances. They denote ways in which identity and belonging are constructed, performed and enacted. Moreover, as will be shown within the chapters, these are the modes of identity and belonging that have been and continue to be essentialised in academic literature and public discourse. For some time all of these modes of identity and belonging were (and often still are) considered biological rather than social, which has made their cultural dimensions a concern for sociological analysis and debate.

In contrast, the patterns of identity and belonging that are unpacked in the second half of the book might be better described as 'sites' as they are more readily associated with physical and social spaces of identity making and belonging. That said, this division between sites and modes is certainly not infallible and there is considerable overlap between them (for instance, as discussed in Chapters 3–5 and 8 spaces like the home, the workplace, the neighbourhood and even the nation can be classed, gendered and, in some cases, sexualised). As such, we have not formally divided the book in this way, choosing to instead take an approach that is grounded in the idea that identity and belonging are increasingly fluid, intersectional and permeable categories in contemporary society. With this in mind, the summary presented below is provided so that you may choose to read the chapters that focus on the modes or sites that fit best with your studies and interests.

The book begins with Chapter 2 – Hawkins's discussion of ethnicity. This chapter charts the development of once popular but harmful conceptualisations of race and, in doing so, provides a rationale for the sociological turn to 'ethnicity' to understand difference. Hawkins shows how ethnic identity is blurry, multiple but also highly regulated. Although 'ethnicity' opens up sociological analysis so that we can account for culture, essentialism still dominates in everyday understandings of ethnic belonging. What is more, Hawkins describes how essentialism serves political purpose; globalisation has brought with it a greater mix of peoples but Hawkins shows how states continue to use ethnic boundaries to manage diversity.

In Chapter 3 Jensen makes use of British case studies to examine models of social class as they relate to identity and belonging and to refute the now commonplace conception that social class is irrelevant for contemporary experience. In this chapter, Jensen describes how class theory has moved from 'objective' understandings of class position to cultural understandings of identities and relationships. Here a connection can be made between Jensen's and Hawkins's chapters – cultural turns within the discipline have allowed for more dynamic accounts of both social class and ethnicity. Jenson shows how class analysis has been revitalised by Pierre Bourdieu's theory in particular and how, despite the popularity of arguments for its decline, social class has become even more relevant in an era of global economies.

As with Chapters 2 and 3, Chapter 4 is concerned with identity as it is constituted through social practice. Huppatz explains gender identity as historically and culturally variable and shows how globalisation has impacted local and global formations of gender as well as feminist politics. She also highlights the difficulties in conceptualising gender as identity – the male/female binary makes it difficult for many to 'belong' – and introduces the reader to several popular theories of gender power and practice that avoid essentialism.

Chapter 5 focuses on a topic that is closely related to gender – sexuality. As with the previous chapters, McKinnon and Gorman-Murray are careful to show how sexuality is culturally produced. They start by mapping the historical emergence of sexual identities and demonstrating how social space has been important for the construction of homosexual belonging. McKinnon and Gorman-Murray show not only how homosexuality has been mobilised as a political identity but also how the global homosexual community has been divided so that Western identities occupy a central position. Global processes have facilitated the imagining of a global queer community, but there is a tension between this imagining and the diversity of lived experiences across different parts of the world as well as an interplay between Western and local sexual identities.

Chapter 6 explores youth identities and documents different approaches that have emerged in the social sciences to examine young people and the cultural practices and performances that they engage in. Exploring age, transition and generation-based definitions of youth, like other chapters in this collection, it charts the shift from thinking about identities in biological or psychological terms to thinking about them as socio-historical and socio-cultural artefacts. In so doing, the chapter turns its attention to historic and contemporary understandings of youth cultures and explores the meanings that are given (by young people and academics) to their cultural performances, lifestyle choices and group interactions. Finally, pointing to the increased heterogeneity and fluidity within youth cultures, Matthews documents the ways in which young peoples' identities and experiences of belonging are becoming increasingly globalised and increasingly complex.

The remaining eight chapters deal with sites that are both 'old' (for example religion) and relatively 'new' phenomena (digital media) – all of which may be just as significant for our social lives as the modes discussed in the first five chapters. The eight chapters examine how these sites are facilitated and/or compromised as modes of identity making and belonging by processes of globalisation.

In Chapter 7 Power examines households and neighbourhoods as 'homes' that exist as both spaces and social practices. She describes how belonging is produced in homes through practices of homemaking and shows how the activities that we carry out within them play a part in making our identities. She also examines the darker side of local communities. While neighbourhoods may be 'homey' and sites of inclusion, their moral dimensions work as 'disciplinary forces', governing the behaviours of their inhabitants and the aesthetics of their houses, which can lead to exclusion. In addition, Power considers the impact of globalisation on neighbourhoods and argues that although anxieties about the effects of globalisation on local communities are common, these effects are sometimes positive and are by no means straightforward.

Chapter 8 moves the discussion from the local to the national. Rowse provides an historical account of the emergence of national identity with global modernity, highlighting the artificiality of nation-states but also their very real impacts on our daily experiences. He makes a distinction between the nation and the nation-state and, in doing so, shows how the cultivation of national identity is a, sometimes unsuccessful, political project of the nation-state. The chapter also highlights how nation-states do not need to be liberal-democratic, despite the efforts nations put into building national identities. Rather, they can foster exclusion if they are, for example, built upon ethnic distinctions. Nevertheless, civil and ethnic belonging can be produced by nations, even if ethnic belonging is sometimes achieved in conflict with global discourses.

In Chapter 9 Possamai-Inesedy examines classical and individualisation perspectives on identity in the sociology of religion. Taking issue with the secularisation thesis, she points to the fact that although some religions may be experiencing a decline in membership, in contemporary society there is equal evidence of other religious groups continuing to grow in popularity. Thus she suggests that religious revivalism and pluralism are evident in many countries today and that, influenced by a global economy where religion is viewed as a consumption choice, religious identity is more likely to be achieved than ascribed. In such contexts, Possamai-Inesedy suggests individuals may adopt syncretic religious identities as an alternative to disembeddedness and disenchantment or seek ontological security in the 'traditions' offered by religious fundamentalism.

Chapter 10 focuses on movement that has been associated with religious pilgrimage and persecution as well as other factors – migration. Hawkins begins by providing an historical account of migration. She describes choice, force, circular and labour migration types and how they have been impacted by de-colonisation, the creation of new polities and globalisation more generally. Hawkins then broadly summarises a range of theoretical perspectives on these movements, from neoclassical to migrant networks approaches. Since the 1990s, and now that migration studies have become a qualitative as well as a quantitative project, theories are 'transnational' in approach, which has allowed social scientists to consider how migrants produce transnational identities and belong to multiple cultures.

In Chapter 11 Huppatz examines what is considered to be a driving force of much migration – the labour market. She maps the impact of industrialisation, feminisation and globalisation on labour market experiences in the global north. As she describes these changes, Huppatz also introduces the reader to a range of classical and contemporary theories of work. Much of Huppatz's discussion focuses on the relationship between gender and work, so there are clear connections between this chapter and Chapter 4. Huppatz shows how gender norms and power relationships have shaped women's participation in both paid and unpaid labour and how globalisation further perpetuates gender inequalities in labour markets. Although global flows of wealth may have altered the work landscape and proliferated consumer society, Huppatz argues that work remains significant for identity and belonging.

In Chapter 12 Matthews highlights the relationship between leisure and work and shows how the line between the two is often blurred. For Matthews, leisure activities are not simply those that are taken up by an individual outside of work; rather, they are activities that are chosen freely. It follows then that leisure might be important for selfhood; it may aid in identity making and remaking and also resisting norms. Yet Matthews highlights that leisure is also experienced within social contexts and so geography, social class, ethnicity and gender may all play a part in structuring and constraining our leisure experiences. Furthermore, as leisure is implicated in evocations of belonging it can produce cohesion (via, for instance, family 'play') or exclusion (as in the case of some sporting practices).

In Chapter 13 Finkelstein and Johnson Morgan explore a mode of identity and belonging that is often taken up in, but not confined to, leisure time – consumption. Finkelstein and Johnson Morgan begin by historicising consumption practices and introducing early theorising on this topic. While consumption is often thought of as a by-product of industrialisation, Finkelstein and Johnson Morgan show that consumption practices and theory began much earlier than this. The authors examine how aesthetic styles of the past and present can demonstrate a willingness to conform and belong. At the same time the symbols on our T-shirts and even our bodies can be fashioned to express our subjectivity. Finkelstein and Johnson Morgan assert that globalisation is implicated in the availability of fashions and the forms they take. Increasingly, processes of globalisation give us the resources and the mobility to control our identities but the more we consume, the more our tastes become part of patterns that are informed by advertising, celebrity and global markets.

Chapter 14, the final chapter, examines what is also considered a site of consumption that is integral to globalisation – digital media. Demonstrating the overlap between many of the sites and modes of identity and belonging, digital media is also linked with leisure (and young peoples' leisure in particular), is often involved in workplace practices and can be approached as an industry. It is also frequently understood as providing space for experimentation, with for example gender and religion, and for the fostering of intra-group belonging and advocacy, as is the case, for instance, with respect to marginalised sexualities and ethnic groups. In this chapter Collin describes the growing significance of digital media for our identities. However, she does not take the position that technology dictates social change or that social change produces new technology; rather she views society and technology as sharing a dialectical relationship. This means that Collin sees identity and belonging but also digital media as social processes. Digital media opens up possibilities for connecting with others and expressing our identities because it enables both face-to-face (via video) and virtual co-presence and it also facilitates identity experimentation and 'bricolage'. However, at the same time, 'old' divisions are reproduced through digital media in that only the privileged tend to have access to this technology and even those who have access to it do not necessarily make use of this resource. Moreover, as our private online activities are actually public events that are monitored by an audience and collected as data, digital media reproduces power relationships by facilitating surveillance of the self as well as corporate surveillance of consumers.

The chapters in this collection are therefore diverse in focus. However they are also clearly connected in that they seek to make sense of the complexities of identity and belonging in late modernity. As described in this chapter summary, there are also many ways in which the chapters' sites of identity and belonging intersect. These intersections have informed their sequence; the chapters are organised in clusters of related topics that, as a whole, provide an overview of sociological understandings of modes of identity and belonging. They may be read as a collective but they may also be read independently, depending on student interests and the teaching focus.

CHAPTER 2

Ethnicity

Mary Hawkins

Introduction

In 1969, a newly formed British pop group, Blue Mink, released a single titled 'Melting Pot'. The song reached number three in the British charts, but a cover version released in the United States, also in 1969, failed to impress North American listeners. Perhaps the song's call for a global melting pot, in which all the races of the world would be stirred up, and then poured out as 'coffee coloured people by the score', was too unsettling for a nation where just one year previously the leader of the African-American Civil Rights Movement, Dr Martin Luther King, had been assassinated by a white man. The race riots which followed King's death certainly rendered the song's injunction to 'take a pinch of white man, wrap it up in black skin' disturbing, if not dangerous, at a time when the US melting pot was on the boil. Listening to 'Melting Pot' today, however, is a slightly embarrassing experience. Not because its vision of a melting pot 'big enough to take the world and all it's got' seems naïve but because the song calls for harmony and unity among all the world's peoples, while at the same time labelling these peoples as, for example, 'curly Latin kinkies', 'Red Indian boys' and 'yellow Chinkies'. To contemporary ears, Melting Pot is racist, even if it is set to a happy, infectious melody.

Can we then conclude that most people today are less racist than was the average person in 1969? Certainly, since the late 1960s, many nations have passed legislation that prohibits discrimination on the basis of race, gender, religion, age and sexual preference. For example, the United Kingdom introduced the Race Relations Act in 1968; in the same year, the United States amended the Civil Rights Act of 1964 to include a provision that made it illegal to intimidate or interfere with anyone by reason of their race, colour, religion or national origin and Australia passed a Racial Discrimination Act in 1975. Legislation, however, is not the only factor to consider. The process of globalisation has brought increasingly more people into contact with different – by colour, race and religion – peoples, both in a virtual sense, through television and new media, and in a literal sense, through migratory movements and cheap package holidays that take even the most insular of folk to foreign lands. At the same time, social scientists and historians have constructed trenchant critiques of race and racial prejudice.

By the late twentieth century, 'race' was understood, both in the university and among many in the general population, as an intellectually moribund and politically suspect concept, and had been replaced, in university courses and government legislation, by 'ethnicity', a concept which stresses group attachment and belonging based on shared culture rather than colour. This did not, however, signal the end of prejudice. Difference, and prejudice based on difference, continues. In this chapter, we will review the meaning of race, consider the emergence of ethnicity and the ways in which it imagines attachment and belonging and assess the strategies deployed by states in their management of ethnically diverse peoples.

The meaning of race

Human beings apprehend the world through their senses, but they communicate that apprehension to others, and build knowledge about the world, through language. Languages structure human perception by grouping that which is perceived into categories of 'like', within which individual terms may be contrasted to another, paired, term as 'unlike': such a pairing is called a binary opposition. Languages include hundreds of such binary oppositions or terms which gain meaning through their pairing with another, opposite term – thus 'order'/'chaos', 'male'/'female', 'good'/'evil', 'black'/'white'. As de Saussure, the Swiss linguist and semiotician whose work on language and meaning laid the foundation for the theoretical approach which we call structuralism, pointed out, the meaning of 'evil' can only be grasped if first one knows the meaning of 'good'. Further, the terms that comprise a binary opposition are related to each other hierarchically: hence 'good' is valued over 'evil', 'order' over 'chaos', even 'white' over 'black'. In this sense, the systemic classification integral to human language, thought and knowledge is at the same time a system which structures difference hierarchically and attaches symbolic meanings to these differences. In many instances, these 'are not simple frameworks of symbolic meaning but they also represent ideologies that are used to grant power to some and to subordinate others' (Rodriguez-Garcia, 2010, p. 256). Rodriguez-Garcia (2010, p. 256) uses this phrase in his review of the ways in which states manage cultural diversity, but it provides a useful starting point for thinking about race, which may be sociologically defined as an ideological system that grants power to some and subordinates others.

In his preface to *The Inequality of Human Races*, first published in France in 1853 and translated into English in 1856, de Gobineau wrote that 'the racial question overshadows all other problems of history ... for a very large number of human beings it has been, and always will be, impossible to take the first step towards civilisation' (1915 [1853], p. 27). For de Gobineau, the three races of the world – black, yellow and white – are natural groupings that may be identified by skin colour, physical type and hair texture, but natural attributes are less meaningful than the mental and moral characteristics he attributes to each type. The black race, for example, is described as:

> the lowest ... if his mental faculties are dull or even non-existent, he often has an intensity of desire, and so of will, which may be called terrible ... to these qualities may be added an instability and capriciousness of feeling ... (he makes) no distinction between good and evil. (1915 [1853], pp. 205–206)

The yellow race, on the other hand:

> is inclined to apathy ... he tends to mediocrity in everything ... he does not dream or theorise; he invents little, but can appreciate and take over what is useful to him. His whole desire is to live in the easiest and most comfortable way possible ... (he is) superior to the black. (1915 [1853], p. 206)

Finally, the white race:

> are gifted with ... an energetic intelligence. They have a feeling for utility, but ... (are) more courageous and ideal than the yellow races ... (they have) a remarkable love of liberty ... an extraordinary attachment to life ... their principle motive is honour. (1915 [1853], p. 207)

The white, according to de Gobineau, lacks the intensity of sensation characteristic of the black, but this is evidence of white superiority: the white are 'less tempted and less absorbed by considerations of the body, although in physical structure he is far the most vigorous' (1915 [1853], p. 207). De Gobineau's entire racial system can be summarised thus: 'black' means dull and terrible; 'yellow' is idle and apathetic and 'white' is simply glorious.

For a contemporary reader, de Gobineau's work is remarkably racist. Nineteenth-century popular and scholarly thinking, however, took racial division to be a phenomenon of nature and assumed an inequality between races. Charles Darwin's work on the evolution of species and the writing of social Darwinists, such as the widely read Herbert Spencer (Connell, 1997, p. 6), were harnessed as scientific evidence of racial inferiority and degradation; the savages were not simply dull and backward, they were also unfit, in evolutionary terms, and like dinosaurs, dodos and other unfit creatures, would eventually die out. Other influential social theorists of the time include Lewis Henry Morgan (1818–1881) and Edward Tylor (1832–1917), both of whom argued that cultures progressed through various stages and that the stages were associated with races. In a number of works published in the 1870s, and most significantly in *Ancient Society* (1976 [1877]), Morgan elaborated a schema of social development that presented human history as consisting of three periods: the Savage, the Barbaric and the Civilised. Savages – de Gobineau's 'black' – included hunter gatherers, such as the Australian Aborigines; Barbarians – 'yellow' – had mastered pottery and iron tool making and the dawn of civilisation – 'white' – was marked by the invention of a phonetic alphabet and writing (Fozdar et al., 2009, pp. 111–112).

What, then, was the role of the supposedly superior white race? According to some, it was to soothe the savage's dying pillow. As late as the 1930s Daisy Bates (1938), an Irish woman who camped on the fringes of the Nullarbor desert in Australia for some 40 years, published *The Passing of the Aborigines*, in which she assumed that Aborigines would die out and decried miscegenation, the 'mixing of blood', as at fault, because it produced nothing but degeneration (a sentiment with which de Gobineau, who abhorred inter-racial sexual unions, would have fully agreed). The most historically significant nineteenth-century white role, however, was to take on the 'white man's burden', as Rudyard Kipling put it in his eponymous poem, of civilising, through colonisation, the savages and the idle barbarians, those whom Kipling calls 'half devil and half child'. Indeed, European colonisation, from the fifteenth-century Spanish voyages to the Americas through to the British annexation, by the early twentieth century, of more than half the world, was consistently justified by recourse to an ideology of racial superiority and consequent racial responsibility. In this view colonisation was not synonymous with enslavement, land appropriation and exploitation; rather, it represented a noble and honourable endeavour on the part of the white race to bring the lower black and yellow races to civilisation (see Hawkins, 2014, pp. 44–50).

The refutation of 'race' and the emergence of 'ethnicity': the Boasian tradition

Not all social scientists of the late nineteenth and early twentieth centuries were happy with the racialisation of humanity. In the United States, Franz Boas – who was born in Germany, studied among Central Eskimo (Inuit) groups in Canada, continued his fieldwork among Native Indians of North America and was Professor of Anthropology at New York's Columbia University from 1899 to 1937 – directly confronted the question of differences between 'primitive man' and 'civilised man'. He challenged racial prejudice in a series of papers that eventuated in his 1911 book, *The Mind of Primitive Man*. In it he broke with the idea of grand scientific laws of cultural evolution, arguing that there was no such inevitable progression but rather that cultures had their own individual histories. He argued that 'race' and the typologies of de Gobineau, Tylor, Spencer and Morgan were constructed without evidence and in explanatory terms were useless:

> There is no fundamental difference in the ways of thinking of primitive and civilised man. A close connection between race and personality has never been established. The concept of racial type as commonly used even in scientific literature is misleading ... achievements of races do not warrant us to assume that one race is more highly gifted than another. (Boas, 1983 [1911])

Boas went so far as to argue that variation within a race was much greater than between races and that racial prejudice 'is the most formidable obstacle to a clear understanding' (1983 [1911], p. 245) of human difference.

Boas's students, who included Margaret Mead, Ruth Benedict and Ashley Montagu, continued to challenge race and racism. Hence Benedict, in *Race, Science and Politics* (1940), asserted that 'in order to understand race persecution, we do not need to investigate race; we need to investigate persecution' (1940, p. 146), and 'if civilised men expect to end prejudice – whether religious or racial – they will have to remedy major social abuses in no way connected with religion or race' (1940, p. 150). For Benedict, race belonged to biology and was in no way associated with culture.

Ashley Montagu took the argument one step further, claiming that the concept of race is itself racist and arguing for the substitution of 'ethnic group' for 'race'. In the 1950 UNESCO Statement on Race, of which Montagu was a principal author, he suggested that:

> National, religious, geographic, linguistic and cultural groups do not necessarily coincide with racial groups: and the cultural traits of such groups have no demonstrated genetic connection with racial traits. Because serious errors of this kind are habitually committed when the term 'race' is used in popular parlance, it would be better when speaking of human races to drop the term 'race' altogether and speak of *ethnic groups*. (UNESCO 1950 Statement on Race, *Man* 220, pp. 138–139)

This wording proved so contentious that it was dropped from the revised 1952 UNESCO Statement on Race. By 1952, however, there was an emerging literature that sought to establish ethnic group, rather than race, as a primary object of study for social scientists interested in group and individual identity, affiliation and belonging. This literature argued that race was a category imposed on individuals and groups and could not be said to constitute an identity or provide a focus for belonging. The earliest contributor was Max Weber.

'Ethnicity' and the contribution of Max Weber

From the mid-nineteenth century onwards, commencing with London's Great Exhibition of the Works of Industry of all Nations in 1851, European, American and Asian cities hosted, variously, World Fairs, World Exhibitions and World Expositions, devoted to showcasing industry, commemorating historical events and celebrating 'progress'. These were, and continue to be, truly international events. In 1904, Max Weber attended the Congress of Arts and Sciences of the Universal Exposition in St Louis, Missouri, and was struck by the diversity of American society, by the sight, as he put it, of 'the Greek shining the Yankee's shoes, the German acting as his waiter, the Irishman managing his politics, and the Italian digging his dirty ditches' (Stone, 1995, p. 392). Weber here echoes David, the Russian Jew in Israel Zangwill's 1901 play, *The Melting Pot*, who views the sun setting over New York and declaims:

> There she lies, the great Melting Pot – listen! Can't you hear the roaring and the bubbling? There gapes her mouth – the harbour where a thousand mammoth feeders come from the ends of the world to pour in their human freight. Ah, what a stirring and a seething! Celt and Latin, Slav and Teuton, Greek and Syrian, – black and yellow – , what is the glory of Rome and Jerusalem where all nations and races come to worship and look back, compared with the glory of America, where all races and nations come to labour and look forward!

David's speech evokes a sense of comradery and equality among America's diverse people, but for Weber it was the differing status of African-Americans, and Native Americans, that was fascinating. In particular, he was provoked to ask why it was that African-Americans were treated with such contempt, and why even the smallest trace of observable African ancestry would relegate an individual to a subordinate status, whereas significant Indian 'blood' did not. He found his answer in slavery and the strength that African-Americans had demonstrated by surviving the traumas, physical and psychological, of slavery. This strength was associated with manual labour, but such labour was held in almost feudal contempt by southern White society (Stone, 1995, p. 393), as were the labourers themselves.

Weber did not entirely abandon the notion of race, but he rejected any equivalence between nature, culture and social status and in the years following his St Louis visit developed a definition of ethnic identity and belonging that remains central to contemporary studies of ethnicity. Hence for Weber, ethnic groups are:

> human groups (other than kinship groups) which cherish a belief in their common origins of such a kind that it provides a basis for the creation of a community. This belief may be based on similarities of external custom or practice or both, or on memories of colonisation or migration. The question of whether they are to be called an 'ethnic' group is independent of the question whether they are objectively of common stock ... the sense of a common ethnic identity is not itself a community, but only something which makes it easier to form one. It facilitates the formation of widely varying kinds of community, but chiefly, judging by the empirical evidence, of political communities. Conversely, it is often the political community, even when formed in a highly artificial way, which gives rise to beliefs in ethnic identity which survive even its downfall, unless there are such obstacles as extreme differences in custom and practice or, most important of all, in language ... the belief in ethnic identity ... sets limits to a community. (Runciman, 1978, pp. 364–365)

Belief, memory, community, limits or boundaries and politics are the key terms in Weber's definition, and they remain key concepts in ethnic studies. Much of the sociology of ethnicity since Weber is devoted to an exploration of one or more of these concepts, from, for example, Roland Barth's work on ethnic boundaries (1969) and Glazer and Moynihan's account of the persistence of ethnic attachment in the United States (1963) and its political deployment (1975); to the many analyses of ethnic belonging and nationalism (see Gellner, 1983; Hobsbawm, 1983; Eriksen, 1993; Rowse, this volume), ethnic cultures (Hall, 1997) and ethnic identity within multicultural states (Collins et al., 2000; Hage, 2000, 2003). Each account poses similar questions about how ethnic attachment is formed, performed, persists and changes over time, but the explanation each provides may be characterised as tending either towards that which Grillo (2003) has called cultural essentialism or towards an interpretation based on the positioning of ethnic groups as interest groups. Thus the essentialist approach imagines ethnicity as primordial, 'in the blood', and is in this sense not dissimilar to essentialist approaches to race, while the interest-based or instrumental approach explores ethnicity as akin to a resource, to be deployed in order to further the political and other interests of individuals and groups.

Modes of ethnic identity and belonging: primordial and instrumental approaches

Stuart Hall has written of the manner in which race functions to constitute a system of equivalencies between nature and culture (1997). Or, more simply, if you know where a person fits in the classification of races, you can from that infer what they think, how they feel, whether they can run fast, whether they are intelligent and so on. Hall is referring here to racial prejudice, but his point about nature and culture is a significant one and is central to an understanding of primordial approaches to ethnic belonging. Primordial accounts, which draw their inspiration from Shils's (1957) work on sacred, civil, personal and primordial social ties, position ethnic belonging as pre-social and pre-cultural – as natural. For the American anthropologist Clifford Geertz, primordial attachment was the most significant problem facing the 'new states' or those formed following the Second World War and usually after the departure of a colonial power. These new states – India, Indonesia and Burma – were peopled by diverse ethnic groups, each of which, at least, according to Geertz, was bound up in their own community and own communal identity, wherein there was no place for an overarching state. Group attachment was primordial, meaning:

> one that stems from the 'givens' – or more precisely, as culture is inevitably involved in such matters – the assumed 'givens' – of social existence: immediate contiguity and kin connections mainly, but beyond them the giveness that stems from being born into a particular religious community, speaking a particular language, or even a dialect of the language, and following particular social practices. These congruities of blood, speech, custom and so on, are seen to have an ineffable, and at times overpowering, coerciveness in and of themselves. One is bound to one's kinsman, one's seignior, one's fellow believer, *ipso facto*; as the result not merely of personal affection, practical necessity, common interest or incurred obligation, but at least in great part by virtue of some unaccountable absolute import attributed to the very tie itself. The general strength of such primordial bonds, and the types of them that are important, differ from person to person, from society to society, and from time to time. But for virtually every person, in every society, at almost all times, some attachments seem to flow more from a sense of natural – some would say spiritual – affinity than from social interaction. (Geertz, 1963b, p. 108)

The notion of primordial ties has been the subject of intense, most often critical, debate within social science (see for a review Grosby, 1994), and there are certainly competing analyses of ethnicity in new states, as this chapter's case study on Indonesia demonstrates. However, it is worth noting that in everyday social interaction, on radio talkback, in social media and on current affairs television programmes, there is frequent recourse to primordial assumptions. The radio commentator who opines in relation to an immigrant group that 'they just don't fit into this country, those people just can't understand democracy', or, 'of course she plays the piano well, she's Korean, isn't she', is invoking a primordial discourse. In an example of 'hyperprimordialism', two different ethnic groups in Mongolia, when asked if a baby boy, who was adopted by the other group at birth, raised by them, spoke only their language and thought of himself as one of them, was actually of their ethnic group or of his birth ethnicity, both groups replied, 'of his birth' (Gil-White, 1999, p. 795). From a primordial point of view, 'blood', or nature, always trumps nurture.

Instrumental or interest-based approaches to ethnic identity do not refute primordial accounts as such but rather seek to demonstrate the manner in which ethnicity is deployed within society. Deriving from Barth's (1969) work on ethnic boundaries, and Glazer and Moynihan's (1963) on ethnic identity in the United States, this approach emphasises the plasticity and fluidity of ethnic group boundaries and identity. As Glazer and Moynihan argued, if it is better in California to be a Mexican than an Indian, then some Indians will style themselves as Mexican, while 'German Jews rose to Congress from districts dominated by East European Jews' (1963, p. 17). In a very different social and historical context, James Scott has argued that the many different ethnic groups of upland southeast Asia – Karen, Hmong, Shan, to name but a few – whose lives, cultures and kinship networks traverse the borders of Thailand, Burma and Laos, possess an entire repertoire of possible ethnic performances (2009, p. 254). In the marketplaces dominated by ethnic Thai, they become Thai; when attending a ceremony, they are Shan; in their fields, they may be something else entirely. Scott cautions against viewing this as some form of ethnic conversion, arguing that multiple ethnic identification is the lived reality of these peoples, and the desire to group them under one name, and assign them one identity, is not the desire of these peoples but of the states that sought to incorporate them: 'a named people and their supposed location (were created) for purposes of bureaucratic order, where an otherwise indistinguishable mass of settlements and peoples without structure had often prevailed' (2009, p. 257).

Blurred ethnic boundaries may well be the lived reality of many of the world's peoples, but, in many multi-ethnic states, ethnic boundaries are strongly maintained, and the 'cultural stuff', as Barth put it (1969, p. 12), that is enclosed within those boundaries is regulated and controlled, precisely because 'culture' is the accepted marker of ethnic distinction and supposedly provides the basis for ethnic belonging. In such states a peaceful co-existence of diverse ethnic groups is often perceived as problematic, because – and this is where primordialism often insinuates itself – ethnic difference is taken to imply innate differences in social values and mores, in culture. Here culture is taking on something of the meaning of 'blood', or what de Gobineau termed 'race'. One solution to the fear of ethnic conflict is to celebrate diversity but to develop government policies that contain its expression within legislation. Another approach is to empty ethnic identity of its cultural stuff, to reduce ethnic culture to a representative song, dance and costume and to create a state culture into which is poured, in varying quantities, elements of all ethnic cultures of the state. Australia provides a good example of the policy-driven, containment approach to the management of ethnic diversity, while Indonesia has excelled in assembling, in a relatively short period of time, a state identity, Indonesian, that is comprised of cultural bits and pieces drawn from the many ethnic groups that populate the archipelago. It is to the Australian and Indonesian approaches to ethnic diversity that we now turn.

Case study 1: Indonesia: the domestication of ethnic diversity

Indonesia's national motto is *Bhinneka Tunggal Ika*, a Sanskrit phrase that may be glossed as 'Unity in Diversity', and its Coat of Arms depicts a *Garuda*, the large mythical bird which carried Vishnu, the Hindu God, and now lends its name to the national airline carrier, Garuda International. *Pancasila*, the title given to the nation's five foundational principles of government and social organisation, is also drawn from Sanskrit, the liturgical language of Hinduism. Hinduism is practised in Indonesia, and the great historical states of the Indonesian archipelago – Sumatran Srivijaya in the seventh to eleventh centuries and Javanese Majapahit in the fourteenth to early sixteenth centuries – were Hindu or Hindu-Buddhist, but from the mid-sixteenth century onwards Indonesia's ethnic groups gradually converted to Islam. Today, of Indonesia's population of nearly 250 million people, some 95 per cent are Moslem, and Hinduism is practised only by 4.2 million Balinese and 600,000 Tengger, a small ethnic group of east Java. Indonesia is home to around 300 ethnic groups, but none of them do, or likely ever did, speak Sanskrit. So why, then, express Indonesian statehood through a language that no Indonesian speaks and via a religion that relatively few Indonesians practise? The answer goes to the heart of Indonesia's management of ethnic diversity. Simply, Sanskrit, and Hindu mythology, was chosen precisely because it was empty of everyday cultural meaning for almost all Indonesians. Belonging to no one group meant that it could belong to everyone.

While early Indonesian nationalist groups were formed on the basis of shared religion (*Sarikat Islam*), or spoke for one ethnic group and not others (*Budi Utomo*), by the 1920s the primary fears held by Indonesian nationalists were that an independent Indonesia might be torn apart by inter-ethnic rivalry or that a state formation which gave prominence to the numerically dominant Javanese – nearly half the entire population of the archipelago – may alienate smaller but economically important ethnic groups, such as the Minangkabau Malay of Sumatra and the Minahasa and Bugis of Sulawesi. These fears were expressed openly at the 1928 Youth conference, attended by, among others, the Javanese-born Sukarno, who a year earlier had founded the National Party of Indonesia (*Partai Nasional Indonesia*) and would become Indonesia's first president, and Mohammed Hatta, the Minangkabau who also would lead a national party and would become the first vice president of the new republic. A topic for debate at the conference was the Indonesian national language or, more precisely, what language that should be. Javanese, spoken by half of all Indonesians, was an obvious contender, but it is a notoriously difficult language to learn, and it was felt to be simply too Javanese: Javanese as a national language might impose Javanese as a national culture. In the end, the conference chose Malay, which was spoken as a mother tongue by relatively few but had spread throughout the archipelago as a trading language and was thus spoken, albeit rather badly, by many (Fozdar et al., 2009, p. 51).

Indonesia achieved independence from Dutch colonial rule in 1947, and its new leadership embarked on a programme of state formation that was secular, and that envisioned an 'utterly new culture, purified of the old feudal traditions and liberated from its specific ethnic roots' (Schefold, 1998, p. 269). A modernist, and probably an egoist, but possessed of significant charisma, President Sukarno viewed ethnic diversity as a threat not only to his vision of a modern Indonesia but also to himself. In 1956 a frustrated Hatta resigned, and under the slogan 'Guided Democracy', and with the backing of the army, Sukarno drew more power to the Presidency. He also actively sought to create a national culture, but this culture appeared to many to be, like Sukarno himself, Javanese: in 1958 revolts in Minangkabau and Minahasa bordered on a civil war that was quelled only with the intervention of the army. By the early 1960s, a now desperate Sukarno, deserted by the army, attempted to retain power by combining nationalist, Islamic and communist forces and playing them off against each other (Schefold, 1998, p. 273), a strategy that would result in an attempted communist coup and the victory of the military leaders. Among these leaders was Suharto, the second president of Indonesia.

Suharto's approach to Indonesia's ethnic diversity was not to quell it, in the Sukarno manner, but to domesticate it. Regional ethnic cultures were not simply permitted to stage cultural events such as ethnic dances; they were all but required to do so. The national television broadcaster – until the early 1990s there was only one, run by the state – offered programmes such as *From Village to Village* (*Dari Desa ke Desa*) which showcased regional culture, defined as dress, dance, song and food. Government buildings in the provinces incorporated elements of local building styles, annual national competitions for the title of Indonesia's exemplary village were staged and in 1975 the president's wife opened a new theme park in Jakarta, Beautiful Indonesia in Miniature (*Taman Mini Indonesia*). This park contains an example of a house from every one of Indonesia's provinces, and each house's accompanying pavilion is used for dance and drama performances. No particular prominence is given to the houses of Java; a visitor ignorant of Indonesia's history and demography may well assume that Indonesia's ethnic groups are of similar population size. There is also a display of wedding costumes from throughout the archipelago, of musical instruments and of the tools of daily life. The message is clear. Indonesia is not riven by ethnic diversity; it *is* ethnic diversity, and its many ethnic groups are, as Schefold puts it, 'glittering prizes' (1998, p. 276). Emptied of troublesome cultural stuff – law, values, morals and religion – ethnicity has been domesticated in the service of the nation (for further discussion of the interrelationship between ethnicity and nation, see Chapter 8).

Case study 2: Australian multiculturalism

On 9 October 1996, a newly elected Queensland senator, Pauline Hanson, rose to give her maiden speech in Australia's Federal Parliament. Claiming that she spoke for 'ordinary Australians' like herself, a mother and a small businesswoman who had seen some 'hard knocks' in life, she proceeded to attack both Australia's Aboriginal and Torres Strait Islander policies and Australia's immigration and multicultural legislation. Both, she contended, were examples of reverse racism, and neither were supported by the majority of the Australian people:

> I and most Australians want our immigration policy radically reviewed and that of multiculturalism abolished. I believe we are in danger of being swamped by Asians. Between 1984 and 1995, 40 per cent of all migrants coming into this country were of Asian origin. They have their own culture and religion, form ghettos and do not assimilate. Of course, I will be called racist but, if I can invite whom I want into my home, then I should have the right to have a say in who comes into my country. A truly multicultural country can never be strong or united. The world is full of failed and tragic examples, ranging from Ireland to Bosnia to Africa and, closer to home, Papua New Guinea. America and Great Britain are currently paying the price.

Within hours, this speech had been excerpted in newspapers, quoted on radio and was the focus of intense debate on television current affairs programmes. Many Australians sided with Hanson, enough so that a year later she could found her own party, One Nation. Equally as many disagreed, and Hanson herself, who had run a fish and chip shop prior to her election to parliament, became the butt of countless jokes, of the 'what sort of fish can't you buy at Hanson's fish and chips shop? Blackfish, yellow fish and jewfish' variety. To be sure, there was a gender dimension to the anti-Hanson rhetoric, but the intense, often strident, debate provoked by Hanson's speech has not lessened appreciably over time. Australians may like to think of themselves as 'laidback', and 'relaxed', but as soon as migration and multiculturalism are mentioned, everyone has an opinion. In multiethnic Australia, ethnic and racial diversity is controversial.

Australia's population is currently about 23,600,000. Of these people, nearly 9 million live in either Sydney, the capital of the state of New South Wales, or Melbourne, the capital of the state of Victoria (http://www.abs.gov.au). One in four Australians is a first-generation immigrant, while 43 per cent are either first or second generation: in Sydney this figure is 61 per cent. Post-Second World War immigration policy was based on the Immigration Restriction Act of 1901, commonly known as the White Australia Policy, which favoured white British migrants over all others, but this policy was progressively dismantled until its abolition in 1973. In practice, immigration has drawn in people from throughout the world to Australia. Although the United Kingdom and New Zealand remain the two largest sources of migrants, in recent years the migrant intake from Asia, Africa and the Middle East has increased considerably (Collins, 2013, p. 134). At the same time, immigration policy has changed significantly, from a focus on permanent family and humanitarian migrant resettlement to an increasing prioritisation of skilled and highly qualified permanent and temporary immigrants. In the process, and despite the antagonism of Hanson supporters and the conservative Coalition Howard government (1996–2007), Australia's policy of managing ethnic diversity through multiculturalism has survived, and Australia rates either first or second (behind Canada) on the global scale of successful integration of migrants (Kymlicka, 2012; Collins, 2013).

In a 1973 speech entitled 'A Multi-Cultural Society for the Future', the minister for immigration under the Whitlam Labor Government, Al Grassby, introduced the term 'multiculturalism' and laid out the basis for a new immigration policy, but it was the subsequent conservative government, led by Malcolm Fraser, that translated the concept into legislation. Fraser was keen to reject the key premises of Australia's previous assimilationist policies: that immigrants should leave their culture behind and that there was no need to establish migrant services or institutions, as these would only be a hindrance to migrant assimilation. In 1977 he appointed an Australian Ethnic Affairs Council, which in the same year provided a submission to the Australian Population and Immigration Council, entitled 'Australia as a Multicultural Society'. This report read, in part:

> In our view, an acceptance of the multicultural nature of Australian society implies that government and established institutions acknowledge the validity of ethnic cultures and respond in terms of ethnic beliefs,

values and customs… What we believe Australia should be working towards is not a oneness, but a unity, not a similarity, but a composite, not a melting pot but a voluntary bond of dissimilar people sharing a common political and institutional structure. (http://www.aph.gov.au)

In 1978, the Galbally Report, presented by Malcom Fraser to the Australian Parliament, set out the requirements for the legislative enactment of multi-culturalism: all members of society should have equal opportunity to realise their full potential; every person should be able to maintain his or her own culture without prejudice or disadvantage; the needs of migrants should in general be met by programmes and services available to the whole community, but special services and programmes should be established to ensure equality of access and provision and services and programmes should be designed and operated in full consultation with clients (http://www.aph.gov.au).

Successive governments would be more or less enthusiastic in their support of multiculturalism, but multiculturalism has become firmly entrenched in Australian culture, not least perhaps because it well accords with how Australians like to view themselves, as open and egalitarian. However, this does not mean that racism has disappeared. Hanson's One Nation party has been re-established, and recent surveys have reported high levels of opposition and intolerance towards migrants (Markus, 2014). For example, Kevin Dunn's Challenging Racism Project, based at the University of Western Sydney (http://www.uws.edu.au/ssap/ssap/research/challenging_racism), has found high levels of racism directed towards, in particular, Muslim Australians, and national surveys in high immigration concentration suburbs of Australia's major cities have found lower levels of trust and community participation and higher levels of negativity than is evident in areas of low ethnic diversity (Markus, 2014). There is also evidence of ethnic discrimination in the Australian labour market – job applicants with distinctly different names but similar resumes to other applicants are less likely to be called to interview than are applicants with more 'Australian' names (Collins, 2013, p. 141). Moreover, rates of employment for more recent immigrant ethnic groups are far higher than the national average, and humanitarian entrants are the most disadvantaged: at the 2006 census the unemployment rate for those from Somalia was 30.7 per cent and from the Sudan 28.2 per cent, at a time when national unemployment was below 6 per cent (Collins, 2013, p. 141).

We might conclude from this that everyday Australian multiculturalism is practised within a society where ethnic difference continues to matter and where assimilation remains an ideal. Migrants may bring their food and festivals to the assimilation table, for the enrichment of all cosmopolitan Australians (Hawkins, 2014, p. 111), but troublesome cultural stuff, such as the wearing of a burqa, should be left at the borders. The definition of 'Australian' has certainly changed since the repeal of the White Australia

Policy but not yet to the point where an Australian-born person of, for example, African or Asian descent is unlikely to be asked, even if in the friendliest of tones, 'And where are you from?' To this question 'Melbourne' is not an acceptable answer.

Conclusion

In this chapter we have reviewed the meaning of race and demonstrated the manner in which it was used to differentiate between human groups and to justify the domination of one group over another. The concept of ethnicity opened new avenues of sociological exploration and furthered our understanding of the political and strategic deployment of ethnic identity and belonging. But, and despite the careful management of difference within multi-ethnic states such as Australia and Indonesia, race and ethnic difference matters a lot. Certainly the attribution of mental and moral characteristics to a cultural or colour group belongs to a discredited science, but essentialist thinking, or more simply, racism, remains an everyday occurrence.

Questions for students

- Read Pauline Hanson's maiden speech (http://australianpolitics .com/1996/09/10/pauline-hanson-maiden-speech.html). What sort of evidence would you require in order to evaluate her claims?
- List the essential characteristics of the US 'melting pot' approach to ethnic diversity (see Glazer and Moynihan, 1963, 1975) and contrast it to Australian multiculturalism. Which in your opinion provides the greatest life opportunities, social, cultural and economic, for immigrant groups?
- Have you ever experienced or witnessed an act of racial prejudice, such as name calling? What caused it, and how did you feel when it happened? Did you do anything about it?
- Is your state multi-ethnic, and if so, how is that ethnic diversity managed? How successful is that management (refer to Collins, 2013)?

Recommended reading

Connell, R.W. (1997) 'Why is Classical Theory Classical?', *American Journal of Sociology*, 102(6): 1511.

Hage, G. (2000) *White Nation: Fantasies of White Supremacy in a Multicultural Society* (Sydney: Pluto Press).

Hall, S. (2000) 'Old and New Identities, Old and New Ethnicities', in Back, L. and Solomos, J. (eds.) *Theories of Race and Racism: A Reader* (London: Routledge), pp. 144–153.

CHAPTER 3

Social class

Tracey Jensen

Introduction

This chapter examines different models for understanding social class as a key facet of identity and belonging. In the eighteenth and nineteenth centuries the 'lower classes' were discussed and categorised largely through moral (and moralising) languages of hygiene, dirt and contamination. By the turn of the twentieth century, social reformers had started to use social classifications to campaign around political issues such as health inequalities, social mobility, education and wealth distribution. Now, well into the twenty-first century the future of class theorising seems to be again at a crossroads. What is social class? How much does it matter? And how does it connect with our sense of ourselves? This chapter examines how social class is experienced in the everyday, how people identify as belonging or 'being' of a particular class fraction, how classed identities are produced through work, locality and education and how we signal our classed identities through taste, consumption and aspirations. Although many social theorists have recently proclaimed that 'class is dead' and many politicians argue that 'we are all middle-class now', this chapter will show how social class is very much alive and remains a key site of social identity and belonging. Drawing on the recent renaissance of research on the issue of social class in the United Kingdom and through a range of case studies, this chapter will ask readers to reflect upon the denials and renewals of social class as a category of identity.

Sociology and social class

The discipline of sociology emerged largely through a concern with the changes brought about by modernity and how this impacted upon the movement of people within society. Would industrialisation, urbanisation and modernisation mean that people would experience more or less social mobility? How did circumstances of birth connect with distribution of wealth and differences in life-chances? How might structured social advantages and disadvantages be measured and theorised? As a result of questions like these, a number of competing systems for defining social class were developed, with most relying upon categories of labour, occupation and employment to locate individuals within specific class categories.

Case study 1: mapping the social classes in nineteenth- century London

Charles Booth's (1889) *Life and Labour of the People in London* charts his expansive surveys into the living conditions of the urban poor. Booth himself saw his research as driven by scientific enquiry, rather than moral concerns, but we can see in his taxonomy clear moral undertones. The eight social classes he mapped out range from 'the lowest class, vicious and semi-criminal' to 'upper-middle and upper classes, wealthy' and his schema sought to complicate both the large antagonistic class theories of Marx (which divided society into labour/capital or proletariat/bourgeoisie) as well as classification systems which divided workers broadly into occupational sectors. Booth saw social class as hierarchically organised and encompassing not only economic or occupation position, but habit, attitude and orientation to the world. He was intensely curious about the poor in particular and they are much more finely scrutinised than the wealthier inhabitants in the notebooks of his researchers; as Ben Gidley remarks, 'for Booth and his associates, the poor were just more interesting' (1997, p. 14). The working class is thus fragmented into minute graduations of poverty and respectability across six of Booth's eight classes. This encounter between bourgeois social reformer and proletarian object of enquiry can be seen as a template for much subsequent sociological research on identity and community.

The process for officially classifying the 'social grades' in Britain began in 1851, and the Annual Report (or census) was first published in 1913 (Roberts, 2011). The 'social grades' (from 1990 renamed 'Social Class based on Occupation') further divided the conventional three classes (upper, middle and working class) into six socio-economic classes, united by occupation and employment status. In this schema, every citizen is allocated to either professional, managerial/technical, skilled (non-manual), skilled (manual), partly skilled or unskilled – on the understanding that within these classes, people have similar lifestyles, as well as social, cultural and leisure behaviour. Similar models – the work of John Goldthorpe, for example, which was particularly interested in social mobility (whether and how far people could change social class over the course of their lives), and the National Statistics Socio-Economic Classification or NS-SEC, which is a modified version of Goldthorpe's social class scheme – use overlapping and intersecting class categories that retain the centrality of occupation and labour. Across these taxonomies, class positions are seen to derive from social relations in economic life or, more specifically, from employment relations: it is the kind of *work* that people do that reveals what their social class is. From this we can understand not only how much they earn or how skilled they are, but also how secure their wage or salary is, how long they are likely to be unemployed in periods of crisis and how much mastery they have over their working week, their economic prospects and their relationship to credit and debt.

How useful are these classification schemes for understanding social class? What they all share is a desire to measure and objectively 'know' social class: to pin individuals to a category with confidence. These models approach social class as a set of groupings to which individuals belong to and from which their social identities emerge. Such an approach to social class was powerfully challenged with the revival of Marxism within the emerging discipline of cultural studies, adjacent to and often overlapping with sociology, elaborated and refined between the 1940s and 1970s in a time often romantically referred to as the 'golden years' of stratification research (Devine and Savage, 2005, p. 4). This revival endeavoured to reconfigure the concept of social class as more than an experience of particular incomes, occupations and employment statuses into a configuration of particular cultural and lifestyle experiences.

Cultural studies, spearheaded by Stuart Hall and the work of the Birmingham Centre for Contemporary Cultural Studies (CCCS) (also discussed in Chapter 6), took seriously the study of popular culture as a struggle for cultural power and as a site for the expression of messy class identities which are at once ideological, eruptive, reactive, deferent and irreverent (see Hall, 1998). The 'cultural turn' in class theory produced a lively body of research which often emphasised the resistance and expressiveness of particular cultures and subcultures, tied into the context of class consciousness and class imagery. Much of this work can perhaps be accused of romanticising working-class figures of resistance (an accusation often levelled at Hall and Jefferson, 1976; Hebdige, 1979; Willis, 1977), but at the same time it persuasively reinvigorated class theory with a sense of struggle. Social class in this body of work is relational and must be understood as a struggle *between* classes and as an antagonism situated within capitalism itself, whereby some groups are socially privileged in structured (though volatile) ways. Importantly, class labels and 'social grades' are themselves newly understood as capitalist instruments. The very idea of class consciousness (and by extension the act of class denial) is deeply political.

'We're all middle-class now': the decline of class theory

The decline of class theory began in the 1980s, curiously a period characterised by, if anything, *growing* socio-economic inequality (Savage, 2000). How could this be? The decline of class theory is complex – connected to the decline of heavy industry and de-industrialisation, the rise of service occupations and new class fractions and the growth and extension of consumer culture. Importantly, in the United Kingdom, working-class communities organised through locality and neighbourhood were undermined with the introduction of the 'right-to-buy' housing policy in 1980. This initially popular policy, which gave social housing tenants the option of purchasing their homes at a large discount, meant that socially housed renters could become private owners. It also led to painful fractures in social housing estates between the upwardly mobile homebuyers and those who remained tenants and decimated the supply of affordable housing available for rent. These changes led to a number of prominent sociologists claiming that 'post-industrial' society was on the way to becoming unfettered by old class loyalties and communities. For these sociologists, contemporary society was better characterised as one of risk and mobility (Beck, 1992) or individualisation and de-traditionalisation (Giddens, 1991). Several intertwined theoretical trends, such as postmodernism, emphasised self-making, choice and plasticity over ascriptive and static ties. Anthony Giddens's work in particular was central to new notions of selfhood which argued that the circumstances of birth and socio-economic position were of declining importance and that individuals were newly able to 'script' themselves by adopting freely chosen lifestyle choices. Stratification research, which was initially blind to those other facets of identity which intersect with social class, such as ethnicity and gender, was gradually eclipsed by research into these other markers of difference.

As 'new' categories of gender, race, sexuality and nationalism began to gather momentum as sources of identity, sites for political organisation and, of course, intellectual opportunities, social class was positioned as out-of-date, irrelevant, embarrassing and even shameful (Sayer, 2002). As Imogen Tyler (2013) documents, this backlash against class theory happened at precisely the moment when class theory was needed – when processes of global neoliberalism were beginning to open up great social divisions and to widen economic polarisation between rich and poor on an intensive and extensive scale. The decade of the 1990s saw British culture riding high on the global wave of 'Cool Britannia', and in this period of outward-facing possibility, the very idea of social class seemed a pedestrian concern. The backlash against class theory dismissed the rich scholarship developed in conjunction with class theory, feminist and post-colonial work and epitomised in the work of the Birmingham CCCS.

Steph Lawler (2005) argues that discourses of 'classlessness', far from abolishing class, are formed in the context of meritocratic principles, whereby class can be transcended through 'equality of opportunity'. Lawler argues that the promise of classlessness is therefore intimately bound up with class, as a promise to conquer the 'problem' of class. Once class is reconceived as a 'problem' with specific solutions, the material foundations of inequality recede and the 'lifestyle choices' of those bearing the burdens of this problem (the working-class) take centre stage. Chris Haylett (2003) argues that the existence of working-class conditions, such as hardship and exploitation, often becomes elided through policy discussions of 'cultures' which need to be transformed.

> [T]arget problems easily become targeted lives, little more than the adjuncts of rationalistic theory ... Working-class cultures are positioned at the apex of these troubles, as problematic, in need and usually 'in receipt' but not capable of giving or teaching anything of worth to dominant centres of value. (2003, p. 57)

Added to this theoretical embrace of 'classlessness', the 1980s and 1990s can also be seen as a time of huge shifts within political discourse in the United Kingdom (and elsewhere), from 'social class' to 'social inclusion'. British Prime Minister (1979–1990) Margaret Thatcher's famous declaration that 'there is no such thing as society' referred to the belief in classlessness and that the structures of stratification held literally no meaning in an age of entrepreneurial self-making. Thatcher's comment is as much a dismissal of the trade unions that attempted to fend off her programmes of de-industrialisation as it is an interpellation of the new ideal citizen, a subject who was above all an individual. Val Gillies (2005) points to the power of this emerging language of individualisation and discusses the ways in which it has reshaped the political landscape, with welfare policy reform substituting the redistribution of wealth with the redistribution of possibilities, and the branding of those who still speak of class loyalties and identities as 'losers'.

> Thus, poverty and privilege, once discussed in terms of wealth redistribution and attached to the concept of class, have been redefined by inclusion exclusion debates, which sideline issues of inequality and foreground individual life-choices and conduct. Lack of material resources is then represented as a symptom of exclusion rather than its cause. (Gillies, 2005, p. 19)

Social class, once understood as being formed through material conditions and economic insecurities, and through the uneven distribution of opportunities and privileges, was now understood as a matter of deficit culture, of problem choices and of the failure to make the right kind of life.

Class renaissance and the return to class

There has been something of a 'renaissance' in class theorising (Gillies, 2007, pp. 20–21), led largely by the revisiting of the work of Pierre Bourdieu by feminist sociologists (Skeggs, 1997, 2004; Reay, 1998; Lawler, 2000). The rise of sociological class theory was, as many theorists have pointed out, really the rise of theory emerging from the study of *working*-class communities. A particular classed body of society became subjected to measurement and categorisation through the use of surveys and statistics and the use of records within spaces of education and medicine in a process Lynette Finch (1993) has termed 'the classing gaze'. There are a number of consequences to this myopic classing gaze, in which middle-class sociologists peer at working-class objects for study. In a kind of parallel to classical anthropology, the 'peer' operates in one direction only, and the gaze cannot be returned or challenged. The fantasy and projection of middle-class gazers onto working-class objects becomes invisible (Skeggs, 2004) and the working class becomes a site for aberration, pathology and inadequacy. Similarly, some have claimed that the focus on structural classification as the mechanism through which class can be understood also leads to a certain myopia about value and morality, and the texture of social distinction itself. Andrew Sayer (2002) discusses the elevation of dispassionate objectification of class as endemic to the learning of 'sociological thinking' itself, pointing to how the unease and evasion of class by sociology students is undervalued:

> While experienced sociologists might put the novices' unease down to naivety about sociology, and feel superior about their ability to confront class dispassionately, I would suggest there is something to be said for inverting that valuation: while the beginning students have not yet unlearned their very justifiable sense (albeit a scarcely articulated sense) of the moral problems of class, sociologists have unlearned them and become de-sensitized to them. (2002, p. 22)

For Sayer, it is sociologists' 'blasé amoralism which is at fault' (2002, p. 1.6) and the reluctance to examine critically the moral and ethical aspects of class which has led to the decline in class theory, as well as the unexamined unease with which people continue to live classed identities whilst remaining uneasy about articulating class. The re-emergence of class theory has been given a fresh lease of life with Bourdieu's concepts, and his impact upon the renaissance of the theorisation of class cannot be underestimated. Bourdieu's interest in how people develop a practical mastery of the world, and how the acquisition and practice of these masteries reproduce inequalities, provides us with a template for understanding social class in much more dynamic and fluid ways than conventional stratification theory can. His conceptual trinity of *habitus*, *capital* and *field* reframes social class as a generative, contradictory and ambivalent set of differences that are neither static nor stable.

Bourdieu's key concepts: habitus

Throughout his work, Bourdieu uses the term *habitus* to refer to a generative scheme of dispositions; these dispositions include bodily practices, improvisations, movements and modes of speaking and walking, as well as orientations towards oneself, culture and the world, such as attitudes and ways of thinking and feeling about the future. Subjects acquire and develop their habitus through socialisation, principally within the home, and their habitus subsequently takes them out into the world beyond. Bourdieu refers to the habitus using many terms, sometimes referring to 'practical habituation', a 'second sense', a 'practical sense' or 'a feel for the game'. For Bourdieu, practical mastery is not simply conscious and theoretical, but nor is it unconscious and repressed; he uses the word *doxa* to refer to the taken-for-granted or experience beyond reflection. This doxic experience and the habitus that underpins it help take class theorising away from conscious reflection. This is particularly important when we remember the problems faced by stratification theorists who struggled to account for social class when it was not consciously spoken of by subjects.

In Bourdieu's terms, when subjects do not demonstrate class consciousness or do not explicitly identify their class location, this does not mean that they exist outside of social class. Indeed, what characterises habitus is the naturalness with which it is inhabited by subjects. It is not spoken because it does not *need* to be spoken; it exists at a pre-reflective, bodily level or, in Bourdieu's terms, 'the habitus makes coherence and necessity out of accident and contingency' (1977, p. 87). The concept of habitus enables us to theorise the natural, comfortable and taken-for-granted aspects of childhood-learned sets of dispositions. Habitus provides a framework for thinking about a socially classed self in terms of an embodied subjectivity that one acquires and which endures, though in a way which is complex, dynamic and symbolic, and not simply an emanation of occupation or wealth. Habitus reorients class theorisation within the world of everyday culture and of ways of living and being within the world, as well as the comfort or unease with which people inhabit the world.

Bourdieu's key concepts: capital

The background experiences and dispositions through which subjects navigate every day shape the ability with which they can play their resources. Bourdieu uses the term *capital* to identify different kinds of resources that may be played. Whilst he has been criticised for relying too heavily on the somewhat economic metaphor of 'capital' (Baert, 1998), Bourdieu's intentions in employing this term was to complicate visions of inequality which focus narrowly upon wealth and assets. Inequalities exist and are perpetuated across landscapes that are never simply economic or pecuniary. They are also deeply emotional: social class animates the interior life and feelings of hope, pride, shame, aspiration, fear and resentment (Biressi and Nunn, 2013). As such, Bourdieu's approach represents a serious challenge to advocates of wealth redistribution and dissociates social class from the stifling and limiting classifications of the occupational scales discussed in this chapter so far.

Bourdieu names four kinds of capital – economic, social, cultural and symbolic – and argues that it is through the inheritance and conversion of these capitals that bodies are able to move through social space and become subjects of value. Economic capital is straightforward enough as a concept, referring to income, wealth and financial assets. The error of conventional stratification theory is to *only* take account of economic capital, and whilst he agrees that the institutionalisation of the economic field tends to determine the remainder of social life, he also argues that if practitioners are to grasp the lived intricacies of social class, attention must be paid to the other three capitals in tandem. Social capital is for Bourdieu the value generated by 'who you know', associations, networks, relationships, connections, communities and groups. Cultural capital is a more complex capital, in that it includes legitimated cultural knowledge and discourses that become embodied as dispositions *as well as* cultural goods and objects. Cultural capital may also be informal (taste or style) or formal (qualifications). Cultural capital thus refers to both cultural competencies at the level of the habitus as well as the cultural goods and practices that the subject demonstrates his or her competency *with*.

Symbolic capital is for Bourdieu a kind of meta-capital, into which other capitals become convertible through legitimation. Symbolic capital is absolutely key to Bourdieu's work and we cannot understand his approach to social class without it. In order for a capital to be transferable into symbolic power, it must be legitimated within the value system, and here lies the rub for Bourdieu. Only certain kinds of capital are legitimated within the value system, and therefore some kinds of capital remain powerless within the wider cultural game. This is one of the ways in which Bourdieu's use of the term 'capital' is distinct from the ways in which it is employed by economists or by rational choice theorists; capitals are not universally exchangeable or equivalent in value; rather they are dependent upon the 'cultural arbitrary', which designates some activities, practices and cultural forms as valuable and others as not. For example, the value generated through physicality, aggression and machismo by working-class schoolboys was not legitimated by symbolic power within the institutional setting of the school (Willis, 1977).

The value generated through 'babydaddy' kin networks is not converted into symbolic power outside the local housing estate (Stack, 1974; McKenzie, 2013). Only particular capitals count.

Bourdieu's key concepts: field

Bourdieu develops the relationship between habitus and capital through reference to the third term in his trinity, that is, *field*. Field refers to the contexts in which capitals may be played. Bourdieu uses the term 'field' rather than 'institution' to draw attention to the nature of conflict, rather than consensus, of social life, and to draw attention to the fact that social worlds may be weakly institutionalised and possess un-established boundaries; in short, the term 'field' implies struggle, in a way that the term 'institution' cannot (Swartz, 1997). Within any number of fields of social space, there are particular rules that may be implicit, unknown or in flux. One's individual habitus, or embodied dispositions, enables or constrains one within the 'field' or external environment. The dynamic between habitus, capital and field results, for Bourdieu, in a range of strategies and possibilities that may be enacted; but importantly, he argues that these strategies are unequally realised, depending upon the specific capitals that the individual can mobilise.

Bourdieu thus invites us to think of social class as a cultural game (albeit one with very high stakes), in which it is possible to convert economic, social and cultural capital into symbolic capital, a kind of meta-capital which delineates power. Only certain forms of these capitals are convertible in this way, whilst others are ridiculed, denigrated or otherwise framed as 'wrong'. Whilst knowledge about, and consumption of, fine art, theatre and classical music are culturally legitimised as valuable, and therefore a capital worth accruing in terms of symbolic power, other cultural practices and the knowledges accrued from them, such as listening to pop music, watching television or playing bingo, are not. In this way, certain forms of capital – middle-class forms – become sanctioned as 'correct', and whilst individuals may accrue other forms, these capitals are not recognised or sanctioned and are therefore null and void in the wider game for symbolic power (see Chapter 13 for a discussion of class and consumption).

New class fractions? 'The underclass' and 'the precariat'

If it is true that the rapid social, economic, political and cultural changes of the end of the twentieth and beginning of the twenty-first century require a new class vocabulary, what terms might we generate for the contemporary class cartography? Assuming that many of these shifts are driven by neoliberalism, globalisation and the intensifying social inequalities between rich and poor, we might wish to reconceptualise the class vocabularies we use for the most privileged: the highly mobile, global elite who have been described as a new 'super-rich' class for whom nationality is of receding importance and who fraternise with one another in gated communities, private clubs and schools and decadent leisure sites that most people are excluded from. The study of economic elites is re-emerging as an urgent research field for sociologists.

However, the new class fractions which have been more readily fleshed out by social theory have tended to be those at the least privileged ends, experienced by the most economically vulnerable and insecure. Guy Standing (2011) proposes the term 'precariat' as a new class formation in the twenty-first century: a youthful reinvention of Marx's term 'proletariat', the worker who has nothing to sell but his own labour and who is readily exploited by the capitalist class. The precariat, like the proletariat, is a subject powerless to resist his own exploitation, but this exploitation has intensified as a result of the movements of global capital, where production (and thus work opportunities) can be transferred to the place with the cheapest labour available. This, combined with weakened labour movements and dwindling union membership, with the marketisation of education and with the dismantling of the welfare state, creates new conditions of insecurity for this class fraction, where work (if you can get it) is low-waged, temporary or fixed-term (rather than permanent) and without entitlements such as sick or maternity pay. For the precarious class, paid work does not offer social mobility or a sense of belonging but, at best, survival and alienation:

> The precariat lives with anxiety – chronic insecurity associated with not only teetering on the edge, knowing that one mistake or one piece of bad luck could tip the balance between dignity and [...] losing what they possess even while feeling cheated for not having more. (Standing, 2011, p. 20, cited in Biressi and Nunn, 2013, p. 68)

Other empirical research conducted by Tracy Shildrick and her colleagues in Teesside, a post-industrial area in the North East of England, has extended Standing's concept of the 'precariat' and documented the constant movement between low-pay and no-pay experienced by the most vulnerable workers who are struggling to make a living with insecure and inadequate work (Shildrick et al., 2012). Shildrick et al. compellingly argue that deindustrialised areas such as Teesside have remained underinvested with meaningful work opportunities and that once-working-class communities are now better conceptualised as precariat areas.

While the concept of precariat retains and develops a meaningful class analysis for contemporary times, more populist concepts of socially and economically marginalised class fragments approach these processes of social exclusion as something that is produced through the poor moral choices of those at the bottom. The concept of 'the underclass' has a remarkably long history (Welshman, 2006) but gained a great deal of currency in the 1980s when American policy analyst Charles Murray visited the United Kingdom and offered a highly problematic but politically popular account of those citizens who were stuck at the bottom of the class scale. In Murray's terms, what produced the disadvantages of the underclass was their moral failings: their idleness, their fecklessness and their abandonment of securing institutions such as the family (lone mothers were a particular preoccupation in his model).

Case study 2: the Great British Class Survey

Even through its periods of intellectual unfashionability, social class has always been a topic of particular salience in Britain. Classifying oneself and others holds it seems a great appeal, as can be seen in the huge interest generated by the Great British Class Survey conducted between 2011 and 2013 by academics in York and Manchester. The web survey, conducted in partnership with the British Broadcasting Corporation (BBC), yielded a massive dataset of 160,000 responses, from which a sample was extracted and explored in more detail. The questions covered economic, social and cultural dimensions of social class and the overlaps with Bourdieu's work can be seen. Mike Savage and Fiona Devine (two principle members of the research team) have stated their aims to revive classic sociological theorising of stratification, while moving beyond questions of occupation and to treat social classes not as 'employment aggregates' but rather as distinctive assemblages which crystallise across the three forms of capital.

Two key claims made by Savage et al. (2013) on the basis of the survey are that first, there are clear patterns of social polarisation between the social classes at the top and bottom, and second, the social classes themselves are fragmenting. They identify seven latent social classes: the elite, whose very high economic capital sets them apart from the rest of the population; the established middle class who have high levels of all three capitals and are culturally engaged; the technical middle class, a new, small class with high economic capital but less culturally engaged and with relatively few social contacts; the new affluent workers, a young and active group who have medium levels of economic capital but higher levels of cultural and social capital; the emergent service workers, another new young and mostly urban class with low economic capital but with high levels of 'emerging' cultural capital and high social capital; the traditional working class, an older group who score low on all forms of the three capitals and the precariat, the most deprived class of all with low levels of economic, cultural and social capital.

How useful is the Great British Class Survey for understanding how social class works in the twenty-first century? Substantive critiques have been voiced by many sociologists concerned with methodological and sampling issues, but perhaps more importantly in terms of issues of identity and belonging, with the ways that the publications so far from this study appear to have emptied social class of the dimensions of power, inequality and exploitation which have formed critical underpinnings of stratification research. The Great British Class Survey invites respondents to detail their economic, social and cultural capital, but the most important dimension of social class in Bourdieu's framework – symbolic capital – is entirely missing from the survey. How can we capture the processes through which some class positions are legitimated as 'tasteful', 'correct', 'aspirational' or 'respectable' while other classed lives are shamed or disciplined through their perceived moral failings? More than anything, the Great British Class Survey appears to empty social class of its deeply relational nature, whereby classes exist in anatonistic struggle with one another: the struggle for value and for power.

Class identification and class disidentification

The renaissance of class theory, which has revisited Bourdieu and this time with an eye on where class intersects with other categories of identity like gender, 'race' and sexuality, has been pioneered by a number of critical feminist sociologists, most notably Beverly Skeggs (1997, 2004) whose research has examined the ways in which social class is not only classificatory but also concerned with strategies of disidentification. In her longitudinal ethnography of white working-class women in the North of England, Skeggs demonstrates how they attempt to defend themselves against the pathologising and stigmatising external gazes and to produce positive value by class denial, evasion and narratives of escape. 'Class', far from providing the sanctity of belonging, evokes powerful emotions of 'doubt, insecurity and unease' (1997, p. 75)

Case study 3: Chav hate on campus

A significant classed caricature emerged in the first few years of the twenty-first century in the United Kingdom, which rapidly inherited the social and cultural baggage ascribed to the 'underclass'. The etymology of the word 'chav' is uncertain, though many theories circulate (see Jones, 2011) and the most popular see it as an acronym for 'Council Housed and Violent/Vile'. 'Chav' is a term which is used to describe young, white, working-class men and women as 'shiftless, tasteless, unintelligent, immoral or criminal' (Tyler and Bennett, 2010, p. 379) and which others have described as a form of 'social racism' (Burchill, cited by Tyler, 2008). Imogen Tyler (2008, 2013) documents the pleasures of hatred contained within the figure of the chav, particularly of the pregnant, uneducated 'chav girl', who is animated across cultural sites (reality TV, web forums, newspaper stories) as a target of mockery, contempt and disgust. The fictional fabrication of 'chav' bears little connection to the actual lives of those at the bottom of social classification; rather they become figures of consent used to justify increasingly punitive economic policies.

Tyler examines how the surge in 'chav hate' took particular hold in universities, with many student unions holding 'chav theme nights' where students could dress up as classed caricatures and play at 'slumming it', students made short films about 'chav zombies' infecting the (middle-class) student body and student web forums are soaked in classed hate and fantasies of violence. As Tyler argues, 'the chav is the polar opposite of the "self-scripting" mobile, flexible and individualised selves... as a neoliberal name for the poor in Britain, "chav" enables those who use, invoke or indeed perform this name to constitute themselves as "other than poor"' (2013, pp. 166–167).

Conclusion

Social class, as this chapter has explored, has had a long and turbulent history in sociology: being theorised variously as an objective description of one's occupational status and associated dimensions of lifestyle; as a marker of taste, consumption and aspiration; as a site of resistance and pride over which cultural and political struggles for power are fought; as a shameful subject that invokes deeply emotional and complex inner lives and as a marker of intellectual irrelevance. It has been a site of belonging, bringing people of similar experiences together under the labels of 'working class', 'middle class' and so on – but has also been a deeply contested site of disidentification, stigma and shame. The processes through which people become 'classified' require us to think about how value is created and bestowed upon subjects in different social, cultural and economic locations. Such processes are always intimately connected to power and as such are deeply political. The conditions of life, the formation of taste and lifestyle, whether one participates in 'legitimate' or 'valued' cultures or not, all show how social class can be not only an identity of belonging but also a site of disidentification. The renewed interest in social class may perhaps point to renewed class solidarities and belonging (and perhaps a new reconfiguration of class struggle), but we should also recognise that classed categories like the 'chav' and the underclass are deployed in ways that naturalise poverty and legitimise social and economic polarisation.

Questions for students

- Can sociological classifications of social class ever be 'transparent'? Is social class 'out there' in objective reality, waiting to be discovered, or is it made through social research and measurement processes?
- What examples can you think of where 'middle-class' values, experiences and tastes are constructed as 'natural', 'normal', 'valuable', 'respectable' and/or 'moral'?
- With the reinvention of class stigma ('the chav' and other terms), is social class becoming less a site of identification and more a site of disidentification?
- As the wealth gap between rich and poor increases, should sociologists concentrate their attention on the two extremes of the class spectrum?
- How does social class connect up with other dimensions of identity (gender, 'race'/ethnicity, nationalism, age, etc.)?

Recommended reading

Biressi, A. and Nunn, H. (2013) *Class and Contemporary British Culture* (London: Palgrave Macmillan).

Roberts, K. (2011) *Class in Contemporary Britain* (London: Palgrave Macmillan).

Skeggs, B. (2004) *Class, Self, Culture* (London: Routledge).

CHAPTER 4

Gender

Kate Huppatz

Introduction

Gender is present in many of our daily activities – in our clothing choices, our eating habits, our employment tasks and the domestic labour we carry out in the home. But gender is more than activities; we also use gender to differentiate ourselves from others and to know 'who we are' in the world. For those of us who, for the most part, 'fit' or appear to fit within the dominant gender order, gender gives some kind of ontological security, a sense that we 'belong'. The perceived importance of gender for personhood has led to the concept 'gender identity' becoming 'perhaps the commonest way of understanding the presence of gender in personal life' (Connell, 2002, p. 85). But what is gender identity exactly? How do we belong to a gender group? How is it that there can be multiple types of masculinity and multiple types of femininity? What happens when we do not belong, when gender identification fails to fall neatly into commonly held understandings? And how have gender practices, identifications and belonging been impacted by the rapid global changes we have experienced in recent times? This chapter attempts to address these questions by drawing on historical and cultural accounts of gender as well as influential theories of gender power and practice.

Identifying gender

The concept 'gender' gives reference to a number of complex and diverse 'arrangements' between men and women and it is also quite a 'slippery' term in that it can mean different things in different contexts (Bradley, 2013, p. 1). For example, we use the term 'gender' to talk about a culturally constituted identity, the organisation of large-scale labour market activities or familial obligations. Moreover, gender is often assumed to operate in a binary, but gender can take multiple forms and this means that the term does not only refer to men and women but also to transgender and intersex identities. Sex further confuses understandings in that sex and sexuality are intimately related to gender and are sometimes interchanged with gender in writing and public discourse (for example, the word 'sex' itself is often used to stand in for gender (Bradley, 2013, p. 1)).

What is more, gender is interpreted in a myriad of ways within social theory. Theorists vary in the extent to which they see the body as significant for gender; some see gender as primarily a political identification, while others are more concerned with how it is articulated in intersection with other social divisions or identities. For example, 1970s feminist theorists objected to the elision between sex and gender. Feminists at this time asserted that there is a sex/gender distinction whereby sex refers to our reproductive capacities and gender refers to our social identities, with the hope that distinguishing the biological from the social would open up space for social change (see for example Oakley, 1972). In contrast, post-structural feminists have questioned the sex/gender distinction. Gatens (1983) argues that this distinction is a social construct; she asserts that from birth male bodies are attributed power whereas female bodies are seen to 'lack'. This means that gender is inscribed upon our bodies and that the corporeal and social are intertwined; 'the imaginary body, the body the mind constructs, that is the metaphoric body, is linked to the differential social value placed on male and female values in our society' (Wearing, 1996, p. xi). Queer theory (discussed in more detail in Chapter 5) also interrogates this binary; the paradigm highlights the disconnect between the ideological construct and lived experience by focusing on the gender practices and identities that are considered non-normative (Valocchi, 2005, p. 753).

The ambiguities of gender as well as the injuries that categorisation can cause have led some theorists to question whether or not it is appropriate to speak of gender 'identity' at all (see for example, Connell, 2002). Within this chapter, gender is frequently referred to as 'identity'; however, unity and stability in identity is not assumed – this chapter examines gender as historical, cultural, multiple and political, produced in practice and via processes of globalisation.

Gender over time and across cultures

Historicising gender

Although gender may have a relationship with the body, the description above suggests that it is historically contingent; we only need to look back several decades to see that gender norms are changeable. For example, as will be discussed further in Chapter 11, at the time of industrialisation women were mostly confined to the home and their gender identities were very much associated with domestic life whereas men's identities were connected to the public realm. Expressions of gender outside of the male/female dichotomy at this point were generally prohibited. However, in the 1950s, as increasing numbers of women began to enter the workforce, perceptions of gender began to change. In her historical analysis of British working-class culture Brooke (2001, p. 775) finds that:

> more complicated and less certain gender identities emerged at the workplace and the home during this period. In this, femininity became less firmly tied to motherhood, while work gradually became accepted as a province of both men and women and masculinity was seen as reformed.

This shift was not always noticeable, however, as at the same time there existed a strong nostalgia for traditional gender norms such as the stereotype of the working-class mother (Brooke, 2001, p. 775).

Discontinuity in gender identities is therefore clearest when we look to the changes that occurred in the 1960s and 1970s. This was a time when extreme social upheaval took place, not only in terms of the politicisation of gender but also in how individuals perceived their own gender identities and practised gender relationships. During these decades even more women entered paid work in the public sphere and became economically independent. The availability of the contraceptive pill and changing views of sexuality also enabled women to exert more control over their intimate lives. Today, as a result of continued feminist activism as well as the queer movements' challenges to assumptions of homogeneity within gender and sexuality communities (see Chapter 5 for further discussion), we have a society which is much more open to gender equality as well as to uncertainty and difference. Nevertheless, deep inequalities remain. For example women are still more likely to experience poverty and domestic violence than men, and, as will be discussed in detail later in the chapter, processes of globalisation both democratise and reinforce traditional gender relations. Moreover, the harmful taxonomies of gender such as the male/female dualism still carry social weight and are evident in various violent social practices such as acts of homophobia.

Gender as culture

Variability in expressions of gender is also evident across cultures. For example, Native American cultures have long considered there to be more than two genders: 'the nadle or nadleeh among the Navajos, the Mohave hwame, and the Tewa kwedo, all of which designate a person who has both male and female spirits within' (Medicine, 1996). The term 'two spirit' (sometimes interchanged with 'Berdache'; however, Berdache is an Arabic term which has been imposed upon Native Americans by missionaries and colonialists and is sometimes considered offensive (Medicine, 1996)) was used, and continues to be used, as an identity marker for those who are part of these cultures and identify as having more than one gender or as third gender. Trexler (2002, p. 616) finds that Spanish soldiers observed two-spirit people to be a significant aspect of the social fabric of indigenous communities:

> Dressed as women, they tended to spend their time in the company of women's work teams, performing domestic labor, weaving, beading, or whatever pertained to women in that particular social world. Because they were taller and stronger than women, they seem at times to have led these women's associations and, for the same reasons of physical strength, they were regularly sought out by men to be their wives. Indeed there is some evidence here ... that boys who were especially pretty were raised as berdaches because that beauty attracted future 'husbands'.

However, strict norms of femininity and masculinity sometimes existed alongside acceptance of two-spirit people. For example, in Lakota society women were expected to follow norms of 'proper' femininity while only warriors or those who exhibited exceptional religious qualities were allowed to take on male leadership roles.

If we look to East Asia's history, masculinities were, again, constructed quite differently. In traditional Chinese culture the ideals of 'wen (mental or civil ideals) and wu (physical or martial ideals)' were key components of masculinity and a balance of these elements equated with a superior masculinity (Taga, 2005, p. 5). However, wen was superior to wu, which meant that intellectual masculinity was valued above brawniness, and in contrast to Western understandings, wen was more likely to be aligned with femininity than wu (Taga, 2005, p. 5). These ideals promoted an understanding of gender that did not necessarily marginalise femininity and homosexuality. For example, Taga (2005, pp. 3–4) suggests that, 'a softness in manner' did not undermine 'manliness', especially in the ruling classes and Confucian communities. Similarly, prior to the twentieth century in China, homosexuality did not threaten masculinity as a strict distinction between homosexuality and heterosexuality did not exist, and within the lower classes at least, women shared relative equality with men as they also took part in breadwinning and both men and women experienced 'sexual freedom outside of marriage' (Taga, 2005, p. 6).

Key differences between East Asian and Western masculinities continue to exist. For example, in Japan, older heterosexual couples tend to share a particular dynamic in that the women are responsible for budgeting and the men are emotionally dependent on their wives (Taga, 2005, p. 20). However, Taga (2005) also goes on to propose that rather than having a liberalising effect (as was the case in Western cultures), modernisation reinforced existing inequalities and created new divisions between women and men in East Asia. Further, he suggests that, more recently, globalisation has Westernised masculinity.

These examples show that what is considered to be a normative gender identity varies from culture to culture and so different articulations of gender can indicate cultural belonging (or not belonging) in different contexts. Examining gender identities across cultures reminds us that gender is not fixed and that the male/female dichotomy is a social construct that is particularly prevalent in Western culture.

Case study 1: troubling gender in colonial Australia

There is evidence that identities existed outside the male/female binary in Western history but with varying levels of acceptance from the broader community. For example, *The Sydney Morning Herald* recently reported that it is possible that Australia's first transgender person was Edward De Lacy Evans (Evans formerly identified as Ellen Tremaye), who arrived in Victoria from Ireland on the Ocean Monarch passenger ship in 1856. Evans married three times and, for the most part, appeared to be accepted by his community for much of his life. However, in 1879 he was committed to hospital for depression following marital trouble. Here, after it was discovered that he possessed female genitalia, he was forced to wear women's clothing and subjected to invasive vaginal and rectal examinations. During his treatment at the hospital media interest in his identity grew and Evans became a public spectacle. After his release he appeared in a travelling sideshow where he was advertised as 'The Wonderful Male Impersonator' and in 1880 a pamphlet was published about him titled 'The Man-Woman Mystery' (Khazandec, 2014). Therefore, although Evans was initially accepted by his community, it appears that the medicalisation of his identity inspired the perception that his genitalia mark his 'true' gender. Gender identification outside of the normative schema was viewed as mental illness, deviant enough to include in a sideshow and finally as a great 'mystery'. Evans's story shows how gender categories can hurt individuals 'who do not fit within their normative alignments' (Valocchi, 2005, p. 752), a point that is reiterated in the gender practice theories described below. Nevertheless, this case study does indicate that gender identities, which sit outside of the male/female dualism, are part of Australia's colonial history. Although Western norms of femininity and masculinity appear to have been stricter in the past, transgender identities are not only a *contemporary* Western phenomenon.

Gendered intersections: working-class femininity

There are, of course, also many different ways in which masculinity and femininity can be articulated within one culture at one point in time. And this is because social differences like ethnicity, social class and sexuality may impact the ways in which gender is lived out. For example, Beverley Skeggs (1997) argues that femininity is classed. Skeggs (1997, p. 99) suggests that the ideal of femininity was developed in the eighteenth and nineteenth centuries – through 'textuality' (in calm dispositions, luxurious aesthetics and so forth) and through the archetype of the 'lady', 'which equated conduct with appearance'. During this period, femininity was aligned with the upper classes, and, by the end of the nineteenth century, 'White middle-class femininity was defined as the ideal but also as the most passive and dependent of femininities. It was always coded as respectable' (Skeggs, 1997, p. 99). White middle-class femininity held value as it sat above other forms of femininity in the social hierarchy. This meant that investments in femininity accrued middle-class women status and distinguished them from others. Working-class women, in contrast, had an ambivalent relationship with femininity; they were seen as 'robust' and 'sexual'.

In her ethnographic research with eighty-three working-class women in North-West England, Skeggs (1997, p. 101) finds that, in the present day, femininity is 'established through historical circuits of signs'. Respectable femininity still holds cultural value while working-class women continue to be framed in an undesirable light. Working-class women are conceptualised as 'deviant', 'undisciplined' and 'excessive', as well as lacking 'taste' in making up their appearance (Skeggs, 1997, pp. 99–100. See also the discussion of 'Chav-girl' in Chapter 3). These distinctions are recognised by the women in Skegg's study and so they invest in femininity by taking up caring practices and working on their physical appearances; femininity is a resource that working-class women attempt to make use of to 'halt any losses' when they lack other assets or 'capital'. In particular, the women aspire to be glamorous as glamour 'is the mechanism by which the marks of middle-class respectability are transposed onto the sexual body, a way in which recognition of value is achieved' (Skeggs, 1997, p. 110). Glamour also produces women as desirable subjects, and desirability confirms that investments in femininity have not been lost. Desirability is therefore reassuring for women; it enables 'one not to be seen as inadequate, undesirable and not belonging' (Skeggs, 1997, p. 111). However, this is a risky method of obtaining worth because it relies on masculine judgements and it legitimates masculine power. Working-class women therefore continue to have an ambivalent relationship with femininity. The women in Skeggs's study reproduce femininity out of necessity but in a limited way; its association with middle-classness makes femininity very difficult for working-class women to inhabit.

Gender identities as power

Skeggs's study suggests that gender plays a role in reproducing social class identities and privilege. A hierarchy exists between men and women but gender also plays a part in producing and reinforcing other forms of social stratification such as hierarchies of class (discussed in Chapter 3) and ethnicity (discussed in Chapter 2). Power is therefore implicated in any social understanding of gender identity. Two concepts that are perhaps most frequently referred to when discussing gender power are 'patriarchy' and 'hegemonic masculinity'.

Patriarchy

Initially, patriarchy referred to the 'rule of the father' in family structures. However, feminists have taken up the term and now use it to describe a system of male dominance that extends beyond the household; the concept facilitates a structural account of gender inequality (Witz, 1992, p. 3). According to feminists, under patriarchal rule, masculinity belong in the public domain whereas femininity does not; feminine belonging is relegated to domestic and private spaces. Today, the patriarchy concept also tends to be used very broadly, to refer to the dominance of men over women but also the dominance of some men over other men.

Very well-known conceptualisations of patriarchy feature in socialist-feminist accounts of gender relations. For example, Hartmann (1976) argues that gender segregation in the labour market is the result of the interlocking systems of patriarchy and capitalism. Under these systems, a cycle of disadvantage occurs where low wages maintain women's dependence on men and force them to marry, this then benefits men in that women take on the burden of unpaid domestic labour which weakens women's position in the labour market. The division of labour in the home and the division of labour in the market therefore reinforce each other. However, because theories of patriarchy tend to focus on social structure, and to see the potential for women's agency as always limited, the concept has been critiqued for sometimes sliding into universalism (as well as ahistoricism and ethnocentrism) (Witz, 1992, p. 3). For this reason, the patriarchy concept has been abandoned by many theorists or used in combination with a focus on social practice or alongside more dynamic concepts such as 'hegemonic masculinity'.

Hegemonic masculinity

Raewyn Connell has formulated an understanding of masculine power that does not universalise experiences as the patriarchy concept often does. Connell proposes that gender power circulates as 'hegemonic masculinity'.

Hegemonic masculinity in its original formulation is 'the pattern of practice (i.e. things done, not just a set of role expectations or an identity) that allowed men's dominance over women to continue', rather than an overarching structure (Connell and Messerschmidt, 2012, p. 255). While masculinity is constructed so that it usually dominates femininity (due to men's higher incomes, and so forth), certain types of masculinity are also more powerful than others. There are therefore multiple masculinities, with certain masculinities subordinated to more dominant formations.

Hegemonic masculinity is a normative rather than a normal type of masculinity in particular historical and social contexts; only a small number of men have access to this masculinity, but it is 'the most honoured way of being a man', other men must 'position themselves in relation to it' and it ideologically legitimates men's dominance over women (Connell and Messerschmidt, 2012, p. 256). While hegemonic masculinity is differently constituted at different points in time and certain types may become obsolete as newer versions struggle for hegemony, it is always aligned with 'complicit masculinity', masculinity that is not necessarily achieved with violence but with 'ascendency achieved through culture, institutions and persuasion' (Connell and Messerschmidt, 2012, p. 256).

Recently, Connell and Messerschmidt (2005, 2012) have reformulated Connell's understanding of hegemonic masculinity so that it might better apply to the complexities of masculine power. First, they suggest that the gender hierarchy is more complicated than it initially appears; power does not necessarily operate in a straightforward way from the top to the bottom. For this reason, the agency of subordinated groups is an important consideration when attempting to understand gender relations, as is the 'mutual conditioning of gender dynamics and other social dynamics' such as social class, disability and ethnicity. Second, Connell and Messerschmidt suggest that hegemonic masculinity operates across different geographies and so masculinities must be understood at local, national and global levels (some of the impacts of globalisation on masculinities will be examined later in the chapter). Third, Connell and Messerschmidt (2012, p. 260) highlight the significance of social embodiment for hegemonic masculinity because they view the corporeal and the social as interwoven. Bodies are not simply constructed by culture, nor are they separate from social discourse; rather, bodies are actively involved in the construction of social practice. This means that embodiments can be an aspect of masculine domination. Finally Connell and Messerschmidt suggest that masculinities are dynamic. Masculinities are layered, internally contradictory and changeable. This means that it is possible for gender relations to become democratised; a 'positive' hegemonic masculinity that is accepting of gender equality can be established. Their reformulation of the concept is therefore a hopeful one; although masculinity is a form of domination, the reproduction of the gender hierarchy is not inevitable.

Case study 2: 'skater girls' doing alternative femininities

Connell contrasts hegemonic masculinity with 'emphasised femininity' (Connell and Messerschmidt, 2005, 2012). Emphasised femininity is a concept that gives reference to women's 'compliance' to their subordination to men. Like hegemonic masculinity, emphasised femininity tends to be the normative version of femininity. In a study with twenty girls who take part in skateboarding culture in British Columbia, Canada, Kelly et al. (2005) find that 'skater girls' participate in an 'alternative girlhood' and even resist emphasised femininity. Although skater girls experience skater culture differently depending on their class locations, for the most part, they 'consciously position themselves against what they perceive as the mainstream in general and against conventional forms of femininity in particular' (Kelly et al., 2005, p. 230). This position taking is achieved through various practices such as choosing to dress in ways that are not sexualised and using their own version of 'skater slang'. The interviewees also critique the normative femininity that circulates amongst their peers as hypersexualised and overly focused on consumption and romantic heterosexual relationships. The authors therefore conclude that: 'The alternative authority of skater girl discourse gave the girls in our study room to maneuver within and against the culturally valued discourse of emphasized femininity' (Kelly et al., 2005, p. 245). This youth culture offers girls the space to express agency and do gender differently. As Connell and Messerschmidt (2005, 2012) suggest, the reproduction of the gender order is not inevitable.

Gender as practice

Connell and Messerschmidt (2005, 2012) refer to masculinity as patterns of practice. While a plethora of theoretical perspectives on gender identity exist, and the biological reading of gender (illustrated in Case Study 1) continues to dominate in many Western societies, an understanding of gender identity as formulated through practice has proved persuasive for social theorists. This approach largely emerged out of a critique of sex role theory, a framework that was very popular in the 1970s, when structural and post-structural theorists began to examine how gender is constituted in relationships (Connell, 2003). One of the first understandings of gender as social practice was formulated by West and Zimmerman (1987) who propose that we 'do gender'. Another highly influential approach that sits within the queer theory paradigm is Judith Butler's understanding of 'gender performativity'. The following section outlines these theoretical approaches.

Doing gender

Upon realising that the sex/gender distinction did not stand up, that our sex is shaped by the social and is ambiguous and that gender identity is not necessarily 'achieved' by the individual but, rather, impacted by social structures and relationships, West and Zimmerman looked for an alternative conceptualisation. In their ground-breaking paper, 'Doing Gender', they suggest that a better understanding of the complexity of gender identities can be formulated if a distinction is made between sex, sex category and gender. West and Zimmerman (1987, p. 127) propose that sex is determined through a social process; it is based on 'socially agreed upon biological criteria for classifying persons as females or males' (these biological criteria include things like chromosomes or genitalia, although chromosomes do not always match with genitalia). At birth, our sex category is determined through these criteria, but, of course, these criteria cannot be applied in everyday life. In everyday life sex category is achieved through an individual's proclamation that they belong to a sex category through 'identificatory displays' (West and Zimmerman, 1987, p. 127). Therefore, sex and sex category are often aligned, but they can also vary; an individual can be known as a woman and at the same time not possess female genitalia. Gender is different from sex category. Gender:

> is the activity of managing situated conduct in light of normative conceptions of attitudes and activities appropriate for one's sex category. Gender activities emerge from and bolster claims to membership in a sex category. (West and Zimmerman, 1987, p. 127)

West and Zimmerman (1987, p. 126) propose that we 'do' gender in interactions:

> We contend that the 'doing' of gender is undertaken by women and men whose competence as members of society is hostage to its production. Doing gender involves a complex of socially guided perceptual, interactional, and micropolitical activities that cast particular pursuits as expressions of masculine and feminine 'natures'.

This perspective therefore sees gender as arising from social situations, rather than existing as internal to individuals. For example, as is discussed in Chapter 11, in the carrying out of unpaid labour in the home, or, as is discussed in Chapter 12, in taking up leisure activities. Although this implies that gender is unfixed and changeable, gender is often done in a normative manner that legitimates and naturalises sex categories and gender hierarchies, and failing to do gender in a normative manner brings suspicion upon individuals. West and Zimmerman (1987) propose that resistance to gender divisions therefore requires an assessment of the institutional and interactional production of gender.

Gender performativity

For Judith Butler, as is the case for West and Zimmerman, a core gender identity does not exist within individuals. Instead, like West and Zimmerman, Butler proposes that gender is 'done'; it is produced in social situations. However, Butler goes further than West and Zimmerman in dismissing the sex/gender distinction; Butler collapses the dichotomy so that sex does not exist outside of gender (Salih and Butler, 2004, p. 91). Butler also departs from West and Zimmerman in that she emphasises repetition; gender and sexual identities are produced through the repetition of performance or what she terms 'performativity'. Gender performativity occurs in two stages. First, the expectation of gender essence produces that which it anticipates. Identities are then made to appear fixed through the repetition of acts: 'performativity is not a singular act, but a repetition and a ritual, which achieves its effects through its naturalization in the context of a body, understood, in part, as culturally sustained temporal duration' (Butler, 1999, p. xv). Norms are internalised through repetitive practice and so hierarchical meaning systems produce gender identities as well as set limits on their formation. For Butler then, gender power operates in a productive manner; like Foucault, she sees individuals as 'self-regulating subjects' (Valocchi, 2005, p. 756). Individuals are not 'free agents'; rather, they are produced as subjects through discourses of gender.

However, change and possibilities for difference are also central to Butler's theory. Butler proposes that drag queens and transsexuals, feminine gays and butch lesbians destabilise binary gender norms and reveal the performative nature of gender. They demonstrate that sexual and gender norms are vulnerable to 'performative surprise' (Salih and Butler, 2004, p. 93). Butler (1999, p. 137, original emphasis) argues, '*In imitating gender, drag implicitly reveals the imitative structure of gender itself – as well as its contingency*'.

Butler and West and Zimmerman's theories of gender have been influential in academia and have even made their mark in public discourse. These approaches provide an alternative to the sex/gender distinction and show how gender identities are produced in everyday social activities. They also point to possibilities for new identifications, for moving beyond gender dualities and hierarchies. At the same time, they highlight the injury that normative notions of gender can inflict; it continues to be very difficult to 'belong' in our communities without a normative gender identity, even though alternative genders may create subversive opportunities.

Globalising gender

The norms and practices that West and Zimmerman and Butler highlight as significant for gender are increasingly globalised via flows of knowledge, technology and people. Local gender practices have also changed in response to the globalisation of culture, a global economy and post-colonial processes. However, for some time theories of globalisation overlooked gender and, in particular, femininity (Freeman, 2001). Feminist writers have redressed this issue and so there now exists a burgeoning field of gender theory that focuses on the relationship between gender and globalisation. For example, Freeman (2001) argues that while femininity is often implicitly theorised as local whereas masculinity is theorised as global, women are central to globalisation. Using the transformations of the Afro-Caribbean figure of the 'higgler', a woman who has historically transported commodities to rural areas, as an example, Freeman shows how women and local customs are very much part of processes of globalisation. Freeman (2001, p. 1021) highlights how there now exists a *transnational* higgler who, in addition to carrying out factory work for multinational companies, travels beyond the 'rural/urban loop' she established during colonialism. On her now transnational route, the higgler translates tastes between her own country and the countries she visits and uses consumption to negotiate her movements and relationships in host countries. She is both an instrument of globalisation (via her employment in a factory) and an agent of globalisation (in that she gives style advice and sells goods). In travelling internationally, the higgler also takes part in a non-traditional gender activity. However, her activities are, at the same time, 'quintessentially feminine' in that she is travelling as she always has and makes purchases that both challenge and reinforce traditional notions of femininity. Freeman (2001, p. 1030) concludes that higglers 'are themselves enacting new modes of globalization; they are not merely its effects' and that 'these engagements in production and consumption as they are configured across space and time have taken shape in ways that foundationally depend upon and redefine femininity and masculinity'. The higgler's movements therefore need to be understood in terms of gender and globalisation. They challenge the dualism of local/global and the association of femininity with the local and masculinity with the global.

Yuval-Davis (2009) further problematises women's relationship with globalisation. Yuval-Davis (2009, p. 1) proposes that 'the social change affecting the position of women in society as a result of globalization is paradoxical'. Globalisation enables women's entry into parts of society that they were once excluded from, yet, at the same time, in reaction to globalisation, there have been movements towards reclaiming traditional cultures and the gender differences that are aligned with them. For example, in India, part of the decolonising process 'has been the redefinition and reconstruction of sexuality and gender relations' (Yuval-Davis, 2009, p. 13). Women are required to be symbols of ethnic, religious and national collective belonging, but at the same time they are 'subject to various forms of control in the name of "culture and tradition"' (Yuval-Davis, 2009, p. 13). Women's movements into the global economy have also provided them with greater resources and autonomy but at the same time, their labour force participation tends to replicate their traditional roles in the domestic realm. So for example, migration has become more accessible to women, but women tend to migrate to participate in labour that is feminised (as domestic workers, carers, sex workers and 'mail brides') (for further discussion of the gendered dimensions of migration, see Case Study 2, Chapter 10). The changes brought about by neoliberal globalisation are therefore complicated and contradictory.

It should also be noted that Connell (1998, 2003, 2005) addresses the relationship between gender and globalisation in her theory of masculinity. She argues that masculinity is shaped by global history and globalisation is enacted within a global context. The various processes and components of globalisation, such as migration, global economies and new media, have impacted the forms that masculinity takes. Connell (2005, p. 5) proposes that to understand masculinity then, we must look beyond the individual to the 'world gender order', that is, 'the structure of relationships that interconnect the gender regimes of institutions, and the gender orders of local societies, on a world scale' (Connell, 2002). This world gender order is constituted by certain 'links'. The first is the interaction of local gender orders via various global processes such as neocolonialism or transnational trading. This process is often unsettling and involves violence but produces what Connell (2005, p. 7) sees as the first level of the global gender order. The second is the creation of 'spaces' beyond nations, such as transnational and multinational corporations, the international state, international media and global markets. For Connell, the result of these links is a 'partially integrated, highly unequal, and turbulent set of relations, with global reach but uneven impact' (Connell, 2005, p. 8).

Connell proposes that masculinities are multiplied by the interaction of local gender orders but at the same time transnational processes and spaces create opportunities for globalising masculinities to occur. For example, the global economy has produced transnational masculinities, such as 'transnational business masculinity', 'the masculinity associated with those who control the dominant institutions of the world economy: the capitalists and business executives who operate in global markets and the political executives who interact (and in many contexts merge) with them' (Connell, 2005, p. 13).

Connell also argues that processes of globalisation have altered local gender orders. This reconstruction occurs with the aid of women (for example, via the feminist movement), and often develops unevenly and from different points across cultures. This argument is affirmed by Taga's (2005) observation, discussed earlier in the chapter, that East Asian gender identities have become less liberal through modernisation and Westernisation (and it should be noted that the Spanish colonial missionaries attempted to end the 'two spirit' tradition as well (Connell, 2005, p. 19)). Connell suggests that this restructuring is most evident in the domestic division of labour, power relations, emotional relations and symbolisation. For example, colonialism and neo-colonialism have introduced a public/private divide where domestic work is unpaid and there is a corresponding division of masculinity and femininity into many cultures.

Finally, Connell (2005, p. 24) proposes that the world gender order has enabled a masculine politics, where women tend to be unequal to men, on a world scale:

> the conditions thus exist for the production of a hegemonic masculinity on a world scale – that is to say, a dominant form of masculinity that embodies, organizes and legitimates men's domination in the world gender order as a whole.

However, she also observes that the world gender order has incited resistance. Similarly, Yuval-Davis (2009, p. 17) states that globalisation has necessitated a response from the women's movement that can be described as a 'transversal politics'. The following section examines some of the articulations of that resistance.

The feminist movement: mobilising gender identities

The hierarchy that has been constructed between masculinity and femininity has necessitated the mobilisation of an identity politics via the feminist movement. The broad aim of feminism is to improve the status of women, to better enable women's belonging within social and political life, and if we reflect on the recent history of Western cultures, as we did earlier in this chapter, it is clear that this movement has propelled change in gender relations.

The feminist movement began in the nineteenth century but has experienced a number of reincarnations: first, second and third 'waves'. First-wave feminism was concerned with women's rights (the right to own and inherit property, the right to attend university and so forth), and women's suffrage (the right to vote) was a key concern. The second wave of feminism was most visible in the 1960s and, because knowledge of the complexities of gender inequality increased and the uneven progress of first-wave feminism was recognised, at this point the aims of feminists became increasingly diverse. While some feminists were concerned with women's political representation and the 'glass ceiling', others were focused on pornography and the cultural exploitation of women's bodies. In the 1990s it became very clear that women do not share homogenous identities and that feminists need to speak for a multitude of voices, particularly across ethnic divides. The insights of queer theorists and black feminists changed the feminist agenda so that recognition of identity became 'a way of naming one's uniqueness' and did not necessarily name 'what is shared' (Connell, 2002, p. 89).

Third-wave feminism also developed in the more equitable and inclusive social context of the 1990s. This was a point at which feminism had succeeded on many fronts, and so third-wave feminism rejects the notion that women are always oppressed and includes men as activists in the feminist agenda. This form of feminism has developed from understandings that were formulated in the second wave and so recognises multiple identities and does not seek a unified purpose. Third-wave feminism may also be differentiated from past waves in that it sees sexuality as empowering, makes use of social media, and is less formalised (Lorber, 2012). This waves' inclusivity and comparatively unstructured formation makes collective action difficult and so is perhaps 'not yet a social movement' (Snyder, 2012, p. 312).

Globalising feminism

Globalisation is implicated in feminism's transformations. Yuval-Davis (2009, p. 16) argues that feminism became truly transnational in the second wave when the United Nations became a meeting point for feminists from different global locales. The United Nations' women-focused conventions, conferences and the 1975–1985 UN Decade for Women made the UN a hospitable launch pad for a transnational feminist community, and new communication technologies further facilitated connections. The UN's human rights focus meant that its objectives aligned with the interests of the feminist movement. This alignment resulted in some feminists reframing their ambitions using the discourse of human rights, and this continues within the third wave. Furthermore, transnational feminist activists connect through national conflicts and wars, and the common aspiration to end conflict supersedes other feminist concerns and a traditional identity politics. Yuval-Davis (2009) therefore suggests that a new type of feminist politics has developed out of globalisation – a 'transversal politics'. For Yuval-Davis (2009) this new politics is formed out of feminist values but is 'dialogical in nature'; it contributes to women's rights but also human rights and local and global change. As globalisation has further entrenched existing inequalities as well as produced new divisions between men and women, feminism continues to be important but it must be based on a solidarity that:

> will be transversal in that it will recognize the intersectional differences in women's 'situated positionings and power, carry out the dialogue within the boundaries of emancipatory value system, encompass discourse of difference with discourse of equality and conviviality, and will not confuse the notion of "women" with that of "feminists"'. This is not the time to go back to identity politics. (Yuval-Davis, 2009, p. 18)

Conclusion

Our understandings of our individual gender identities as well as theories of gender identity have profoundly changed throughout time and are shaped by culture and processes of globalisation. Many social theorists have moved beyond the sex/gender distinction and see gender identity as something that is 'done' through social practice rather than an essential attribute. While gender is now experienced and understood in more fluid and open ways, gender power and domination continue to exist, with globalisation both enabling new possibilities and rearticulating and reinforcing traditional gender relationships and norms. The feminist movement has played a key role in opening up gender possibilities and gaining freedom and belonging for women; in its transnational and 'transversal' form perhaps it may help us to move even further beyond gender binaries and hierarchies and to better accommodate difference.

Questions for students

- How is social practice relevant to our gender identities?
- What is hegemonic masculinity? Can you think of ways in which hegemonic masculinity operates in your culture?
- How relevant is your gender identity to you? How is it impacted by other modes of belonging (for example, your social class, ethnicity and age)?

- This chapter provides some examples of the ways in which gender identities vary across culture and time. Can you think of any more examples? Perhaps you have even witnessed changes within your own lifetime.
- How has feminism changed over the years? What role has globalisation played in its reincarnations?

Recommended reading

Butler, J. (1999) *Gender Trouble: Feminism and the Subversion of Identity* (London: Routledge).

Connell, R. and Messerschmidt, J. (2012) 'Hegemonic Masculinity', in Lorber, Judith (ed.) *Gender Inequality* (Fifth Edition) (New York: Oxford University Press).

Jackson, S. and Scott, S. (eds.) (2002) *Gender: A Sociological Reader* (London: Routledge).

Kimmel, M. and Aronson, A. (eds.) (2004) *The Gendered Society Reader* (New York: Oxford University Press).

CHAPTER 5

Sexuality

Scott McKinnon and Andrew Gorman-Murray

Introduction

This chapter investigates sexuality as an individual and collective identity category. The notion of sexual identity is a particularly modern mode of identity and belonging originating in the West in the late nineteenth century and proliferating and transforming over the twentieth century. In this chapter, we explore how sexuality operates as a point of identity and belonging by, firstly, tracing the emergence of sexuality as the basis of personal and collective identities in the West. Once seen as behaviours or acts, sexual desires would gradually be framed in discourse as a critical and innate element of one's being. This discursive framing has seen the emergence of spatially enacted communities of desire in which a sense of belonging is derived from shared sexual identities. We then discuss how globalisation has worked on and through sexuality as an identity category, noting the possibilities and problems in interactions between the local and the global. We conclude with an examination of the website of the International Lesbian, Gay, Bisexual, Trans and Intersex Association (ILGA). By exploring ways in which this site both encourages and embodies a sense of belonging to a globalised community based on minority sexual and gender identities, we consider the political potential and inherent complexities within such an imagined online community.

The emergence of sexuality as a form of identity

Same-sex sexual desire and romantic attachment are, of course, nothing new. As argued by Robert Aldrich, 'Since time immemorial and throughout the world, some men and women have felt a desire for emotional and physical intimacy with those of the same sex' (Aldrich, 2010, p. 1). What are new – or, at least, relatively recent in historical terms – are the forms of collective identity developed by people who feel these desires. What were once seen simply as sexual acts have become the basis of personal identities and feelings of belonging to a larger community. A significant shift in understandings, experiences and discourses of sexuality has seen a set of behaviours become the basis of forms of identity (Foucault, 1976). These identities are historically and geographically constituted, emerging in different ways at different times and substantially shifting and re-forming since they first became apparent in the Western world (Weeks, 1981). Homosexual behaviours have become critical indicators not only of what we may do, but of who we may be. The emergence of 'the homosexual' as a category of person has equally seen the emergence of its binary opposite, 'the heterosexual'.

These identity categories initially emerged in the West in the late nineteenth century. During this time, a number of British, European and American researchers began to posit the idea that the homosexual was a distinct category of person. The word 'homosexuality' was not used until the 1860s, gaining increased prominence in the writings of Havelock Ellis in the 1880s and 1890s (Weeks, 1981). In Ellis's native Britain, sex between men was criminalised and harshly punished but had generally been seen as a temporary aberration rather than an indicator of belonging to a distinct social category. Although small subcultures existed, a public identity based on same-sex desire was not available.

Through the late nineteenth and into the twentieth century, terms such as 'homosexual', 'invert' and 'Uranian' came to be applied to men who sexually desired other men, with some beginning to self-identify within these categories. Medical discourses framed inversion, for example, as a congenital condition, creating a distinction between those who chose to participate in homosexual behaviours ('perverts') and those who experienced homosexual desire as an innate and essential element of their being ('inverts') (Houlbrook, 2006). Homosexual sex continued to be viewed as morally wrong, sinful, criminal and/or pathological, but for some the desire to participate in such acts was now seen as beyond their control. It remained a behaviour in which one should refrain from participating but was now also described as a desire some could not avoid experiencing and an element of a categorical human type. Implicit in any such framing was a specific distinction between normal/heterosexual and abnormal/homosexual.

By the 1950s, 'the homosexual' was firmly established as a distinct identity category. Into the second half of the twentieth century, another distinct shift saw increasing numbers of men and women in the West willing both to self-identify as homosexual and to protest against the framing of that identity as an indicator of perversity or criminality. In the United States, groups such as the Mattachine Society and the Daughters of Bilitis began to frame homosexual men and lesbians as members of an oppressed group who deserved better treatment by the broader society (D'Emilio, 1989). Critical to the arguments of such groups was the notion that sexual identity was not a matter of personal choice. From small and uncertain beginnings, a progressively more assertive and vocal activist movement – which would adopt the label 'gay' – emerged on the basis of individual identities increasingly connected to a broader coalition or community of similarly identifying men and women.

In many large Western cities, emerging alongside these activist groups were urban communities that became publicly visible as homosexual spaces (Levine, 1979; Brown, 2013). A collective sense of belonging was spatially constituted, often in inner-city areas that underwent a process of gentrification through their colonisation by gay men (Knopp, 1998), in particular, but also lesbians, albeit less visibly (Rothenberg, 1995). These areas acted both as residential neighbourhoods as well as housing a range of commercial and community organisations that specifically – and openly – catered to varied lesbian and gay clientele (Collins, 2004). In Sydney, Australia, for example, from the 1960s onwards, Oxford Street and the neighbouring suburbs of Darlinghurst, Surry Hills and Paddington became known as home to lesbian and – especially – gay communities (Wotherspoon, 1991). These spaces represented a collective sense of belonging based on sexual identities. Living as gay or lesbian now incorporated a great deal more than a simple preference for sexual or romantic partners of the same gender. It was now possible to perform those identities through participation in a shared culture.

It is important to note that while we have depicted in broad brushstrokes the development of modern sexual identities, a more detailed examination would locate specific differences, meanings and identity formations in particular locations across the globe (Browne et al., 2007). As argued above, sexual identities are geographically and historically constituted and will therefore shift across both place and time. Although homosexuality became a widely discussed and controversial topic in Britain in the 1950s, for example, and sex between consenting male adults was decriminalised there in 1967, any such discussion was extremely limited in 1950s Australia where decriminalisation would only occur on a state-by-state basis over the course of three decades from the 1970s to the 1990s (Willett, 1997). While, as we will discuss below, globalisation would encourage a sense of belonging to a global or international homosexual community, local factors have been critical in how, when and why sexual identities have emerged in specific locations around the world.

Into the 1990s, it is arguable that minority sexual identities experienced both consolidation and splintering, a contradiction perhaps reflected in tensions between modernist narratives of progress and the postmodern rejection of such narratives. In the West, lesbian and gay identities were increasingly included within consumerist discourses (Willett, 2000). Advertisements specifically targeted towards lesbians and gay men, for example, aimed to reach what was considered a potentially lucrative market. For some, this was seen as an indicator of progress and a point of success for activists whose goal was to create visibility for (and acknowledgement of) lesbians and gays in and by the broader society. To others, this represented the death of radical lesbian and gay cultures (Duggan, 2002). Such advertisements may have represented a form of belonging to society, but this belonging was predicated on the ability – and desire – to participate in a consumerist society (for further discussion of the links between identity, belonging and consumption, see Chapter 13).

Thus, what may present as progress for some represents a failure to others, a contradiction which may call into question a sense of belonging based on sexual identity. Queer theorists have, in fact, worked to disrupt identities and to complicate what may otherwise be seen as essentialist categories (Jagose, 1996; Sullivan, 2003). Emerging initially in the 1990s, queer theory is a field of critical inquiry which specifically resists definition but which can be seen as a means of challenging and questioning fixed notions of sexual or gender identity. Although 'queer' has come to be used by some as an identity label, queer theory seeks to highlight fluidity and complexity, suggesting broader possibilities than the binary of heterosexual/homosexual and resisting sexual and gender labelling. Queer theory also challenges heteronormativity, encouraging analysis which seeks out difference and which, rather than placing non-heterosexual identities as an alternative 'other' that differs from a fixed heterosexual 'norm', instead investigates fluid processes of identity performance.

Although queer theory has successfully encouraged greater complexity and diversity in the ways in which academics and others discuss sexual identities, the fact remains that many people continue to self-identify within a particular category (Hammack and Cohler, 2011). In recent years, acronyms such as LGBTI (lesbian, gay, bisexual, transgender, intersex) have been enacted as a means of describing a community (or coalition of communities) of non-heterosexual and gender-diverse populations. Absent from these labels are a range of identities developed in non-Western contexts, again suggesting the importance of understanding sexuality as geographically and historically constituted (Johnston and Longhurst, 2010). Below, we consider how these identities operate among processes of globalisation.

Globalised identities

If we understand sexual identities as spatially constituted the question then arises as to how sexuality operates as an identity in an increasingly globalised world. Is it possible to feel a sense of identity and belonging to a minority sexual or gender community that is imagined globally, rather than – or as well as – locally? If so, what form does such an identity take? And how does it – or can it – accommodate the diversity and complexity of identities developed in different local, national or regional contexts? Jon Binnie has argued that 'the notion that lesbians and gay men across national borders share a common identity and sense of solidarity has a very particular appeal to many' (Binnie, 2004, p. 37). However, Binnie finds this notion ultimately unsustainable in the face of global differences. A tension exists, therefore, between a shared sense of identity and belonging as imagined by many global queers and the operation of sexuality as a mode of identity experienced differently across territories and scales.

Political theorist and activist Dennis Altman noted in 1996 that, across various parts of the globe, 'in the past two decades there has emerged a definable group of self-identified homosexuals – to date many more men than women – who see themselves as part of a global community, whose commonalities override but do not deny those of race and nationality' (Altman, 1996, p. 424). To Altman, this form of sexual identity was adopted from Western – most particularly, American – gay identities and then adapted in various regions in specifically local ways. As a result, growing numbers of people were expressing a desire to 'live as homosexuals in the western sense of that term' (Altman, 1996, p. 425). To Altman, this was not occurring through the simplistic replication of Western models but through potential adaptations of Western identity politics into 'something new and unpredictable' (Altman, 1996, p. 433).

Altman's arguments have been highly influential in encouraging ways of thinking about globalised sexual identities and in seeking nuanced means of understanding the adoption or adaption of Western modes of being, becoming and belonging. The argument that modern homosexual identities reflect the influence of Western ideas on non-Western 'traditional' sexual values has, however, been the subject of substantial critique and debate, most recently from queer theorists who seek a decentring of the West as the origin point of sexual globalisation.

As stated above (and discussed in Chapter 4), queer theory seeks to disrupt and complicate any binary division between, say, heterosexual/homosexual, male/female and, in this case, Western/non-Western. Natalie Oswin has critiqued Altman's work in these terms, arguing against distinct lines which position Western and modern sexual identity models as dominant over non-Western and traditional views (Oswin, 2006). To Oswin, by decentring the West, 'the supposition of a universal gayness manifesting itself in locally relevant forms is replaced by the recognition of distinct differences between modes of being queer in various locales' (Oswin, 2006, p. 782). Oswin argues that the globalisation of sexual identities should be understood as processes of emerging and merging which reflect less the dominance of one particular territory as they do mutual constitution across territories.

A critical element of globalised (or globalising) sexual identities is the concept of queer mobilities (Binnie, 2004; Gorman-Murray, 2009). With advances in technologies has come the ability for many global citizens to travel – either physically or virtually – across, within and through national borders. Sexual identities often play a central role in how or why people travel, thus enabling or constituting particular modes of mobility while also setting specific limitations to mobility. Persecution of sexual minorities may cause people to flee their home state, for example, while certain nation-states maintain border control policies that deny access to openly queer individuals (ILGA, 2013).

Studies of international migration have recently taken what Mai and King have described as a 'sexual turn' (Mai and King, 2009, p. 296). Heavily influenced by queer theory, this sexual turn has placed migrants as sexual beings, noting the influences of sexual identity (including heterosexual identity) on processes and experiences of migration. Such a framing allows for the importance of sexual and emotional desires as factors in decisions to migrate or in how people experience the places and spaces in and through which they migrate (Gorman-Murray, 2007; Waitt and Gorman-Murray, 2011). Critically, such studies may highlight migrations from or within non-Western nations, thus disrupting any framing of sexual identities as only ever flowing out from the West (Yue, 2008, 2012; Smith, 2012).

Tourism studies have similarly noted the importance of sexuality within processes of global mobility (Waitt and Markwell, 2006; Waitt et al., 2008). Jasbir Puar, for example, has noted tensions between the expectations of mobility by queer Western tourists and the framing by some nation-states of homosexuality as a pernicious element of colonial or neo-colonial Western influences (Puar, 2002). When a cruise ship carrying 900 gay and lesbian passengers was denied docking privileges by a British territory, the Cayman Islands, a substantial controversy arose which eventually involved British prime minister Tony Blair. Puar sees the gay and lesbian populations involved – both those on the ship and local Cayman Island residents – as pawns in 'an oppositional conflict between postcolonial and former colonizing governments' (Puar, 2002, p. 127). While Puar argues that the circumstances of this conflict 'may or may not be about sexuality' (Puar, 2002, p. 127), the differing experiences of sexual identity between Western tourists and local residents would seem to highlight the complexity and tensions within globalised queer identities.

The operation of multinational companies in a globalised economy may also at times highlight these tensions. Internet technology company Google, for example, announced in 2012 the launch of a campaign titled 'Legalize

Love: LGBT Rights Are Human Rights' (Google, 2012). As described by Google, the aim of this effort was 'to ensure that all of our employees have the same inclusive experience outside of the office as they do at work'. The campaign specifically targets nations that criminalise same-sex behaviours, bringing the weight of its substantial economic power to bear on governments around the globe. A Google representative has reportedly explained the company's targeting of Singapore, for example, by stating, 'Singapore wants to be a global financial center and world leader and we can push them on the fact that being a global center and a world leader means you have to treat all people the same, irrespective of their sexual orientation' (Peirano, 2012). Thus, a globalised economy and globalised sexual identities become specifically interwoven as configured by a multinational company.

Such efforts have, at times, placed queer identities as points of conflict in nation-states resisting globalising forces by projecting a specific nationalist identity (Binnie, 2004). The nation-state in these instances becomes defined by its refusal to admit non-heterosexual citizenship within its identity as a nation, thus basing that identity on the heterosexual family (Oswin, 2012). European unification is a prominent case in point (O'Dwyer and Schwartz, 2009). Accession to the European Union (EU) is predicated on acceptance of the European Charter of Fundamental Rights, which includes antidiscrimination protections for LGBT individuals. In countries such as Poland and Latvia, a significant anti-LGBT backlash has resisted these laws, invoking nationalised identities (defined as local, traditional and heterosexual) in opposition to the regionalising forces of the EU (defined as foreign, modern and queer) (see also Waitt, 2005, on sexual citizenship and gay geographies in Latvia).

Global experiences of HIV/AIDS represent another critical element of globalised sexual identities. As argued by Jon Binnie, 'The global AIDS pandemic had been crucial in bringing questions around the globalization of sexuality to the fore in debates within social theory' (Binnie, 2004, p. 109). This pandemic encompasses many of the issues central to globalised sexual identities. As a sexually transmissible illness frequently described in terms of its ability to spread across national borders, AIDS signifies sexual mobilities and challenges to the nation-state. Binnie describes AIDS as a 'postmodern virus' because of its challenges to discourses of progress and development, including medical and scientific progress; paths towards gay liberation by modern gay identities and the development strategies of developing nations (Binnie, 2004, p. 113).

Significantly, AIDS has also prompted and encouraged the development of coalitionist sexual activism across national borders, thus encouraging a sense of globalised sexual identity and belonging (Binnie, 2004). Among disparate sexual and gender minority populations, global queer activism can inspire feelings of participation in a common struggle against a common enemy.

The relevance of issues such as national legislative environments and locally constituted understandings of gender and sexual identity may mean, however, that queer activisms will differ substantially across the globe. Same-sex marriage, for example, has become a central focus for activism in countries in which homosexual sex has been decriminalised, including the United States, Great Britain and Australia. In areas of the Global South, the criminalisation of homosexual acts means that activists work in very different environments and must target their activism in different ways. Recently passed legislation in Uganda, for example, has resulted in the possibility of life imprisonment for 'serial offenders' found guilty of participating in homosexual sex (Karimi and Thompson, 2014). Below, we examine the significance of an international LGBTI rights organisation, arguing for both the value and complexity of global activisms which embody a particular vision of identity based on sexuality.

The International Lesbian, Gay, Bisexual, Trans and Intersex Association (ILGA)

The Internet is a global technology with the capacity to compress distances and to foster a sense of shared identity among geographically diverse populations. This is particularly the case for sexual and gender minorities who often fear reprisals if they reveal their identities in offline spaces and who may therefore seek connection, information and relationships online (DeHaan et al., 2013). As argued by Jon Binnie, 'Cyberspace offers the utopian prospect of escape and self-realization, a means of experimenting with sexual identity and searching for community' (Binnie, 2004, p. 42). Online spaces targeted at or created by LGBTI communities may include dating or sex 'hook-up' sites, LGBTI news publications, activist sites, community health information and social media. In this section, we examine the Internet presence of the International Lesbian, Gay, Bisexual, Trans and Intersex Association (ILGA), highlighting the ways in which such an online space may embody and encourage a globalised sense of belonging based on minority sexual or gender identity. We argue that the creation of such a space is both politically valuable and inherently problematic. In encouraging a sense of solidarity, ILGA allows potentially isolated and marginalised individuals to feel part of a larger community. It remains important, however, to acknowledge the privileges and inequities that exist within this community and to allow for complexity and diversity in the way that community is imagined into being.

Founded in 1978, ILGA currently declares itself the 'only worldwide federation campaigning for lesbian, gay, bisexual, trans and intersex rights'

(ILGA, 2013). While the ILGA Secretariat is based in Belgium and Switzerland, the organisation asserts its claim to global impact and influence through its 1044 member organisations located in 117 different countries. According to the ILGA website, the federation's aim is to:

> work for the equality of lesbian, gay, bisexual, trans and intersex people and their liberation from all forms of discrimination. We seek to achieve this aim through the world-wide cooperation and mutual support of our members. (ILGA, 2013)

ILGA pursues its mission through diplomatic advocacy, political activism and provision of information and support to LGBTI and 'mainstream' populations.

The ILGA website is a significant information portal which details legislative impacts on LGBTI lives across the globe, links to current news articles, provides services to ILGA member organisations, seeks donations, promotes participation in activist events and campaigns and encourages individuals to share their own stories of LGBTI life.

On many of the pages of the ILGA website, it is possible for readers to post a comment via the social networking site Facebook. This facility encourages a sense of participation and solidarity, through which users can participate in a global activist community based on sexual and gender identity. On 9 October 2011, a Facebook user identified as 'Lloyd Love' posted a comment to the 'About ILGA' page of the site that read in full, 'We are as ONE'. The brief comment can be read in a number of ways but seems most clearly to suggest a globalised sense of identity, through which the struggles, experiences, activisms and desires of all LGBTI people are understood as an element of a singular and cohesive community.

In many ways, this post sums up a particular vision of belonging based on a specifically globalised sense of sexual identity. It also suggests both how an organisation such as ILGA may encourage such a sense of belonging and how that organisation is imagined into being by members of the online community it forms. Throughout its publications, including its website, ILGA stresses its internationality and inclusivity, encouraging a feeling for the reader that – no matter their national identity – they are part of a common struggle based on their minority sexual or gender identity. Significant tension exists, however, in what would seem at first to be a simple yet powerful statement of unified goals and dreams. A politically potent voice may be developed through such unity, but for whom does it speak? Who is the 'we' in that statement? Does this unified voice allow for complexity and difference within its vision of solidarity or does it enforce a particular set of normativities?

These tensions have led to critiques of ILGA by activists and academics who fear that, in encouraging a uniform sense of identity and belonging, the organisation is in fact enforcing Westernised values and opinions. Martin Manalansan, for example, has argued that ILGA, through its publications and conferences, has displayed 'a tendency to deploy monolithic constructions of gayness and gay liberation' (Manalansan, 1995, p. 429). To Manalansan, this reflects a Eurocentric imagining of 'gay' which fails to include or acknowledge the full range of minority sexual or gender identities experienced by many of the people for whom ILGA claims to speak.

ILGA's organisational structure, as displayed on its website, appears to respond to such critiques via divisions into particular regional and gendered groupings. The website includes separate pages for each of ILGA's regional groups (Africa, Asia, Europe, Latin America and Caribbean, North America and Oceania) as well as its Women's and Trans Secretariats. While maintaining a goal of global cooperation, these organisational groupings allow for at least some degree of difference and complexity by suggesting, for example, that the experiences of sexual and gender minority populations in Africa will be different from those in Europe. Differences within each of these regions may be less successfully catered for through such a strategy; however, ILGA's news postings and legislative updates do highlight national specificities and diversity of experience.

The difficulty of both encouraging solidarity and acknowledging diversity is noted on the 'Your Story' page of the ILGA site. This page encourages users to contribute posts describing their own stories of 'What LGBTI life is like in reality'. ILGA's request for users to add stories to the page states, 'Let others know what it's like to be LGBTI in your country! If an experience is meaningful for you, it will probably be meaningful for someone else' (ILGA, 2013). This request acknowledges that national differences will create diverse experiences by specifically asking about 'your country', while simultaneously encouraging a feeling of belonging by asserting that these experiences may also 'be meaningful for someone else'. Thus, nationally or regionally diverse experiences may find commonality of meaning when read in the context of this site based on the shared sense of belonging encouraged within the site.

Uniformity may also be encouraged or enforced through the use of the identity label LGBTI, a label which may not be applicable or uniformly understood within diverse regions. In a study of tensions between global discourses and local 'realities' in Bangladesh, Dina Siddiqi argues that 'global identity categories such as ... gay/lesbian are too narrow to capture the fluid and highly context-specific ways in which gender and sexually nonconforming persons understand themselves' (Siddiqi, 2011). The use of LGBTI by ILGA, while designed to be inclusive of diverse experiences, may in fact exclude some who feel no attachment to such labels.

Peter Nardi argues for the possibility that, rather than seeking or enforcing a uniform homosexual identity, ILGA instead seeks a form of political unity that allows for societal pluralism (Nardi, 1998). Writing in 1998, Nardi frames the goals of global LGBTI activism as an attempt to uncover 'the inequalities linked to the privileges and assumptions of hegemonic heterosexuality' (Nardi, 1998, p. 584). Framed in this way, ILGA's goals can be seen less as an attempt to enforce a particular, uniform imagining of LGBTI identity and more as an attempt to disrupt a global imagining of universal heterosexuality. Rather than suggesting that a global LGBTI community will or should experience non-heterosexual identities in similar ways, ILGA instead seeks space to advocate for the needs of non-heterosexual citizens within diverse global constituencies.

Nardi's argument acknowledges the potential political value of an organisation such as ILGA; however, acknowledgement should also be made of the privileges and inequities that will be present in any such organisation. As argued by Jon Binnie and Christian Klesse, 'Because solidarity needs to bridge unequal territories of power, ... everyday experiences of activism are rarely free from tensions' (Binnie and Klesse, 2012, p. 456). Within a global LGBTI community, certain members will experience privilege based on issues such as race, ethnicity, class and gender. Potential exists that within globalised activism the privileged 'speak for' the voiceless, rather than creating a space in which the previously silenced are now able to speak for themselves.

Hakan Seckinelgin has highlighted potential problems with the feeling of solidarity that can be generated by the news media and Internet technologies (Seckinelgin, 2012). Seckinelgin argues that 'cosmopolitan intimacies emerge at the juncture of events unfolding and the people observing them from a distance' (Seckinelgin, 2012, p. 542). News garnered through a venue such as the ILGA website may, therefore, encourage a feeling of solidarity with people we imagine to be sharing identities and experiences similar to our own. The distance between their lives and ours is compressed and simplified, viewed through an imagining of sexual or gender identity that is more relevant to us than them. Although such solidarity has the potential to create positive change, it is also possible, as argued by Seckinelgin, that 'the solidarity created from a distance creates challenges for those who are constructed as people *like us*' (Seckinelgin, 2012, p. 542).

In terms of a sense of belonging fostered in a venue such as the ILGA website, it is also important to note that particular technologies – such as computers or other devices with Internet access – are necessary in order to participate in the site as a forum. Whether through insufficient incomes required to afford technology, an absence of necessary local infrastructure or censorship regimes which monitor and restrict access to particular sites, many of the members of the global community seemingly embodied by the ILGA website are, in fact, unable to access that site. In seeking to understand how a globalised sense of sexual or gender identity may be embodied or encouraged through the Internet, it is important to remember that the Internet is inequitably accessible across the globe (for further discussion, see Chapter 14).

Nonetheless, ILGA's online presence performs a potentially important role in providing information, connection and a feeling of belonging to and among geographically diverse populations. The site can be seen as embodying the problematic interplay between the political (and emotional) value of solidarity and the critical importance of acknowledging privilege, diversity and complexity. Ultimately, it is likely that when seeking a sense of belonging and identity through this site, each user brings their own vision of sexual or gender identity understood through and constituted by local contexts. A global community is imagined into being in a way that provides a feeling of belonging and assumes similarities across and through distance, difference and diversity.

Case study: heterosexual identity and the 'straight ally'

Scholarly interest in sexuality has tended to focus on desires and identities that sit outside what might be considered the heterosexual 'mainstream'. Researchers have, however, begun to take an increasing interest in how heterosexuality itself operates as a form of identity and belonging (Hubbard, 2000; Little, 2003). As argued by Hubbard, there is value in exploring 'the many possible articulations of heterosexual desire that are included or excluded within a dominant construction of heteronormality' (Hubbard, 2008, p. 645). Once positioned as a cohesive norm, the label 'heterosexual' is increasingly understood as covering a broad variety of identities that are regulated and performed in diverse and complex ways.

The 'straight ally' is an interesting case in point. This identity label may be adopted by or applied to 'straight identified individuals who are supportive advocates for the LGBT Community through their activism, involvement or their nature to speak out against oppression and inequality' (LGBT Resource Center USC). A range of campaigns, often focusing on social media, have encouraged heterosexual people to publicly identify as a straight ally, including 'Straight for Equality' (PFLAG, 2012) and 'Straight but Not Narrow' (SBNN, 2010, http://www.straightbutnotnarrow.org/).

As an identity marker, 'straight ally' reveals the inherent complexity of (hetero)sexual identities. By including the word 'straight' the label acts as a specific and public identification as heterosexual. However, the label equally suggests a sense of identity and belonging developed through alliance with LGBTI groups and in opposition to some heterosexual people. There is an implicit suggestion that some heterosexual identities incorporate or are defined by anti-LGBTI attitudes. The 'straight ally' rejects such attitudes while still firmly declaring a heterosexual identity. This is a form of heterosexuality defined as both different from and aligned with LGBTI identities, which is at once the same as but in opposition to some heterosexual identities. The heterosexual/homosexual binary is simultaneously perpetuated and complicated in a process that emphasises fixed sexual and gender identities while also creating a sense of belonging across difference.

Conclusion

Although ostensibly defined by the gender of our sexual object choice, sexuality as an individual and collective category of identity and belonging has come to represent far more. Through sexual identity we may participate in a community enacted materially within particular urban spaces or virtually in the online world. Sexual identities may constitute our place as citizens of a nation-state; as migrants across national borders; or as members of a global activist coalition. Sexual identity may enable a sense of belonging to a community of shared desire or may represent an exclusion from nationalist mythologies. The rights of minority sexual and gender identity populations remain contested and controversial across the globe. Nonetheless, the emergence and (re)formation of these identities since the nineteenth century has significantly altered how sex and sexuality are placed in discourse and enacted as sites of identity and belonging.

Questions for students

- Thinking about your own sexual identity, in what ways do you feel a sense of belonging with people who share that identity? In what ways do you feel a sense of difference?
- Do you perform your sexual identity differently as you move through different spaces? If yes, how? Are there spaces in which you feel freer to identify in particular ways than in other spaces?
- What role do governments play in regulating identities based on sexuality (including heterosexual identity)? How does sexuality operate differently across nation-states?
- In what ways does sexual identity operate differently for people of your generation as opposed to, say, your parents' generation?

Recommended reading

Binnie, Jon. (2004) *The Globalization of Sexuality* (London: Sage).

Brown, Michael P. (2000) *Closet Space: Geographies of Metaphor from the Body to the Globe* (London: Routledge).

Browne, Kath, Brown, Gavin, and Lim, Jason. (2007) *Geographies of Sexualities* (Ashgate: Farnham).

Johnston, Lynda and Longhurst, Robyn. (2010) *Space, Place and Sex: Geographies of Sexualities* (Plymouth: Rowman and Littlefield).

CHAPTER 6

Youth

Amie Matthews

Introduction

> We saw it [going travelling] as just, the only time before mortgages, before kids, before anything else. To just … *leave*.
>
> (Emily, age 23)

> I wanted to go overseas before I had any commitments. Many of my friends just want to find Mr Right, settle into a good job and pop out a couple of kids. And that's great for *them*. I just want a few more experiences before I settle down.
>
> (Erin, age 22)

> One of the things that really influences me is a fear of settling down and waking up years later, not having done the things that I want to do. Travel sort of prevents me from falling into this 'trap'.
>
> (Scott, age 22)

The above statements, which are extracted from interviews with young Australian travellers, are demonstrative of the types of reflexive identity construction many young people are engaged in today. Drawn from studies of the global backpacking culture, which examine travel as a rite of passage in the lives of contemporary Western youth (for further discussion see Matthews, 2008; Matthews, 2014), these interviewee reflections associate global mobility with an accumulation of experience and, simultaneously, the deferral of responsibility. What is clear from this is that international travel is seen as a means of embracing opportunity and crafting a future personhood, or adult self, which is both experienced and, importantly, fulfilled. One gets the sense that such future fulfilment rests on making the most of youth by making the 'right' choices. Indeed, travel is constructed here as a youthful choice – as an alternative to 'settling down' or to the decisions (mortgage, house, career and kids) that are deemed symbolic of adult status. These observations hint then not just at the cultural significance of travel for members of the backpacking culture, but at some of the social meanings attached to youth and by exten-sion adulthood. Where youth is characterised as a period without responsibil-ity and as a time for experimentation and the development of self, adulthood is understood to be what results once that experimentation and self-work has been carried out and responsibility takes hold. While not all young people may see youth and adulthood in this way, such discourses are undoubtedly significant when it comes to understanding youth, identity and belonging.

Though tourism is the domain from which I have approached the study of youth, not all young people have, of course, the opportunity or inclination to engage in travel. It is not everywhere a positively sanctioned leisure activity, and it can require significant amounts of both time and money. Nonetheless, I would argue that many young people (travellers and non-travellers; Australian and otherwise) are actively involved in deciding for themselves (or at least pondering) the sort of life experience they wish to accumulate and who it is that they wish to become. In such cases, young people develop, reflect upon and refine their identities through their social networks and their leisure, education, work and/or consumption choices. In youth, these choices are often being made independently, for the very first time. It is these choices then, the contexts in which they are made and the meanings that they are given, that are of central concern to youth studies. Drawing on this multi-disciplinary field, this chapter will examine what youth is and how identity and belonging are experienced by young people. More specifically, the chapter will examine age, transition and generation-based definitions of youth and how they influence our understanding of young people and their identification practices. As many of these practices are not undertaken in iso-lation, the chapter will also explore youth cultures, providing as it does so an overview of the history of youth cultures research and of the ways in which youth cultural practices (and researchers' assessments of them) have changed over time, thanks in large part to globalisation.

Defining youth on the basis of age-based transitions

As this book demonstrates, identity and belonging are issues central to our individual *and* social lives. These topics have long been a concern in the social sciences, and researchers have repeatedly focused on how different aspects of peoples' lives – their gender, sexuality, religion, ethnicity, social class, work, families and neighbourhoods, for instance – influence who they are and who they strive to be. Another key aspect of our lives that is often deemed to have a significant impact on our experiences of identity and belonging is age. At the heart of much youth studies research is an assumption that age or, per-haps more aptly, life stage has significant bearing on how we see ourselves, the opportunities available to us, how others see us and how we interact with social institutions. So what then is understood by the term 'youth' and who do we define as being 'young'?

According to the Australian Bureau of Statistics (ABS), 'youth' can be defined as 'the transitional phase between childhood and adulthood' and as pertaining to individuals falling 'between the ages of 15 and 24 inclusive' (ABS, 2007). This designated age range is based upon that used by the United Nations General Assembly, which was first introduced during International Youth Year in 1985 (ABS, 2012). On the other hand, according to Allison (1999) and the Australian Clearinghouse for Youth Studies, the World Health Organisation and the Australian Medical Association adopt the age range of 10–24 when referring to youth, demonstrating in the process the increasingly blurred boundaries between childhood and youth. Opening up the scale at the other end, in the late 1990s, the Southern African Zonal Youth Forum, in recognition of the impact of extended schooling on the lives of young people, extended their 18–26 youth age range to 18–30 years (Allison, 1999). More generous still (and favourable to this thirty-something author!) is the Federated States of Micronesia's definition of youth as a period of life between the ages of '6 and 35' (Allison, 1999). What becomes clear from this brief examination of youth as an age, or range of ages, is how variable such definitions are. What are less variable are the meanings that are associated (at least in Western societies) with being in the life stage between childhood and adulthood and the reasons (academic and empirical) for treating this as a separate category of life.

As argued by Rob White (1999, p. 1), 'age has a major bearing on where young people fit within the broad range of social institutions … Furthermore, how the young are faring in relation to these institutions also has a major influence on perceptions of the health and wellbeing of the society as a whole'. It is for these reasons that issues like teenage pregnancy, youth suicide, juvenile crime and the so-called generation gap are common causes for concern, if not moral panic. As youth are understood as being the next generation of adults, or as 'the future', they (as individuals and as a group possessed of unique identification and cultural practices) come to be seen as important social markers – of who we are as a society and where we are heading.

The socio-cultural or, more accurately, socio-temporal positioning of youth impacts the way in which they are perceived and understood. It also influences the power they are deemed to wield. On the one hand, as noted above, young people are often designated as harbingers of what is yet to come. On the other, they typically have limited influence over the present, which has ostensibly been created by those who came before them. It is not surprising then that many young people feel they are subject to the social, economic and political influences of adults (Harris et al., 2007). Indeed, youth is frequently understood not just in terms of age, but in terms of transition, and young people are commonly defined as much by what they are not – not a child, yet not quite a fully-fledged adult – as what they are. It is not surprising then that for some thinkers, this is a period of not only transition but also tension or conflict.

Certainly, this is one of the key ideas that has been maintained since Erikson proposed in the 1950s that personal identity – or one's sense of who one is – develops during adolescence. It was Erikson (1994) who established the oft-quoted idea of an 'identity crisis', arguing that this was a key characteristic of the shift from childhood to adulthood. By his argument, it was only through this conflict and the turmoil associated with adolescence that individuals could and would seek out, test and establish their adult identity. Certainly, adolescence (and youth more broadly) is a significant time for identity construction, and there is much research to indicate that during this time it is young people's engagements (and sometimes conflicts) with various socialisation agents, as well as involvements in risk-taking behaviour, which contribute to this process. However, the idea of there being one true or singular identity that results from this process is not, under late or liquid modernity, as convincing as once it was. Further, some authors have argued that because so much social change has occurred in recent decades that it is more useful to talk about youth in terms of generation than as transition.

Understanding youth in generational terms

According to Wyn and Woodman (2006) one of the key issues with the transitional model of development is that it is frequently attached to psycho-social and biological perspectives, meaning that young peoples' movements to adulthood are measured against standardised goals or benchmarks. As a result, ideas about appropriate (and inappropriate) modes or rates of transition develop, with the effect that 'young people's own views become less valid than adult-centred measures of young people' (Wyn and Woodman, 2006, p. 498). This is especially problematic, they argue, when those adult-centred measures are based on linear constructions of youth and adulthood, which correspond primarily with the experiences of the 'baby boomer' generation.

In a context where extended periods of study, increased costs of home ownership and changes in interpersonal relationships mean that youth is becoming more prolonged, and where engagements with youth cultures may be extended (Nilan and Feixa, 2006a), it is argued that the baby boomers' experiences of youth are no longer strictly relevant, nor in fact available to young people today. Suggesting that such pathways to adulthood are, in fact, 'historical artefact', Wyn and Woodman (2006, p. 498) argue for a generational approach to youth, which takes into account the social and cultural context in which young people are transitioning to adulthood. They contend that 'generation' provides an opportunity to examine the historical and social ties that bind different cohorts of young people together and craft for many of them a shared consciousness or sense of unity. Which is not to suggest that they are all *one and the same*, but that they 'belong to a common period of history' or that their 'lives are forged through the same conditions' (Wyn and Woodman, 2006, p. 496) and social forces.

One such force that has been presented as having significant influence on young people today, those who we might characterise as Generation Y (born in the 1980s and 1990s), is the rapid development of technology, particularly in the fields of computing and communication. According to those who maintain that young people today are the most familiar with and adept at information and communication technology, they have become, because of the time in which they were born, a 'Net generation' or 'Digital generation' (Prensky, 2001). Certainly, such formulations take into account the increasingly networked society in which we live (for further discussion, see Castells, 1996). However, I would argue that in focusing on *one* aspect of the social context in which young people are positioned, such explanations can have the effect of limiting, rather than expanding, our understanding of youth today.

Case study 1: the digital generation and a (so-called) digital divide

Over the last 10–15 years there have emerged a number of claims highlighting young people's technological savviness and, at the same time, the apparent lack of technological literacy amongst older people. Marc Prensky (2001) has famously argued that there exists today a 'net' generation or generation of 'digital natives' and that education needs to adapt in order to better cater for this new generation of students. According to Bennett et al. (2008, p. 776), the term 'digital natives' was used by Prensky (2001) to describe 'the generation born roughly between 1980 and 1994' who have grown up with a 'familiarity with and reliance on ICT [information and communication technologies]'. Also referred to as the 'net generation', 'generation Y' and 'the millenials' (Kennedy et al., 2008), this group of young people is apparently distinguished from earlier generations (termed 'digital immigrants') on the basis of their desires for, and skills with, technology.

Personally, as a member of this digital or net generation, who also happens to be a university lecturer, I find Prensky's assumptions about digital nativism and a digital generational divide particularly interesting. I can't help but wonder if I am an imposter amongst my millennial counterparts (possessing neither an iPhone or an X-box) because of the fact that I exist on the cusp of generations X and Y or because I have been teaching in tertiary institutions now for some 10 years and have thus been influenced by my 'digital immigrant' colleagues. I am also unsure how to explain my older brother's ability to work as an IT consultant, my father's infatuation with computers and my grandparents' (who are well into their eighties) use of email. Further, I cannot explain – based on Prensky's (2001) model – why many of my younger students struggle with using online learning technologies and information databases. What I find more troubling still though is the fact that Prensky (2001) fails to take into account an even bigger digital divide that exists today, not between generations but between different social classes, neighbourhoods and, in fact, nations.

Holderness (2006, p. 251) notes that there is a 'general and serious tendency [of researchers] to overlook the needs of *digitally disadvantaged* children and young learners living in lesser developed countries' arguing that there is a stark contrast 'between First and Third World countries with regard to technology access and utilization' (a point also made in Chapter 14 of this volume). Of course, the issue of Internet accessibility is not restricted solely to divisions between developing and developed countries. It also arises in the 'developed' world, most commonly, as a correlate of social class and/or differences in geographic distribution and educational levels of the broader population (for an early discussion of these gaps, see Lash, 1994; Castells, 1996). Further, even where access to ICT is not an issue, a number of studies have emerged showing that there is significant diversity among young people in their use of technology and that young people do not necessarily engage with *all* technologies equally (Kennedy et al., 2007, 2008). Thus, while Prensky's (2001) arguments (and others like them) can be read, on the one hand, as a generational account of young people's lives, needs and desires, it seems that by only taking one aspect of their experience or historical and social circumstances into account (technology), and assuming that it is experienced in the same way by all young people, what emerges is a caricature of youth and an over-exaggerated distinction between generations.

While generational approaches have merit then, we must be careful that they are crafted in a nuanced fashion – taking into account the *multiple* priorities and subjectivities of young people and considering them alongside the *multiple* priorities and subjectivities of those who come before and after them. After all, as Wyn and Woodman (2006) point out, terms like 'baby boomers', 'Generation X' and 'Generation Y' are not exact. But it is not the years of birth, or the ages, attributed to members of each generation that are as important as the social forces that they have experienced. These shared social forces are what mark these groups of people or, more rightly, their lives as being distinct in some way – as being different from the lives and social worlds of their parents or their children (Furlong et al., 2011). However, even within generations, those social forces will be experienced differently (Furlong et al., 2011), depending for instance on factors like nationality, social class, ethnicity and the country and neighbourhood in which one resides.

Irrespective then of the definition of youth that we adopt – whether we see youth as referring to a particular age, generation or transitional life stage – what I am especially concerned with in this chapter, focused as it is on identity and belonging, is the way in which youth operates as a distinct period of meaning, making and identification. For this is something, it seems, that most if not all young people encounter - a need, as White and Wyn (2004, p. 186) put it, 'to do the work of making meaning of life and ... of answering the question "Who am I?" in this life'. The remainder of this chapter will examine how different young people have done and are doing this against a variety of local and global backdrops and how academics have approached the study of the cultural practices and performances that have resulted.

Youth subcultures and the emergence of youth studies

Some of the earliest studies of young people and their social and cultural practices have been tied to urban ethnographies carried out in the first half of the twentieth century by researchers at the University of Chicago in the United States of America. Though these studies were not always youth specific, many of them, like Cressey's (2008) *The Taxi Dance Hall* (first published in 1932), involved examining cultural practices that were seen as existing outside of the norm (or outside of 'decent' society). In the case of *The Taxi Dance Hall*, the music, dance and alcohol consumption, and 'promiscuous' behaviours of marginalised men and women, many of whom were *young* men and women, were the focus. Much of the urban sociology that was carried out at this time, and that is associated with the 'Chicago School', involved studying the urban poor, their lifestyles, communities and cultural practices. These practices were seen as a threat to mainstream society and values and, as they either involved or had the potential to involve (and 'corrupt') young people, they were subject to scrutiny. Due to this focus, though the Chicago School is often associated with the beginnings of subcultural research, it and the more criminological strains of youth subcultural studies that it inspired have since been critiqued for positioning young people as a problem to be solved (for further discussion see Williams, 2007).

Marking a departure from the Chicago School's apparent problematising of youth was the Centre for Contemporary Cultural Studies (CCCS) at the University of Birmingham in the United Kingdom (also discussed in Chapter 3).

Frequently regarded as marking the next major development in youth subcultural studies (for more on this history, see Williams, 2007) and more broadly as having made significant contributions to British cultural studies, academics from the 'Birmingham School' argued that there was a need to avoid making assumptions about the deviance of youth and to instead examine the structures or social forces that produced subcultures (see for example, Clarke et al., 1993).

Taking the emphasis away from the supposed deviance of youth subcultures, researchers at the CCCS instead drew attention to the way in which young peoples' cultural practices could be explained with reference to social class and consumption. This was in part the result of an overarching concern with explaining social phenomenon with respect to social and cultural (including symbolic) structures (Hall and Jefferson, 2006). It is also an historical artefact, in that while youth cultures were not new in the 1950s and 1960s, they had taken on new characteristics as a result of increased youth employment and subsequent affluence and consumerism after the Second World War (see Roberts, 2013). According to Clarke et al. (1993) it was the increased affluence, consumerism and consumption, as well as increased optimism witnessed after the Second World War (also discussed in Chapter 13), which contributed to the development of a specific youth consumer market. On top of this the development of mass media and popular culture, the increase in post-secondary education and opportunity for choice or decision making aided the development of a more attenuated gap between childhood and adulthood, a youth culture to fill this gap and subsequently youth subcultures (for further discussion of this history see Roberts, 2013).

Like cultures, subcultures consist of shared interests and meanings, shared rituals, styles, modes of behaviour and language. They are designated as 'sub' cultures though because they emerge within, or in reaction to, the confines and constraints of a dominant culture (what we might refer to as mainstream culture) or a broader cultural grouping such as that envisioned as occurring at the level of class, ethnicity or nationality. In short, subcultures can be understood then as cultures within cultures. According to Clarke et al. (1993, p. 47), as members of subcultures young people:

> explore 'focal concerns' central to the inner life of the group: things always 'done' or 'never done', [and engage in] a set of social rituals which underpin their collective identity and define them as a 'group' instead of a mere collection of individuals.

Furthermore, they demonstrate that they belong to this group through the 'adopt [ion] and adapt[ation of] material objects – goods and possessions', which they 'reorganise ... into distinctive "styles"' (Clarke et. al., 1993, p. 47).

Style, comprised of things like dress, appearance, music and comportment (the way one behaves, walks and talks), was deemed to define different subcultures (Hebdige, 1979; Clarke et al., 1993), having an impact on individual and group identities. The idea was that each subculture had a unique style and that those different styles held specific symbolic meanings for their members. Studying punks, ska and Rasta subcultures, 'Teddy Boys', mods and rockers, the drug cultures of the 1960s and 1970s and the hippie countercultural movement, CCCS researchers (see for example, Hebdige, 1979; Hall and Jefferson, 1993) saw in each, different behaviours, different consumption patterns and importantly different forms of resistance.

One of the key aspects of the CCCS approach was to see the cultural practices of subcultural groups as acts of creative resistance to the constraints of hegemony. They argued that:

Members of a sub-culture may walk, talk, act, look 'different' from their parents and from some of their peers, but they belong to the same families, go to the same schools, work at much the same jobs, live down the same 'mean' streets as their peers and parents. In certain crucial respects they share the same position ... [However] Through dress, activities, leisure pursuits and life-style, they may project a different cultural response or 'solution' to the problems posed for them by their material and social class position and experience. (Clarke et al., 1993, pp. 14–15)

In other words, young peoples' subcultural practices were viewed as emerging from the cultural and social milieu of their parents, in response to dominant (or hegemonic) culture and, the shape they took was understood therefore, as being influenced by social class. For Clarke et al. (1993, p. 53) it is (or was) 'at the intersection between the located parent culture and the mediating institutions of the dominant culture that youth sub-cultures arise'. Thus, subcultures were often seen as a means by which young people could create cultural and social alternatives for themselves: new systems of meaning, alternative beliefs or ideologies, new forms of cultural capital, lifestyles and, importantly, social and geographic spaces. Youth subcultures were seen as possessing a radical potential for transformation or social change, and that radical potential was embodied in style.

Case study 2: punk and the significance of style

In the classic text *Subculture: Signification through Style*, Dick Hebdige (1979, p. 101) argued that subcultural styles were employed as a form of 'intentional communication', used by members of subcultures to signify both distinction from mainstream society and belonging to the subcultural group. One of the key aspects of Hebdige's (1979) argument was that these stylistic representations or ensembles were created through bricolage, meaning that different items and objects, as well as stylistic practices were juxtaposed, layered upon one another and melded together, in such a way as to create new, often subversive, meanings. Of interest to Hebdige (and other youth subcultures theorists) was the way in which various groups appropriated consumer goods for their own purposes. Consumption then became an act of power, an act of resistance and a conscious means of crafting a specific identity and signifying group belonging.

This was most notable in punk where objects not typically valued (everyday objects, even disposable 'rubbish' items) were converted into clothing and items of adornment; challenging and subverting common ideas about taste, fashion, consumption and even gender. As Hebdige (1979, pp. 106–107) notes:

> punk style was defined principally through the violence of its 'cut ups'... the most unremarkable and inappropriate items – a pin, a plastic clothes peg, a television component, a razor blade, a tampon – could be brought within the province of punk (un)fashion. Anything within or without reason could be turned into part of what Vivien Westwood called 'confrontation dressing'... [offering] self-conscious commentaries on the notions of modernity and taste.

At the same time, 'taste-defying' music and accompanying styles of dance were also produced and performed, challenging various social and cultural norms. Situating themselves firmly outside of mainstream genres like rock and pop, punk artists purposefully celebrated their non-commercial or amateur status and embraced shocking names, lyrics, album titles and album covers (Hebdige, 1979). DIY (do-it-yourself) was a dominant theme in punk culture, one that continues to wield influence today. As Muñoz and Marín (2006, p. 132) observe:

> In the history of punk, the 'do it yourself' slogan, to which is added; 'anyone can', was a response to the dominant belief that the act of musical creation required lots of money, education, influence and luck to distribute one's own creations through established corporate mechanisms ... the DIY spirit inspired many young second-generation British punks to go against the commercialization of their culture ... [and] DIY has remained in punk culture... as a reminder of the fact that individual thinking does not seek the acquiescence of others to exist.

We see in punk then, as with other subcultures, a careful crafting of identity. Interestingly though, at the same time, we also witness an ethos of *individualised* belonging.

Moving beyond subcultures: youth identities as hybridised, fluid and globalised

While work produced by the subcultures researchers belonging to the Birmingham School is considered ground-breaking, as the youth cultural landscape began to change, becoming more fluid and individualised, arguments about distinct, discrete subcultures came into question. Subsequently in the 1990s and early 2000s, a number of alternative (post-subcultural) concepts and frameworks, like 'neo-tribe', 'lifestyle' and 'scene', were introduced (for more on this history, see Hall and Jefferson, 2006; Williams, 2007; Bennett, 2011). According to Bennett (2011, p. 495), who was one of the key proponents of the idea that we had entered a post-subcultural landscape (see for example, Bennett and Kahn-Harris, 2004), these new frameworks were devised in response to an increased 'proliferation of youth styles' (brought about by the global circulation of cultural products), a 'pick and mix approach' to those styles and an increased focus on individualism and associated fragmentation of youth subcultural practices.

As Roberts (2013, p. 338) observes, in such a context, 'rather than groups predefined by locality, and/or social class acquiring distinctive tastes, the tastes have created their own scenes and crowds composed of young people from diverse backgrounds'. Subsequently, concepts like 'scene' were devised to accommodate young people from diverse backgrounds coming together (whether virtually or in 'real life') over a shared interest. Employed initially with reference to music-based affiliations, the scene, like neo-tribe, captured looser forms of collectivity and sociality and identified youth groups with more fluid membership and permeable boundaries. Indeed, it was easily envisioned within the scene model that individuals might move between different groups, belong to more than one scene at the same time and perhaps only engage in scene membership at specific times of the week or year (such as, in the case of club or rave culture, the weekend). Ultimately, what these models emerged in response to then was an increased focus on 'individual subjectivities' (White and Wyn, 2004, p. 189) in late modernity.

Related to this increased focus on individuality, one of the other key criticisms of the CCCS was for sensationalising youth by only focusing on spectacular group identities or the spectacular *elements* of a subculture in their analysis (for an overview of this critique, see Hall and Jefferson, 2006; Williams, 2007). Interestingly though, the CCCS acknowledged this propensity themselves, noting in *Resistance through Ritual* that they were focusing on very specific aspects of youth culture, 'those sections of working-class or middle-class youth where a response to their situation took a distinctive sub-cultural form' (Clarke et al., 1993, p. 16). Indeed they were at pains to make clear that:

> The great majority of working-class youth never enters a tight or coherent sub-culture at all. Individuals may, in their personal life-careers, move into and out of one, or indeed several, such sub-cultures. Their relation to the existing sub-cultures may be fleeting or permanent, marginal or central. The sub-cultures are important because there the response of youth takes a peculiarly tangible form. But, in the post-war history of the class, these may be less significant than what most young people do most of the time. (Clarke et al., 1993, p. 16)

Such sentiments have been echoed more recently. White (1999, p. 2) has noted for instance that while all young people may be involved in cultural practices and performances, 'not all youth activity can be captured by the phrase "youth subcultures", nor are all young people engaged in what traditionally could be seen as subcultural activity'. In fact, he argues that 'most young people more often than not tend to identify with fairly conventional attitudes, aspirations and behaviours' (White, 1999, p. 2). It is an argument that is supported by Roberts's (2013, p. 336) historical approach to youth subcultures and leisure practices, in which he contends that 'most students in the 1960s never took part in a sit-in or demonstration ... just as most early school-leavers did not become Teds, skinheads, mods or rockers'. Additionally, others have also pointed out that even where spectacular subcultures still exist, it must be recognised that their spectacular elements may have distinct meanings to the group, but that overall they are informed by very similar concerns. As Hodkinson (2012, p. 569) points out:

> Comparisons of non-content-specific aspects of goths, metallers, punks, clubbers, skaters and others are liable to reveal marked similarities with respect to the values and group ideologies espoused by participants and their practices of identification and distinction. Discursive espousals, for example, of distinctiveness, creativity, authenticity, self-expression and open-mindedness, alongside disavowals of a perceived trend-following, undiscerning and commercialised dominant culture, have been reported and deconstructed by a host of studies of different groups in different times and spaces.

So where does this leave us then in trying to understand young people, their individual and group identities? What these critiques of youth subcultures theory and new developments point to is that though there remains an understandable focus on some of the more spectacular elements or lifestyle practises of young people (with research on, for instance, punk, goth, rave, skate, metal and surf culture), there is a need to continue tying those practices to their structural specificities, a point that members of the CCCS made, incidentally, quite strongly (see for example, Clarke et al., 1993; Hall and Jefferson, 2006). There is also a need to provide accounts that partner ethnography and insider perspectives with textual, outsider readings so as to avoid, as Hodkinson (2012, p. 568) argues, 'reducing the underlying significance of youth cultural groups to the looks, sounds, texts and practices which make them most obviously, unique or extra-ordinary'. Such holistic approaches are more likely to result in nuanced understandings of youth cultures – understandings, which can better accommodate internal inconsistencies and contradictions within youth cultural practices and ideologies (see for example, Brill, 2007), as well as more fluid and globalised identification practices and group dynamics.

With this in mind, a body of work (see for example, Nilan and Feixa, 2006b) has begun to emerge examining how young people are responding to the pressures of globalisation and ever-increasing individualism and the way in which youth cultures and identities are negotiated in the local/global nexus. This work argues that, rather than youth cultures simply being spread across the globe in a homogenous fashion, they are adopted, adapted and 'negotiated' (Butcher and Thomas, 2006) in local contexts, resulting in more creative and complex outcomes, hybridised identities and cultural practices.

Case study 3: youth cultures – local and global

In their analysis of the influence of music subcultures (particularly punk and hip-hop) in Colombia, Muñoz and Marín (2006) acknowledge that while marketing and global media may have an influence on the spread of youth cultures across the globe, this should not be assumed to equate to the importation of subcultures from elsewhere and the subsequent loss or homogenising of local youth culture. They argue that such concerns are informed, in part, by the erroneous notion that youth cultures are themselves singular and discrete, when in fact they are by their nature experimental, and therefore heterogeneous, open and evolving systems. Thus in Colombia, they note that the adoption of punk in the late 1980s was one means by which young people could voice their concerns about prominent local social and political issues – namely, the violence, corruption, poverty and loss associated with the cocaine trade. Hip-hop, skinhead and rap cultures were also used not just to give expression to young peoples' concerns about local issues, but also as a means of disseminating information, which could counteract the stereotypes and singular, dominant, views propagated in (according to the authors) a corrupt mainstream media. In a similar fashion, Feixa (2006), through a cross-cultural comparison of punk in Mexico and punk in Spain, demonstrates that youth subcultures are influenced by and interpreted according to local needs, as well as local customs, cultures and histories. To this end he writes:

> although youth cultures always emerge from a distinctive national and socio-cultural economic context, there exist multiple means of transnational communication, so youth from far distant places come to identify themselves with similar styles. However, rather than signalling imitation and conformity, attachment to these styles is mainly symbolic – the deep meanings encode local tensions and resistances. (Feixa, 2006, p. 164)

Conclusion

Commencing with examples of the way in which young Australian travellers – members of the global backpacking culture or 'scene' – are engaged in a purposeful and highly reflexive construction of self (tying their youth identities to the accumulation of experience, the deferral of responsibility and non-adulthood), this chapter has examined how youth is commonly understood in contemporary society – by young people themselves and by academics. More specifically, it has provided an overview of some of the key debates that emerge in youth studies today – debates about what youth is, as well as how young peoples' cultural practices and identities should be approached. While many of these arguments continue, what is clear is that young peoples' identities and experiences of belonging play out in very specific ways. They may be influenced by age and life stage or the generation that they belong to. However, they are not the result of age, life stage or generation alone. Rather, the choices that young people make, the identities they construct for themselves, the cultural practices that they engage in and the groups that they belong to, are also influenced by factors such as social class, ethnicity, gender, sexuality, education, religion, their neighbourhoods, leisure practices, media consumption, families and peer networks. Subsequently, it is no surprise that young peoples' identities (whether collective or individual) are incredibly diverse. Thus, age is not the sole influence when it comes to young peoples' identities or experiences of belonging; rather, youth identities are formed and experienced in ways both related to and separate from age, which play out on both local and global stages.

Questions for students

- How important is age or life stage to your own identity? Do you think you are a different person now from what you were when you were younger? Do you anticipate that you will be a different person when you are older? Why/why not?

- How convinced are you by Prensky's (2001) argument about digital generations? Considering other discussions of media use in this volume (see for example, Chapter 14) do you think that there is a digital generational divide? Why/why not?
- Have you been or are you a member of a youth subculture? If so, can you define members of that group according to a distinct style or is it something else that unites these individuals?
- It is argued in this chapter that youth identities today are increasingly constructed as hybrid identities – melding together different local and global influences and formed in conjunction with intersecting aspects of everyday life (like gender, ethnicity and social class). What influences shape your own identities and are they local or global?

Recommended reading

Bennett, A. (2011) 'The Post-Subcultural Turn: Some Reflections 10 Years On', *Journal of Youth Studies*, 14(5): 493–506.

Hall, S. and Jefferson, T. (eds.) (2006) *Resistance through Rituals: Youth Subcultures in Post-War Britain* (Second Edition) (London: Routledge).

Hodkinson, P. and Deicke, W. (eds.) (2007) *Youth Cultures: Scenes, Subcultures and Tribes* (New York: Routledge).

Nilan, P. and Feixa, C. (eds.) (2006) *Global Youth?: Hybrid Identities, Plural Worlds* (New York: Routledge).

CHAPTER 7

Households and neighbourhoods

Emma Power

Introduction

This chapter explores two very familiar sites, households and neighbourhoods, and discusses the importance of these sites for senses of identity and belonging. The chapter will show that there is a two-way relationship between identity and household/neighbourhood: while social identities impact on the ways that people experience households and neighbourhoods, the experiences that people have within their households and neighbourhoods also impact upon their sense of identity and belonging. These ideas will be explored through case studies that examine the ways that people 'make homes' and interact within neighbourhoods. Importantly, households and neighbourhoods will be explored both as places and sets of practices, that is, the practices of homemaking (through which home is created and maintained) and neighbouring (the interactions between people who are neighbours and through which neighbourhoods are constituted). Through this focus on practice we can start to ask how houses are made into homes and how neighbouring relations shape the nature of different neighbourhood spaces. The chapter also reflects on the ways that global cultures, processes and relations are impacting on the sites and practices of home and neighbouring, starting at the home before expanding in scale to consider the space of the neighbourhood.

Home

Home is a place that has both material and imaginative dimensions; it is both a physical place and a space that is associated with feelings of comfort, security and belonging. Places do not simply exist as homes. Rather, 'home' is made through homemaking practices that transform places (such as houses) into homes. Homemaking practices involve relations of belonging and exclusion that actively separate home from undesirable and 'unhomey' spaces and connect it to desirable and 'homey' spaces, objects and ideas. This is an ongoing, relational process where, as Blunt and Dowling (2006, p. 22) remind us, 'the material form of home is dependent on what home is imagined to be, and imaginaries of home are influenced by the physical forms of dwelling'. In other words, what we think of as being 'homey' impacts upon the ways that we make home as well as the places that we make and imagine as home.

There is a strong connection between home and identity. Our social identities can affect our sense of home and impact the ways that we make home. Further, what we consider to be 'homey' is shaped by our culture and our social location. Likewise, identity is shaped by home: the experiences that we have at home and the ways that we make home are connected to the performance of different social identities. For example, in Western cultures an historical understanding of women as homemakers connects women's social identities and everyday practices to the home and the tasks of homemaking and childrearing (this is explored further in Chapter 11).

Locating home

While the domestic house or household is the site most commonly associated with home, home can also be made and experienced in diverse places such as parks, favourite holiday spots, pubs, bars and so on. For some gay men and lesbians commercial places like bars that welcome gay and lesbian patrons can be an important home space, affording a sense of belonging that is not available within other public spaces or, sometimes, the family home (Holt and Griffin, 2003). For people who are homeless, home can exist in particular public spaces or multiple spaces across cities. May (2000), for example, shows that for some people who do not have fixed housing, home can instead be connected to a familiar place or town. For these people, the experience of homelessness is not simply about the lack of fixed housing, but also the feeling of estrangement and of no longer fitting within places that have been 'home'. Similarly, Hodgetts et al. (2008) show that for some homeless people public libraries come to be experienced and used as home-like spaces. For men in their research, borrowed books were important 'personal anchorage points that foster[ed] a sense of connection and belonging' and, sometimes, an overt connection to a previous homeland or network of relations (Hodgetts et al., 2008, p. 946). Phil, a Maori homeless man who was interviewed in the research, used a book about his *iwi* (tribe) this way, using it to narrate a story of himself that emphasised a connection to his homeland and family. The library and this particular book became core to Phil's sense of belonging in the world and through locating Phil in a homeland and family context also helped him to reassert his identity as a Maori. On the other hand, while attachment to home can afford a sense of belonging, the loss of home and experience of homelessness can give people a sense of being lost, as explored in Case Study 1.

Case Study 1: homelessness

In her 2011 book, *Beside One's Self: Homelessness Felt and Lived*, Catherine Robinson explores the connection between home and senses of self and security amongst young homeless people in Sydney and Brisbane. She argues that homelessness, being without place, has deep implications for young people's sense of self and well-being. Describing this connection between home and self in scholarly terms Robinson explains:

> Not only do homeless people experience traumatic places but they experience the trauma of being without places of 'sanctuary'. Places of memorial and habitual connection, places that open a sense of safety and familiarity such that the self can be at once reinforced and forgotten, are vanquished. It is the struggle for home and for place, the tiring transience of 'the experience of being unplaced', [...] which remains always central to homelessness felt and lived. (2011, p. 79)

For many young people in Robinson's research homelessness was characterised by mobility, both the movement away from a family home and movement through 'countless street-living sites and temporary forms of accommodation, through suburbs, cities, and across state borders' (p. 80). Although typically motivated by particular tasks or needs this constant movement gave rise to feelings of dislocation and isolation.

Robinson's participants described their efforts to identify places of shelter and security within which to pass time. Ben, for example, described his preferred sleeping place: 'On the trains ... usually the 12.09 a.m. Lithgow, 'cause it leaves at 12.09 a.m. and gets back into Central at 6 a.m. I used to get the 1.30 a.m. to Springwood'. These long-distance trains offered Ben a place to be and to pass time. However, the transience of the space also challenged Ben's ability to settle and 'become at home in place' (Robinson, 2011, p. 93).

Some young people also found and created spaces of stability that they could return to and in which they felt a sense of belonging and connection. Paul, for instance, described a couch that he and his friends had set up in an isolated location that he regularly visited to spend time with old friends who were not homeless. Although not allowed to return to his family home, he was able to spend time in this familiar location and there experienced a sense of being at home. The experiences of these young homeless people highlight the powerful connections between home and identity. For these individuals home was much more than a shelter; it was a place of memory, belonging and self. As such the loss of home was associated with a deeper loss of self and belonging. These connections point to challenges for home-lessness policy makers and service providers about how senses of self and belonging can be fostered even as people inhabit transient spaces.

In addition to being found in diverse places, home is also multi-scalar. It can be made at many different scales from the house to the neighbourhood or local community, the region, the state and even the nation. It is also made through relations that are multi-scalar. For example, images and objects that represent distant homelands can be used to create a sense of connection, belonging and home, just as Phil's library book connected him to his traditional homelands. At its many sites and scales home is not just the material site, it is also a feeling. In Western cultures, we often talk of feeling 'at home', of the comfort, security and belonging, associated with a space. On a personal level this feeling might be experienced when returning 'home', for example, when arriving in a particular house or neighbourhood after time away or coming through the border security zone when returning from an overseas trip. As Hetherington (2003) reminds us, 'home' is an active and embodied experience. At the scale of the house it is a feeling that is found when we slip our feet into our familiar slippers or turn the key in the lock of our front door. It is in the feelings of connection, belonging and security that we experience in our home places.

Making the house-as-home: everyday practices of homemaking

The place most commonly associated with home is the domestic house. Through homemaking practices residents transform houses into homes. At the most simple level, people fill their houses with items that make the space feel like home. These can be objects such as furniture or colours and textures that are appealing. These choices are often culturally specific, with different cultural groups preferring different furnishings and colours. They are also often influenced by fashion. For participants in McCracken's (1989) North American study, particular colours (orange, gold, green and brown), building materials (wood, stone, brick) and fabric types (unfinished natural fibres) and objects with a personal significance were experienced as homey. These very specific aesthetic and textural choices worked together to make the house feel comfortable and welcoming to its residents and visitors. The diversity of these practices and choices means that what feels like home to some people may not feel like home to others. For example, for some people openness and lightness coupled with sparse, tidy displays of household objects is essential to the feeling of home (Dowling and Power, 2012), while for others an overt sense of cosiness through limited lighting, or what others might perceive as 'clutter', is preferred.

Home, belonging and identity

The act of making home is a process of identity construction and performance. Through the process of homemaking, including choosing objects and furnishings for the home, people project and perform their sense of belonging to particular groups, including ethnic or cultural groups and even, at a smaller scale, of being part of a family. Choices of objects are also a way that people can perform a sense of self, choosing furnishings, colours and textures that represent their interests and how they feel or would like to be seen. Noble (2004) describes this as a process of 'accumulating being'. This is a dynamic process where a sense of self is accumulated over time through objects that are collected and retained across the lifespan. Significant objects can narrate a sense of who people feel that they are at a particular point in time, or a sense of where they have come from, of their life story. These objects do not simply tell a linear life story but rather when retained together tell a story about the life stages that individuals have gone through and the experiences and senses of self that have accrued over time through these experiences.

The use of objects that have a personal significance or connection is an example of 'accumulating being' through homemaking. These types of objects are often highly valued and an important part of what makes a house feel like a home, as reflected in McCracken's (1989) research, discussed above. Objects that are connected to family and friends can play a particularly important role in creating a sense of home and belonging. This reflects the dominant association between ideal 'homey' homes, families and children in contemporary Western understandings of home (Blunt and Dowling, 2006). Important objects can include items such as furniture that is inherited from the family home or gifted by family members and friends. They can also include photographs of familiar people such as family members, or depict friends and special occasions. When displayed in the home these types of objects and images work to remind residents of significant people and events and therefore create a sense of belonging and connection to broader networks of relationships beyond the home. Participants in Noble's (2004) research emphasised objects that narrated this type of connection. For example, Cathy and Nick identified a cabinet of objects that held particular significance to them. Containing objects received from their daughter for Cathy's birthday and Christmas, a wedding present, Cathy's mother's 21st birthday present, gifts that they had given each other over time and even a gift from a previous employer it was 'a microcosm of their familial and interpersonal world' (Noble, 2004, p. 240). Photographs were also important to many participants. Dagmar spoke about his family photos, saying 'they're your history really', while Jack described them as 'a record of your growing up and your family' (Noble, 2004, p. 241).

Homemaking choices are made in relation to others that inhabit the house. They are therefore often much more than simply an individual choice. For couples in cohabiting households the process of combining possessions and sharing decisions about the design and decoration of the house is an important way that houses are made into shared homes and that couple identities are established (Gorman-Murray, 2006, see also Clarke, 2002). Gay men interviewed by Gorman-Murray (2006) described this process. Stephen, for example, explained that home is 'a place that is part of the physical embodiment of my relationship with my partner. A place we share and shape together'. Stephen and his partner moved 'somewhere new for both of us' when they moved in together, 'as part of creating a new, shared life together'. Other couples described how they combined possessions, or bought new domestic items together, as a way of establishing their identity as a partnership. As Noble (2004, p. 241) suggests, these objects are significant in 'providing evidence of genealogical links, both across time and space'. In locating people within a network of relations such objects work to establish a sense of identity and belonging that is central to the sense of home.

In an increasingly global and mobile world where people travel for work, for holidays and also to live internationally, objects in the house-as-home can provide a sense of connection to distant people and homelands. Participants in Rose's (2003) research explained that displayed photos of distant family members helped them to feel more connected and close to these important people, locating the home within a broader set of familial relationships. Material objects and images can also connect people to distant places. For example, when people have moved home, including to another country, objects, furnishings and images associated with previous homelands can help to maintain a connection to the previous home and at the same time help establish a sense of belonging in the new home (Noble, 2004; Tolia-Kelly, 2004). For Sheetal, a participant in Tolia-Kelly's (2004) research, a photograph of a rock formation in the area that she grew up provides a powerful reminder and connection to her former home in Tanzania. Looking at the photo, which is displayed in her home, connects Sheetal to significant events that took place at the rocks when she was growing up and helps her to 'inhabit' that place through her memories of it.

The exterior appearance of housing can also connect immigrants to their homeland. For some, carefully chosen and familiar garden plants evoke memories and recreate the types of landscapes seen 'at home' (Brook, 2003). Greek migrants from Sydney's Marrickville who participated in Graham and Connell's (2006) research valued Greek plants which they grew for medical purposes and grew familiar vegetables to maintain cultural food traditions. Housing can also be altered to reflect a familiar and more culturally 'homely' aesthetic. However, just as home interiors are often shaped by the different residents that cohabit a home, home exteriors can be impacted by others who live in the street or local neighbourhood. Immigrants who change their home exterior to reflect aesthetic traditions unfamiliar in the new country can face disapproval from others living in their neighbourhood (Allon, 2002). While the familiar architecture may provide a sense of belonging, the disapproval of neighbours may give rise to a conflicting feeling of being an outsider and of not belonging within the neighbourhood. Neighbourhood relations are discussed in more detail in the next section of this chapter.

Neighbourhood

As well as being shaped by the social and cultural identities and relationships of those who inhabit them, practices of home and homemaking are also influenced by the neighbourhood context and neighbouring relations. The remainder of this chapter explores the house-as-home in its immediate context of the neighbourhood. In this section I will examine the concept of neighbourhood and explore the relations of 'neighbouring' that take place within neighbourhoods. The subtle ways that neighbours regulate and discipline each other's behaviour and the impact of globalisation on neighbouring practice will also be explored.

Defining neighbourhood

The term 'neighbourhood' is most widely used to describe the local area or community within which a person or group of people live. As with homes, the neighbourhood is a physical space but is also a set of practices. Neighbourhoods are defined and produced by the people that live in them as well as by groups and institutions operating at other scales. For example, property developers often use the idea of a 'neighbourhood' as a marketing tool to sell a particular locality as distinct from others that surround it. 'Neighbourhood' is also associated with a set of relationships between people who live in the area – neighbours, who take part in 'neighbouring' activities. The idea of neighbouring is similar to the idea of community. Neighbouring and community are sets of practices or relationships between individuals and/ or groups of people that share an interest; they can have multiple benefits such as generating a sense of belonging and providing access to resources that 'may be more or less tangible, ranging from cash remittances and material gifts, to favours, information, emotional support or even status and respect' (Clark, 2009, p. 1568, and see Richards, 1990; Laurier et al., 2002). The key difference between 'neighbouring' and 'community' relations is their spatial definition. Whereas communities can be spatially undefined (for example, we could think about an Internet based community that is spread globally), neighbouring is a practice that retains a stronger spatial dimension, concerning the relationships between people or households who are also (spatial) neighbours.

Neighbourhood and neighbouring in a globalised world

In the late twentieth and early twenty-first century there has been growing moral concern about the loss of locally based, or neighbourhood-based, community. The growing physical and virtual mobility of people in this era, in line with 'growing distances travelled to work, greater use of telecommunications, and greater access (and attachments) to people living in other locations' (Martin, 2003, p. 366), is widely held to blame. For example, it is often argued that technologies such as the Internet that allow people to affiliate with others at greater distances mean that people no longer depend on local community as a space of affiliation and belonging but rather join broader, geographically dispersed and even global networks with others who share the same interests (for examples of such communities, see Chapters 5 and 14). However, despite this moral concern, it is clear that neighbourhood-based community relations continue to be significant for many individuals and groups. Locally based relationships can have particular significance for groups such as 'the elderly, ethnic minorities, the unemployed, women and children' whose everyday lives are more likely to be carried out within the space of the local neighbourhood (Meegan and Mitchel, 2001, p. 2174). Globalised technologies such as the Internet are also widely used to connect people within neighbourhoods, for example, through Facebook groups that encourage locally based activism or provide a network for residents to communicate and share resources. More advantaged communities also frequently value locally based social relations. For example, research on the gentrification of neighbourhoods points to a strong valuing of locally based community amongst elite gentrifying households. For these people community belonging and neighbourhood identity are central components of the production of appropriate classed identities in the same way as more material practices such as home renovations (Butler, 2007). Rather than simply signifying the erosion of neighbourhood scale relationships, the differential valuing of locally based community instead reflects the needs, interests and experiences of different social groups (see Case Study 2).

Case study 2: neighbourhood gentrification

Gentrification describes a process of renewal in inner-city neighbourhoods, where houses in previously undesirable and often run-down neighbourhoods are purchased and renovated by upwardly mobile professionals. Gentrification impacts on housing stock as well as local amenities such as shopping strips, which benefit from an influx of higher-income residents. These processes are connected to economic globalisation and are witnessed across global cities including London, New York and Sydney. In Sydney economic globalisation has shaped different sections of the city in different ways. While some residents with lower levels of education and skill risk unemployment and transient work when manufacturing and other low-skilled industries move offshore, other residents with higher levels of education and skill gain employment in the new economy, their incomes providing a high level of purchasing power enabling them to own and renovate property and to take part in lifestyle-based consumption such as regularly eating out. Gentrifiers consist of this latter group of upwardly mobile professionals.

Often when people think about globalisation they imagine a world where local difference is erased in favour of a dominant, homogenised global culture. However, the relationship between the local and global scale is much more complex. The huge diversity apparent across gentrifying neighbourhoods is evidence of this complex relationship and of the ways that local cultures can influence global processes. The diversity of gentrifying neighbourhoods also highlights the importance of neighbourhoods to gentrifiers and directly challenges those who argue that we are seeing a demise in the importance of local community. Bridge and Dowling's (2001) research into the 'microgeographies of retailing and gentrification in Sydney' was the first Australian research to comprehensively identify this diversity. The authors examined the streetscapes of Balmain, Rozelle, Glebe and Newtown, four gentrifying neighbourhoods in Sydney's inner west, conducting an inventory of retailing on the high street of each neighbourhood.

Bridge and Dowling's work showed that the streets shared many of the same types of shops such as restaurants and local services like real estate agents and dry cleaners. Alongside the common trends, however, they identified differences between the four neighbourhoods. Newtown, for example, had a higher proportion and diversity of 'exotic' cuisines available emphasising consumption of diverse and international food, whereas Balmain was dominated by 'modern Australian' restaurants emphasising a 'sophisticated' Australian identity. Retail stores also differed. While all suburbs had significant amounts of home-focused retailing, Rozelle had more second-hand shops than Balmain, its closest neighbour, and a greater number of child-focused stores than any other neighbourhood. Newtown on the other hand had more 'trendy'- and 'ethnic'- focused homeware stores, while Balmain favoured higher end and designer stores (Bridge and Dowling, 2001, p. 104).

Retail diversity reflects differing demographics (for example, the greater number of families with children in Rozelle) as well as the different cultural preferences of residents. For Bridge and Dowling these 'increasingly localised consumption landscapes' are evidence of the 'geographical variation in gentrification and its consumption markers' (2001, p. 105). Resident cultures shaped each of the retail strips; at the same time local residents performed distinct identities through their consumption practices in each space, for example, performing different modes of cosmopolitan and classed identities. A penchant for 'exotic' cuisines in some streets shows a preference for exotic cuisines that has been observed across gentrifying neighbourhoods internationally. For locals the consumption of 'exotic' cuisine is part of the construction of a cosmopolitan identity and a means of distinguishing the locality and its inhabitants from residents of outer lying, less desirable areas (Hage, 1997 in Bridge and Dowling, 2001). These four inner-city communities demonstrate the continued importance of local neighbourhood and consumption practices in gentrifying localities.

Like home/homemaking, neighbouring and community are practices: they do not simply exist but rather are relations that are performed between people and/or households. A fundamental component of the production of community at any scale, including at the scale of the neighbourhood, is a process of boundary making, of defining who belongs and does not belong within the community. As Cowan and Marsh (2004) explain, this involves a process of 'othering' through the identification of 'us' (community) as opposed to 'them' (not our community). This is a process of inclusion (about who is considered to be part of community) as much as it is about exclusion (decisions about who is not considered to be part of the community) and means that neighbourhoods are often fragmented and characterised as much by social cohesion as by conflict and separation (Clark, 2009). Processes of inclusion and exclusion can result in the exclusion of minority groups within local neighbourhoods which leads to divided neighbourhoods and unequal opportunities (Davidson, 2010). However, community can similarly involve the formation of communion amongst marginalised groups, or groups that perceive they are under threat, and it can also provide a protective fortification (Cowan and Marsh, 2004). For instance, the formation of local community groups can be an effective method to challenge an undesirable proposed development within a neighbourhood. An example of this is the effort by residents of Tecoma, a small town in Victoria, Australia, to oppose the global fast-food chain McDonalds' proposal to develop a drive-in store on the town's main street. Forming a community group called 'Burger Off' the group have fought the development locally through sit-ins and flash mobs, in addition to sending representatives to McDonalds' headquarters in

Chicago. Although not all residents oppose the development, the large-scale and long-running dispute has worked to consolidate a sense of community and community identity amongst many residents (Milligan, 2013).

Everyday relations of neighbouring

Community relations in local neighbourhood areas have a strong moral dimension and can work to discipline the ways that individuals and households act and interact. These disciplining processes tend to operate informally and are dependent on individuals self-regulating based on their fear of social exclusion if they do not meet community norms or expectations (de Certeau et al., 1998). These disciplining forces function through unspoken moral codes and normalised practices that shape the ways that people interact in local neighbourhoods. Laurier et al. (2002) identify five key rules or codes of neighbouring that are common across suburbs in Western nations. These rarely spoken rules outline the responsibilities and expected forms of behaviour between neighbours and are as much about bringing neighbours together as they are about ensuring an 'appropriate' social distance that does not disturb the privacy of others. The five rules include an expectation (1) that neighbours will be provided with opportunities to meet existing residents in ways that allow them 'to mark social distances, shared interests, and conversational mentionables and unmentationables' that will form the basis of an ongoing relationship; (2) that households will 'maintain [their] property in a similar state to those of [their] neighbours'; (3) that 'Where it is acceptable, [people will] pass [their] neighbours on to other neighbours or acquaintances, especially if they are seeking help'; (4) that neighbours will 'Watch the neighbours and the neighbourhood. [... but where] this rule of thumb is balanced between being reasonably aware of what neighbours are doing – knowing your neighbours and being a nosey neighbour' and, finally, (5) that neighbours' privacy is not intruded upon (Laurier et al., 2002, pp. 349–352). These moral codes shape the ways that people interact within a local neighbourhood setting and are arguably central to the production of successful and harmonious neighbourhood-based sociality. These are culturally based norms that can work to both discipline and exclude individuals and households that do not perform within expectation.

Community and neighbouring relations can also be more formally mobilised as disciplining forces. A range of research examines the ways that such capacities are mobilised in a neoliberal context to constitute a form of de-centred, locally derived governance that 'neatly fits the predominant motif of neo-liberalism – rule without ruling – for it enables individuals to be governed through their associations' (Cowan and Marsh, 2004, p. 846).

Flint and Nixon (2006), for example, show that local neighbourhood, and in particular housing, has become a key site through which civility is regulated in the United Kingdom. In this context the promotion of 'civil' behaviour is framed as a key function of responsible citizens, and neighbours and community members are encouraged to monitor and report uncivil behaviour. McGuirk and Dowling (2011) observe similar relations in an Australian context, pointing to the contractualisation of community and neighbouring in apartment buildings and new master-planned estates. In these places strata and community by-laws codify the 'material and behavioural elements of middle-class respectability' (McGuirk and Dowling, 2011, p. 2623), outlining 'common sense' behavioural expectations such as the importance of keeping a clean property and not impinging on the right of others to the quiet enjoyment of their property. Central to the success of these formal codes is the self-disciplining of resident behaviour, reinforced by the potential for other residents to complain and take formal (anonymous) action through the strata committee.

Disciplinary relations within neighbourhood settings foreground important interconnections between home and neighbourhood. Neighbourhoods are more than just a site or setting for home but instead can influence the ways that residents think about and make their house-as-home. The appearance and presentation of the front of the house and garden are often felt by residents to represent the household to others within the local community. Ensuring that the house and garden fit with others in the neighbourhood is an important way by which people can signal their willingness to be part of the local community. In some communities community rules go as far as requiring that houses appear a certain way, for example, through rules about garden or house design, or colours and plants that can be used in the neighbourhood. These types of rules are common in master-planned estates, such as those discussed in McGuirk and Dowling's (2011) work and are part of how these neighbourhoods are maintained within an appropriate 'middle-classed' aesthetic. In a UK social housing context Saugeres (2000) has shown that judgements about property upkeep can have an even more disciplinary tone. In the estates that she visited housing managers described messy houses and gardens as evidence of the unrespectable status of the inhabiting household.

Conclusion

In this chapter we have explored households and neighbourhood as sites and sets of practices. These very familiar and intimate sites afford us a sense of belonging and are also connected to the ways that people imagine and construct their identity. The chapter has highlighted two important trends. The first is the way that practices of home and neighbouring contain disciplinary elements, where people's identities are shaped and judged according to the ways that they make home or relate in a neighbourhood setting. Second, the chapter has explored the impact of global processes on households and neighbourhoods. We have seen that home and neighbourhood are constructed in relation to these processes; for example, senses of home and family can be created through the maintenance of global ties. Likewise we have seen that neighbourhood can become both less and more important as a result of global processes. While technologies such as the Internet are widely cited as challenging the importance of neighbourhood, neighbourhood continues to be valued and asserted by many.

Questions for students

- List three places that are 'home' for you. How do you feel when you are in these places? What makes these places feel like home?
- Are different spaces in your home associated more with one gender? Which spaces are associated with masculinity and which with femininity? Do the people in your household adhere to these distinctions or do they reject them?
- Do you know and interact with others in your neighbourhood? Do these interactions prompt you to behave in certain ways?
- Is there a neighbourhood association or group in your neighbourhood? Why did this group form and what sort of activities do they perform? Have they worked together to oppose something that is happening in your neighbourhood?
- Are there any residents in your local area who are not included in neighbourhood activities or who are seen as not belonging in the community? Why is this group seen as not belonging? What does this tell you about the identity of your local neighbourhood?

Recommended reading

Allon, F. (2002) 'Translated Spaces/Translated Identities: The Production of Place, Culture and Memory in an Australian Suburb', *Journal of Australian Studies*, 26(72): 99–110.

Gorman-Murray, A. (2006) 'Gay and Lesbian Couples at Home: Identity Work in Domestic Space', *Home Cultures*, 3(2): 145–168.

Wood, L.J., Giles-Corti, B., Bulsara, M.K., and Bosch, D.A. (2007) 'More Than a Furry Companion: The Ripple Effect of Companion Animals on Neighborhood Interactions and Sense of Community', *Society and Animals*, 15: 43–56.

CHAPTER 8

Nation

Tim Rowse

Introduction

This chapter historicises the concept of national identity. It argues that 'national identity' is unique among group identities because it can exist only in a world that has come to be politically organised as an ensemble of nation-states whose functions include the cultivation of national identities. The chapter narrates briefly how such a world system came about, before reviewing some important sociological theories of 'nation' that sensitise us to the possible variety of political alignments of a sense of national identity.

'National identity' is a kind of social identity. According to social identity theory, individuals have 'multiple ways of describing and categorising themselves' and 'in different contexts, different identities become "salient"' (Billig, 1995, p. 69). Billig has argued that to understand *national* identity we must observe how the category 'nation' is institutionalised within a global system of sovereign political entities and how it is then routinely represented in our daily life, such as in a sports commentator addressing one as a member of a particular national community. As anthropologist Katherine Verdery writes:

> In the modern period, nation has become a potent symbol and basis of classi-fication within an international system of nation-states. It names the relation between states and their subjects and between states and other states; it is an ideological construct essential to assigning subject positions in the modern state, as well as in the international order. (Verdery, 1996, pp. 226–227)

Systems of classification are shared representations, reproduced in our daily interaction. These interactions occur not only between individuals but also between nation-states and between elites and masses within those nation-states. Thus, we can agree with Billig that 'national identity' is not a psycho-logical condition and that it is not 'functionally equivalent with any other type of "identity"' (Billig, 1995, p. 65). 'National identities are *forms of social life,* ... caught up in *the historical processes of nationhood*' (Billig, 1995, p. 24, emphases added) that are global in scale.

Two points follow from Billig's argument. First, the fundamental unit of analysis for the sociology of national identity is not the individual and his/her consciousness but the global system of states that present themselves daily as 'nation-states'. Second, this global system is a historically contingent phenomenon; Billig opens a door between the sociology of identity and the history of humanity's political forms.

A leading writer on national identity Anthony Smith is sceptical of historians' accounts of its emergence. Historians have overemphasised 'the inherently absurd and destructive tendencies of nationalism', the 'artificiality' of nationalism, the prominence of elites in its fabrication and the 'modernity' of nationalism – 'a product of the late eighteenth century' (Smith, 1996, pp. 190–191). These historical themes inform this chapter, but let us be clear that to argue that nations are 'artificial' is not to imply that they are illusory. On the contrary, nation-states can tax your income, replace your hip for no cost, punish your boss for bullying you, deport your neighbour, build a skateboard park for your son, sanction your sister marrying her boyfriend but not her girlfriend, conscript you to fight wars against other nation-states, fill potholes in your street and (in states with capital punishment) legally deprive you of your life. Nation-states could not be more real. How we come to have them is an important question for history, and how we imagine belonging to them is an important question for sociology.

The nation-state and the 'contagion of sovereignty'

A world made up of nation-states came about partly through the breaking up of empires. Pointing to the longevity of empire (and of particular empires), Burbank and Cooper remark that 'the nation-state appears a blip on the historical horizon, a state form that emerged recently from under imperial skies and whose hold on the world's political imagination may well prove to be partial or transitory' (Burbank and Cooper, 2010, p. 1).

How did humanity make 'the long transition from a world of empires to a world of states' (Armitage, 2013, p. 191)? Within that question there is another: how did the 'nation-state' emerge as the ideal modern form of 'state'? The first blow against a European empire was struck by the people living in the European region that we now know as the Netherlands in the late sixteenth century; the Dutch violently abjured the Habsburg (Spanish) Empire in 1581 and were recognised henceforth as the Dutch Republic. For the following two hundred years, the empires of Europe remained undisturbed (apart from their occasional bloody contests with one another) until the American Revolution (1776–1783). The revolt of British colonists (with Indian allies) against British rule in North America demonstrated that it was possible for new states to declare themselves and then to win the ensuing fight with their outraged imperial masters. From the late eighteenth century, intellectuals and political elites on both sides of the Atlantic began to argue that political relations between states and within states should be grounded not in the supposed laws of nature and not in clerical interpretations of God's will but in the negotiated consent of human parties, stated in the form of explicit and mutable laws such as treaties, constitutions and statutes. The American Declaration of Independence became an example of a better way to give moral foundation to a state; the relations between the United States of America and other states and the relationship between the United States government and its citizens were henceforth to be defended and judged (and often found wanting) according to emerging ideas of human rights. The French Revolution, commencing in 1789, gave further impetus to the idea that government was the work of states enacting the desires and interests of 'the people'.

Reflecting on the subsequent history of nation formation up to the Second World War, Hans Kohn made a distinction that has become influential. 'Western nationalism' had been associated with movements for popular sovereignty in states that already existed – England in the seventeenth century and France in the eighteenth century; 'Eastern nationalism' had occurred later, seeking to make new states by addressing subject populations not in terms of shared civic values but by appealing to their supposed shared ethnicity, common descent, religion and language (Kohn, 1944). 'Eastern nationalism' was commonly the way that certain nations broke out of empires such as the Ottoman and the Austro-Hungarian, in the period 1880–1920. Kohn's ideal types – Western/civic versus Eastern/ethnic – remain useful to a sociology of national identity, and this chapter will come back to them.

In 2006, the United Nations had 192 member states. Now, with the exception of the European Union (which can be seen as a state that is not a nation-state; it performs many of the state functions listed by Wallerstein (2004)), there are few states that are not nation-states. Their political elites each present themselves as speaking for each 'people' whose culture is recognised as being different from the national cultures represented by the political elites of other nation-states. In breaking away from empires, the idea that each 'people' should decide its own destiny has justified new sovereign political formations: to each 'people' its own nation-state. 'Peoplehood' has usually been evoked in terms of 'ethnicity', that is, a people's collective memory of being of one blood, one tongue and (usually) one faith. Smith has concluded that while 'not every modern nation can point back to an ethnic base', for political elites to recite a story of shared ethnicity has been a prominent theme of enduring nation-hood (Smith, 1991, p. 41) (see Chapter 2 for further discussion). However, feminist scholars have pointed out that evocations of ethnicity have also implied or stated explicitly that men and women belong to a nation in different ways.

Case study 1: national identity as masculine identity

At the end of the First World War (1914–1918), the victorious nation-state (United States of America) and allied empires (the British, French and Belgian) at the Paris Peace Conference (1919) had plans for the territories of the defeated empires – Ottoman, German and Austro-Hungarian – in Europe and the Middle East. They sought the alignment of national identities with state boundaries – that is, to authorise new states that were nation-states, each democratically rooted in an ethnically defined people that asserted entitlement to govern itself. Sixty million people in eastern and central Europe were to become 'self-determining'. Czechoslovakia, Hungary, Austria, Yugoslavia, Romania and Bulgaria were among the nation-states formed on this principle. According to Glenda Sluga, however, 'self-determination' was 'masculinist' in that women were denied equality of participation in the politics of not only the new nation-states but also the old nation-states and empires that were implementing 'self-determination' (Sluga, 2000).

Nineteenth-century nationalism had been gendered male, according to Sluga: 'By the late nineteenth century, representations of women's difference legitimated masculine agency and subjectivity, and designated the capacity for self-determination as contrary to women's feminine nature' (Sluga, 2000, p. 502). Thus, 'democratic-minded peace negotiators and experts' did not expect 'that women would vote in any plebiscites held in the post-war period, or that any international decision-making regarding women's political status should override national precedents' that excluded women from political life (Sluga, 2000, p. 498). Even the delegates in Paris who personally sympathised with votes for women declined to raise this issue; it was diplomatically easier not to challenge the assumption that male voters spoke for 'the people'. Rather, each nation would determine for itself whether and how women would participate in its 'self-determination'.

How did women take this? Was their 'national identity' weak relative to men's or just different? When the Irish Free State won independence from Britain in 1922, both national narratives and the constitution cast women's role in the nation as that of mothers and homemakers, active in the domestic but not in the public sphere (Cusack, 2000, p. 547. See also Chapter 3 for further discussion of the gendered public/private divide). It is likely that many Irish women were able to experience their national identity in these terms, as if their domesticity were as natural as their biological difference from the male. However, masculinist understandings of the national public sphere provoked some women to be more 'international' than 'national' in their politics – to understand themselves as makers and members of emergent non-national political communities. Within their international organisations, they could practise forms of 'national identity' (in clothes, for example) that did not undermine their 'international' campaigns (against coerced labour, for example).

> In a period that saw increasing emphasis on nationality as a feature of citizenship, women negotiated existing discourses of sexual and national difference by forming international organisations which attempted to side-step the limits of women's agency within nations, to launch challenges to those limits from an international base, and to reconceptualise the international as a more "feminine" sphere. (Sluga, 2000, p. 501)

For example, the Pan-Pacific Women's Association, founded in 1928, regularly assembled women from many nations in pursuit of social reform, including anti-slavery and anti-racism campaigns (Paisley, 2009).

States, nations and nation-states

Wallerstein answers the question 'What do states do?' from the point of view of 'entrepreneurs operating in the capitalist world-economy'.

> States set the rules on whether and under what conditions commodities, capital and labor may cross their borders. They create the rules concerning the property rights within their states. They set rules concerning employment and the compensation of employees. They decide which costs firms must internalize. They decide what kinds of economic processes may be monopolized, and to what degree. They tax. Finally, when firms based within their boundaries may be affected, they can use their power externally to affect the decisions of other states. (Wallerstein, 2004, p. 46)

In addition, most states, claiming to be 'nation-states', must address subjects/ citizens *as a people* sharing certain characteristics that set them apart from the peoples of other nation-states. They cultivate national identity.

To study the state promotion of 'national identity', we can pursue two research programmes. We can look at public and private institutions whose actions – broadcasting news, deploying the national football team, administering elections, conducting a census, marketing motor vehicles, devising school curricula and building roads – routinely address each individual as a member of a nation. And we can study – through ethnographies and surveys – how individuals receive what these institutions address to them and how in their daily life they reproduce (or undermine) the national identities that state actions make available.

In the sociology of national identity, it is useful to distinguish between 'nation-state' and 'nation'. A nation-state *is a state* that makes a certain claim about the cultural composition of the people that make it up: the people as 'nation'. It is always contentious to make that claim. From the point of view of the individual practising his/her 'identity', 'nation' is a 'partial' source of identity (it is only one of many possible senses of identity with others) and it may prove to be 'transitory'. Cultivating national identity is a continuing and not necessarily successful political project that states undertake. In post-Sadam Iraq, it is hard political work for a 'nation-state' to substantiate that it is not just a state, that is, to persuade its members (and the members of other nation-states) that collectively the Iraqis are a 'nation'. The fracture of Iraq into many peoples – strongly identifying with regions, ethnicities and religious communities within and beyond Iraq's borders – is an extreme example of a predicament facing many of the world's nation-states, especially those born in the era of decolonisation (late 1940s to early 1970s).

'Making state conform with nation is a recent phenomenon, neither fully carried out nor universally desired', Burbank and Cooper remind us (2010, p. 1). Studies of decolonisation confirm the significant role of native elites in the design of post-colonial states; such studies point to the possible disjuncture of the emerging *national* identities of elites from the identities of those on whose behalf the elites have bargained post-colonial sovereignty. In Malaysia, Sri Lanka and across sub-Saharan Africa the de-colonising powers (such as Britain, France and Belgium) and the indigenous political elites tended to come to agreement (sometimes after armed struggle) that the borders that the colonial powers had determined would remain, without reference to popular conceptions of ethnicity or customary association (White, 2006, p. 274). In Francophone Africa, according to Cooper, there were other possible political forms than the states that emerged. He points to 'pan-Africanism' and to 'regional federation' (which, he notes, had been the basis of French administration and of the mobilisation of trade unions and political parties). In grooming African elites for post-colonial sovereignty, the French discouraged sub-national identities such as tribes and ethnicities. They 'found it easy to imagine the colonised as a nation-in-the-making, even if they were not entirely convinced that "nations" were all that were emerging' (Cooper, 2003, p. 36). The successful African nationalists imagined the colonial state to be their chief adversary, but once that adversary had yielded formal sovereignty the new states had then to deal with 'the people' as if they shared a national identity, 'a transformative project at which European powers had failed' (Cooper, 2003, p. 37). These supposed nation-states were 'politically fragile and ideologically brittle, their insistence on unity for the nation and development denying legitimacy to the social movements out of which political mobilization had often been achieved' (Cooper, 2003, p. 37).

If nation-states strive to form national identities, but do not necessarily succeed, then it makes sense to distinguish 'nation' from 'nation-state'. This distinction then allows us to consider the mirror image of the scenario of a state failing to be a nation-state: a 'nation' that does not succeed in becoming a 'nation-state' but remains encompassed within a wider nation-state and subject to that nation-state's more successful project of identity-making.

Case study 2: the Métis of Canada – a 'nation' or a 'population'?

The Métis are descended from lineages formed through the many sexual liaisons between Native Americans and French colonists, occasioned by the North American fur trade from the seventeenth century to the mid-nineteenth century. When Canada was established in 1867 the Métis were 'an indigenous nation of nearly 10,000 people possessing a history, culture, imagined territorial boundaries, national anthem and, perhaps most importantly, a sense of self-consciousness as Métis' (Andersen, 2008, p. 350). A mixed economy of fur trade employment, independent trading, farming and buffalo hunting had sustained this nation in the Red River region. Métis territory (in what is now western Canada) was invaded by non-Métis ('Canadians') in the late nineteenth century. In 1869, when creating the Province of Manitoba, Canada responded to Métis objections by setting aside 1.4 million acres. Poor implementation of this territorial concession led to some Métis' exodus and to further conflict and Canadian repression in 1885. The terms 'Métis' and 'métis' now refer to peoples in two locations in Canada: the Red River region (in the Province of Manitoba) and the upper Great Lakes region.

Andersen points to three ways that Métis have been recognised: narratively, constitutionally and demographically. Historians refer to the Red River communities as they have long referred to themselves, that is, as 'Métis'. People of mixed descent in the upper Great Lakes region did not – as far as historical records show – refer to themselves as Métis. Official accounts of this second population have referred to them as 'half-breeds' and 'mixed-bloods'. Recently, historians have begun to refer to both groups as 'Métis', arguing that such a term is necessary to give dignified recognition to all those Canadians who are not 'Indian' or 'White' or identified with one of Canada's many immigrant ethnicities. The upper case 'M' concedes their people-hood. Along with First Nations and Inuit, Métis are recognised in Section 35 of the Constitution Act, 1982. The demographic recognition of Métis is through the census: recent census practice has allowed a respondent to identify as 'Métis'.

As Ben Anderson has pointed out, a national census is a crucial tech-nology in the state's contribution to imagining a national community (Anderson, 1983). A census is an identity machine, offering terms by which an individual can identify as a member of a category *within* a national pop-ulation – but what kind of category? Andersen argues that the Canadian census recognises a Métis aggregate but this does not recognise Métis as a nation; the census represents them merely as a 'population'. Anyone who, on the basis of their mixed ancestry, does not see themselves as belonging to the other categories offered by the census may tick the Métis box; the number of such ticks may grow, but to tick the Métis box a respondent need not be saying anything more than that their ancestry is mixed. To choose this population category is devoid of political or his-torical meaning; the census is unable 'to differentiate between racial and national constructions of Métis' (Andersen, 2008, p. 361). In particular, the census places in the same category those who look back to the Red River Rebellion as defining their 'national' heritage and those who are merely of mixed French-Indian descent. The Canadian census, by coding a *Métis population*, is an instrument for the continuing symbolic repression of the *Métis nation*. The cultural work of Canada's census is to solicit 'Métiness' but to render it as a genealogical or racial identity, not as a national-political identity.

Ethnicity and civility in national identity

Nation-states are an element of the package that arrived with 'modernity'. A respected recent historical account of global modernity says that changes within the period 1789–1914 were 'rapid, and interacted with each other ... profoundly.' They included:

> the rise of the nation-state, demanding centralization of power or loyalty to an ethnic solidarity, alongside a massive expansion of global commer-cial and intellectual links. The international spread of industrialization and a new style of urban living compounded these profound developments. The merging of all these trends does point to a step-change in human social organisation. (Bayly, 2004, p. 11)

Although the classic sociological theories of Karl Marx (1818–1883), Friedrich Engels (1820–1895), Emile Durkheim (1858–1917) and Max Weber (1864–1920) arose as efforts to understand the distinct features of modernity, they did not produce a sociology of 'nation', even though each of these men lived through a period of vigorous and politically successful national move-ments and nation-state formation, in Europe and the Americas (James, 1996).

However (as discussed in Chapter 1), the intellectual legacy of these founding fathers of sociology – our understanding of capitalist modernity – informs the contemporary sociology of identity.

Marxist perspectives on 'national identity' inform the writings of Eric Hobsbawm and Tom Nairn. Hobsbawm invites us to see as myths the stories that powerfully engage our sense of national identity: communities that imagine themselves to be 'nations' usually project their solidarity back into 'primordial' pasts that historians can question on empirical grounds. Nations 'invent traditions' (Hobsbawm and Ranger, 1983). Hobsbawm admires national identities that implicate the national subject in 'revolutionary-democratic' and 'liberal' political programmes; the stance of such identities towards the past is critical of bigoted religious and ethnic solidarities, and it is possible to give democratic content to popular senses of national destiny. Hobsbawm deplores and fears national identities that highlight ethnicity as the basis of solidarity with others; ethnic identity is politically shallow, manipulable and likely to mandate the exclusion of other 'ethnics'. Nationalists who promote self-determination based on ethnicity are laying the basis of political movements that may threaten democracy. The better national identities are those that accommodate many different senses of ethnic loyalty within the one political frame (for further discussion of this approach see Case Study 1, Chapter 2). Tom Nairn agrees that national identity may be either democratically inclusive or exclusive of and hostile to 'the other'. He reminds us of Lenin's concept of 'uneven development' (expounded in *Imperialism: the highest stage of capitalism*, 1916), where in the history of capitalism, some regions have prospered at the expense of other regions that they have exploited. Scottish national identity, Nairn has long argued (Nairn, 1968), can be understood as a response to England's political and economic domination of the British Isles. Nairn is sympathetic to national identities insofar as they express, in terms that people find familiar, inspiring and democratic, the claims of their exploited region against the institutions and ideologies that secure another region's domination over them.

In the Durkheim-Weber tradition we consider 'national identity' not in the context of class struggle under capitalism but as one of the functional requirements of modernity – defined by the complexity of its division of labour, by the impersonality of its social relationships and by its unprecedented technical ability to standardise human phenomena across space and through time. The nation-state is the typical political unit of 'modern' society. Interpreting post-war decolonisation sociologically in the early 1960s, Lucy Mair drew on Durkheim's contrast of (modern) 'organic solidarity' with (pre-modern) 'mechanical solidarity' (for further discussion, see Chapter 1) in order to imagine a person belonging to a 'small-scale' society challenged to become a person belonging to and identifying with a 'large-scale' society, a 'new nation'.

> Every member of the large-scale society is party to a greater number of relationships, some ephemeral, some lasting, which do not overlap. Outside his immediate family he maintains few close bonds all through his life. This kind of loosely organized society, held together partly by impersonal transactions and partly by a great number of organisations for the pursuit of specialised ends and interests, contrasts strongly with the closely integrated village or kin-group that we find among peoples of simple technology. (Mair, 1963, p. 13)

Ernest Gellner also drew on the Durkheim-Weber tradition to argue the evolutionary necessity of the nation-state. Human society has shifted (in some regions perhaps is still shifting) from an agrarian to an industrial basis, and knowledge of nature has raised productivity. Economic success has become the principal test of a state's legitimacy, and knowledge is the basis of productivity. Because an educated population – able to manage and manipulate information – has become essential to productivity and legitimacy, modern states must train their populations; thus programmes of universal literacy and prolonged education emerge. '[T]his kind of society not merely permits but positively requires homogeneity of culture' (Gellner, 1996, p. 109). As a culture-maintaining instrument, an effective modern state conducts itself as a 'state-culture' and propagates its national identity as both its imagined unity of purpose and its actual technical competence, ensuring that citizens who are strangers to each other can transact across space and through time in mutual intelligibility and on a platform of trust. Any modern society is compelled to express and to organise itself as a 'nation-state' lest it become economically dysfunctional and thus vulnerable to stronger nation-states.

The demands of modernity may require the cultivation of 'national identity', as Gellner argues, but they do not require nation-states to be liberal-democratic. As the People's Republic of China demonstrates, an authoritarian nation-state can be modern, functional and effective.

Case study 3: belonging to a new national culture

Gellner died in 1995, probably too soon to see a remarkable example of the nationhood that he theorised. The acceleration of China's 'cultural' nation-building has been described by anthropologist Andrew Kipnis:

> at the same time that China is industrializing at the fastest rate it ever has; it is also urbanizing at the fastest rate ever; it is also expanding and

standardizing its education system at the fastest rate ever; it is also building up its transportation and communications infrastructure at the fastest
rate ever; it is also seeing its citizens move around the country in search
of work, love, and/or excitement to a (vastly) greater extent than ever
before; and its population is speaking a standardized national dialect to
a greater extent than ever before. (Kipnis, 2012, pp. 732–733)

The result is that for a new generation of Chinese the entire territory can
be a familiar place. 'This breaking away from more local structures may be
experienced as a form of liberation or loneliness or individualism and can
result in numerous forms of singularity; but, at the same time, it involves
embodying and engaging with the standardized forms of Chinese nationhood that produce the Chinese nation as a form of social fact' (Kipnis, 2012,
p. 752). And this re-imagined national space is functionally continuous with
global society, argues Kipnis. Thus 'at the subjective level of individual
Chinese youth, the construction of commonality across the Chinese nation'
may be experienced as liberating. The very standardisation of Chinese
modernity 'is an invitation to break away from the local structures of family,
community, and school to enter the broader labor markets, cultural communities, marital markets, and competitive arenas for social recognition of
the nation' (Kipnis, 2012, p. 752).

Ethnicity, civility and globalisation

Jurgen Habermas shares with Marxists an interest in whether national identities are historically progressive; at the same time, he draws on the Durkheim-
Weber concern with solidarity and belonging in 'modern' society. He sees
the nation-state as a political solution to two problems of modernity. One
is the problem of legitimation: what can justify the authority of a state once
the idea that such authority was appointed by God had failed to prevent the
carnage of war? The other is the problem of social integration: as societies
grow larger in territory and population and more complex in their interlocking parts, how can a person transact with strangers and be confident that the
stranger understands the transaction in the same terms? The nation-state, at
its best, has addressed both problems. A democratic nation-state is a 'community of empowered citizens who actively contribute to its maintenance'
(Habermas, 1996, p. 285). To realise this ideal in global history, strong political emotions combined with high-minded rationality in popular movements
that overwhelmed and dismantled older forms of tyranny. National identity –
a sense of the importance of 'common history, language and culture' – fuelled
the hearts and minds of those who forged the liberal democratic nation-state;
it enabled citizens 'to see themselves as parts of the same whole' (Habermas,
1996, p. 286).

Habermas helps us to distinguish ways of 'belonging' to a nation-state. Citizenship is both a common set of rights vis á vis legitimate authority *and* a shared culture; citizenship unites 'republican self-understanding' with 'nationalist' self-understanding (Habermas, 1996, p. 286). However Habermas warns that 'republicanism' and 'nationalism' are *not necessarily* complementary and mutually reinforcing: they may come into tension. This is because each nation-state strives to assert itself among other nation-states. Thus, for the sake of the nation-state that I am born into and to which I belong, I may feel obliged to kill those who were born into and belong to yours. National identity understood as a destiny and involuntary obligation thus may become a more powerful sense of belonging than national identity understood as a choice of certain terms of association. This distinction between 'ethnic' and 'civic' belonging recalls Kohn's distinction of 'Eastern' from 'Western' nationalisms. Thus, national identity may be felt or imagined as belonging to a community defined by *civic values* that are understood as aligned with global values and with universal human rights. Alternatively, belonging to a national community may be a sense of shared *ethnicity*, whose values and outlooks are cherished because they are understood to be unique, ancestral and unaccountable to the outlooks and values of outsiders to the nation. In this second perspective, human rights norms may be resisted as the 'globalisation' of the liberal West, an assault on the defining traditions of one's nation. The contemporary assertion of 'Gay Rights' is being resisted by many Russians as a liberal Western assault on Russian moral tradition.

Sociology is itself a global discipline; thus in so far as national surveys of popular opinion and values have standardised their questions, we may pursue the comparative empirical study of national identity and belonging.

Case study 4: an empirical study of globalisation and national identity

Drawing on the World Values Survey (2005) and the National Identity modules of the International Social Survey Program (2003), Gal Ariely collated data from 116,562 respondents in sixty-three countries. Ariely broke his dependent variable 'national identity' into six dimensions. He measured: national identification with the item 'How close do you feel to [country]?'; patriotism ('How proud are you of being [country] member?'); nationalism ('Generally speaking, [respondent's country] is a better country than most other countries' and 'The world would be a better place if people from other countries were more like the [country of respondent]') and ethnic national identity (items asking if people of a named ethnicity were more 'truly' members of the respondent's country). In addition, he used a question about respondents' willingness, should there be a war, to fight for their country.

Globalisation was Ariely's independent variable. Defining 'globalisation' as increasing cross-border flows of goods, services, money, people, information, and culture, he asked how these flows affect senses of belonging to a nation-state. He distinguished between countries according to how 'globalised' they were, combining such quantifiable indicators as the number of McDonalds restaurants, Internet hosts, Internet users, membership of international organisations and international trade. Thus he was able to test statistically whether 'globalisation' (the independent variable) was related to each dimension of 'national identity' (a series of dependent variables), and he was able to examine how closely related were the six dimensions of national identity.

Ariely found that the more 'globalised' was the country, the lower the proportion of respondents who: (a) declared that they would fight for their country in a war, (b) expressed national pride and (c) supported ethnic criteria for being a 'true' member of their nation.

> On average, in those countries that benefit from a relatively more free spread of ideas and information, flow of goods and capital, people are less likely to be very proud of their country, less willing to fight for their country and less likely to support ethnic criteria for national membership. Therefore, these results support the argument that globalisation is related to the decline of national identity. (Ariely, 2012, p. 474)

However, Ariely's findings are also consistent with the idea that a 'civic' national identity is not threatened (and may even be enhanced) by globalisation. Measured national identification and nationalism were not related to a country's level of globalisation. 'The spread of globalisation does not reduce people's identification with their national group or their view of their country as better than other countries' (Ariely, 2012, p. 476). A person might even take pride in their nation's lack of ethnic chauvinism and martial spirit and its openness to what are seen as cosmopolitan values.

Conclusion

This chapter has presented national identity as more a political than a psychological phenomenon. National identity is possible to the extent that humanity has become organised politically into many nation-states, each of which is motivated to cultivate its subject population's distinctive unity. The instruments of such cultivation may be obvious (rituals involving national symbols, such as flags) or subtle (the terminology of internal difference in the wording of a census). Some states have been more successful than others in the cultivation of nationhood, and, even in successful cases, the terms in which a national culture may be expressed and experienced remain open to contestation – by women reacting against masculinist terms of belonging, by ethnic minorities reacting against the subtle or overt presentation of a particular ethnicity as defining the nation. Imagined national communities exist in the context of global flows of people, ideas, goods and money. To imagine one's national belonging raises the question of what is 'outside' one's national community and whether that 'outside' is contrary to or continuous with what is 'inside'. Although the sociological classics – Marx/Engels, Durkheim and Weber – did not produce a sociology of the 'nation', their legacy is evident in writings about the implication of national identities in global class struggle about the competitive dealings among states and about the terms in which national identity is credible to the subjects of state authority. Finally, sociology has itself become both global and national: the nation-state is a unit of analysis, and international methodological standardisation enables comparative study of national identity. The sociology of national identity can proceed empirically by studying both the projects of political and commercial elites and the perceptions and identities of respondents to surveys; ethnographies of national identity are also possible.

Questions for students

- Applying Kohn's distinction, is the nation-state from which you come an example of 'Eastern' or 'Western' nation formation? If neither 'Eastern' nor 'Western' fits your nation-state of origin, can you think of a third category that fits your case?
- In what terms does 'multiculturalism' offer a shared national identity?
- How is it possible for the structures that reproduce gender difference to offer men and women 'national identity' in different terms?
- What identities are likely to undermine or weaken 'national identity'?
- Is it easier to establish a shared national identity if the nation-state governs through democratic institutions?
- Imagine that you are in charge of a survey focused on 'national identity'. Write a question that you think would measure the strength or weakness of the respondent's 'national identity'.

Recommended reading

Hobsbawm, E.J. and Ranger, T. (eds.). (1983) *The Invention of Tradition* (Cambridge: Cambridge University Press).

Kiernan, V. (1976) 'Nationalist Movements and Social Classes' in Smith, A.D. (ed.) *Nationalist Movements* (London and Basingstoke: Macmillan Press), pp. 110–133.

Smith, A. D. (1991) *National Identity* (London: Penguin Books).

White, Philip L. (2006) 'Globalisation and the Mythology of the "Nation-State"' in Hopkins, A.G. (ed.) *Global History: Interactions between the Universal and the Local* (Basingstoke: Palgrave Macmillan), pp. 257–284.

CHAPTER 9

Religion

Alphia Possamai-Inesedy

Introduction

Bauman (2009) argues that the social production of our identity and individuality is a trivial truth. Regardless, when approaching the question of religious identities, contemporary social theory presents us with a problem. What does it really mean to claim a religious identity? Within pre-modernity, religion was presumed as a core to the society and the ascribed religious identity shared by a collective. Within contemporary society, we are faced with not only a multiplicity of belief systems but also the ability to pick and choose amongst them and to decide how central our chosen belief system will be to our life. Religious identity has moved from one of shared determinism to one of individual choice. These changes necessitate new understandings of religion, for the notion proposed by Durkheim ([1915] 2001) and other scholars that religion is 'social glue', is difficult to apply in a landscape that is characterised as plural and where the individual is seen as a consumer. This chapter contends that it is more useful to view contemporary religion in terms of consumer choice and consumer identity.

The current emphasis on choice, and consumer choice in particular, has created new life trajectories for individuals that Bauman terms (1996) 'dis-embedded biographies' – biographies that are unencumbered by traditional roles and obligations. Paradoxically, the shift from the embedded to the dis-embedded biography leads to a preoccupation with the notion of identity. As the individual moves from the security of traditional spaces and patterns of relationships that regulated our lives to the daily construction (often through consumption) of a chosen biography, the question of who we are and where we belong becomes more central (Bauman, 1996. See also Chapters 1, 11 and 13 in this volume). In this context, social theory points to the problem of maintaining a religious identity, regardless of the research in the field which points to its continued role in individuals' lives.

A functional definition of religion, that is defining it for what it does for the individual and society, links religion to the personal identity process. For example, it has been argued that two central functions of religion are the provision of meaning and belonging (McGuire, 1992), clearly linking religion and identity. This chapter will look at this interplay and examine the achieved role of religious identity through the examples of fundamentalism and consumer religions. This focus helps to explain the conditions in which individuals orient themselves towards religious realities and identities in contemporary, globalised society. In doing so, this chapter will make use of the theories of individualisation (Beck and Beck-Gernsheim, 2002) and risk society (Beck, 1992). These frameworks provide the lens with which to better understand the project of the self and how it can be connected to religion.

The epistemological tale of sociology of religion

Sociology of religion has been dominated by extremely contentious methodological terrain since its conception. Although this field of research has changed dramatically from its base of nineteenth-century positivism, it is still dominated by definition, insider-outsider and scientific objectivity debates. The basis of these contentions may well relate to the spiritual or transcendental referent of the research, which has led some to argue that religion is a distinct category of study that calls for unique methodologies.

The discipline of sociology is embedded within a time period of social change that would have impacted its methodological approach. As Pfeuffer Kahn (1995, p. 16) states: '[r]ooted in sciences as a truth-bearing discourse, in a fascination with the industrial process and in a puzzlement over the social location of "men" due to urbanization and social revolution, sociology set about mapping the new social order' – a social order that was based upon the rise of rational thought and the 'decline' of religion. This can go some way in explaining the dominance of literature dedicated to the concept of secularisation; a great deal of energy and time has been dedicated to substantiating the demise of religion.

Interestingly, although identity has relatively recently become a central concern within the sociology of religion, the interplay between religion and identity can be seen as an underlying theme in sociology of religion since the classical period (although, as noted in Chapter 1, scholars such as Durkheim and Weber could not have used the term 'identity' as it was not available to them as a social scientific term (Greil and Davidman, 2007)). An example is Durkheim's ([1915] 2001) work on the role of the sacred and of ritual in fostering personal and social identity. Nonetheless, the assumptions of secularisation focused scholars' attentions on the measurements of decline in religiosity rather than measurements of belonging and identity.

A further obstacle to the study of religious belonging and identity is the neglect, on the part of sociology as a whole, to understand the link between religion and the individual's emotions, perceptions and feelings. Indeed McGuire (1996, p. 102) argues that '[o]ur discipline has been impoverished by an uncritical acceptance of an epistemological tradition in which things of the spirit have been radically split from material things and in which the mind is treated as utterly separate from the body'. The impoverishment that McGuire presents to us is one that would have devalued the key markers of the achieved religious identity – that is reflexivity and individualisation (further discussed below).

With these points in mind, it should be noted that the majority of sociologists of religion today argue that the theory of secularisation has been falsified. This includes early proponents of the theory such as Rodney Stark (1999), who famously proclaimed the theory's 'RIP' in the late 1990s. If we examine contemporary Western society we witness, not secularisation, but rather what can be seen as revivalism and pluralism (this will be further explored below). This explosion of religious movements has included the growth of forms of fundamentalisms as well as what can be termed consumer and hyper-real religions (Possamai, 2009). Examples of these forms of religion will be discussed in the case study below, through which we will further examine the connections between religion and identity. Prior to this it is useful to consider the religious landscape of contemporary society as well as clarify the concept of pluralism.

From secularisation to pluralisation

It is difficult to present a snapshot of the global religious landscape. Although religious revivalism is apparent throughout much of the world there are exceptions. The dominant exception is the geographical space of western and central Europe where there are clear indications of a decline within church-related religiosity, most markedly among Catholics and Protestants. Religious/spiritual activity found outside of these groups is most notable within the 'spiritual revolution', which Heelas et al. (2005) make reference to but also within an upsurgeance of charismatic movements. These groups, most strongly linked with Pentecostalism, are classified as Christian literalist fundamentalist groups who emphasise the work of the Holy Spirit.

Alongside revivalism, a further area of interest for scholars of religion is the connection between the increase of religious pluralism and what can be termed consumer religions. The religious landscape of multiple worldviews denotes personal choice as well as consumption. Debates have been raised, however, about the impact of choice on the religious identity. Theorists such as Berger (1967, 1974) and Giddens (1991) argue that the chosen religious identity loses its ascription and taken for granted character and could result in the weakening of religious commitment. Alternatively, research carried out by Warner (1993) and Hammond (1988) asserts that choice strengthens religious identity by adding agency and meaning to one's commitment.

The cultural significance of the consumer lies with the authority and autonomy it provides to the individual; we have moved from identity ascription to achievement and consumption is central to this (see Chapter 13 for further discussion). Scholars (for instance see Roof and McKinney, 1987; Possamai, 2009; Lyon, 2013) point to how individuals increasingly choose their belief system and indeed how they can construct this belief through picking and choosing in an 'a la carte' manner from a variety of belief systems and creating their own unique version. Zygmunt Bauman (1998) noted that it was these forms of religion that would thrive under the conditions of high/ post modernity. The connections between identity, religion and conditions of high modernity will be more thoroughly explored below. First, an examination of what is meant by plurality is necessary – as it is through its existence that we witness not only the concept of choice within religion but also the emergence of anxiety.

If secularisation has not eventuated, the question is then raised – what has? Not only has religion failed to disappear, we are witnessing its revival. If we examined the religious characteristics of a country such as Australia we would note its changing nature. The colonial religious heritage of Australia is of an Anglican-Protestant majority. The change in the religious landscape of Australia and therefore its identity transformed drastically from 1971 (with the rescinding of the White Australia policy in 1972). This saw not only an increase in religious diversity but also the shift to a Catholic majority. Data from the Australian Bureau of Statistics (ABS) indicates that Anglicans dropped from 39 per cent in 1947 to 22 per cent in 1996 and in 2006 sat at 18.7 per cent – with clear indications that this downward trend will continue. Meanwhile the growth of Catholicism was marked during this time period (from 20.7 per cent in 1947 to 27 per cent in 1996 and 25.8 per cent in 2006), although recent statistics reveal a slight decline of those who identify as Catholic. Areas of growth outside of this Christian majority (at 63.9 per cent in 2006) can be found in a number of religions, but significantly in Hindus and Muslims where the growth rate from 2001–2006 is recorded at 55.8 per cent and 20.6 per cent respectively. The 'no religion' category has also demonstrated significant growth with 27.6 per cent over the same period (Bouma et al., 2011). There has accordingly been a shift from the Anglican-Protestant hegemony of early colonial Australia to a Catholic-Anglican hegemony (Bouma, 2006). This has occurred with the simultaneous growth of those who declare no religion as well as a rise of New Religious Movements (NRMs), including groups that can be categorised as consumer religions.

The argument is then made that modernisation, rather than producing sec-ularisation, has produced plurality (Maclure and Taylor, 2011). Pluralisation, simply the co-existence of various religious groups in one geographical space, has led to a number of changes to the institution of religion as well as the individual's response to it. On the one hand, the co-existence of these many forms of religion/spirituality creates choice, and as Bauman (1998, p. 68) argues, '[p]ostmodern men and women, whether by their own preference or by necessity are choosers'. Plurality is reflective of the consumer culture of our time period (further outlined in Chapter 13); this is witnessed by the common colloquialism in the United States of speaking about 'religious pref-erence' rather than religious affiliation (Maclure and Taylor, 2011). On the other hand, the ability to choose – to have religion available within the mar-ketplace – suggests instability. Choice denotes the voluntary character of one's religion as well as its doctrines. This in turn can create uncertainty within the individual. It can also contribute to further movement away from religion as a primary identity to one that is more peripheral. This highlights the increasing complexity of identity construction, particularly that of the religious identity.

Individualisation, religious consumption and identity

In the light of a plural high modernity, Beck and Beck-Gernsheim's (2002) analysis of individualisation in a risk society would seem to provide a particu-larly apt theoretical tool through which to examine the connections between religion and identity. For Beck, individualisation refers to the breakdown of traditional norms, beliefs and expectations, which in turn frees the individual from these 'constraints' and allows more flexibility in their personal life course. This disembedding component of individualisation implies a freedom from the ties of religion and of class, gender and ethnicity (categories which, as discussed in Chapters 2, 3 and 4, have been conceived of as static and ascribed or as 'essential' at various points in time). This 'freeing' indicates, as Bauman (2009, p. 3, original emphasis) states, that human nature could no longer be seen as a given:

> Instead, it turned into a *task*, and a task which every man and woman had no choice but to face up to and perform to the best of their ability. 'Predestination' was replaced with 'life project', fate with vocation – and a 'human nature' into which one was born was replaced with 'identity'.

This life project, or what Giddens (1991, p. 5 emphasis added) terms 'the reflexive project of the self' 'consists in the sustaining of *coherent*, yet continu-ously revised, biographical narratives'.

As outlined above, in the atmosphere of plurality individuals are burdened and shackled with choices and responsibilities:

> on the one hand, that means an expansion of the radius of life, a gain in terms of scope and choice. Life becomes in many respects more open and malleable. But it also means that new demands, controls and obligations fall upon the individual. (Beck-Gernsheim, 1996, p. 140)

It is only within his more recent work that Beck acknowledges the need to recognise the role of religion within what he terms a 'risk society'. His earlier work assumed the argument of secularisation, which in turn meant that he dismissed the importance of religion/spirituality within contemporary society at both the macro and micro level. Beck (2010, p. 82) now argues that religions have become individualised since 'faith now becomes optional and is tethered to the authority of the religious self'. This markedly different relationship of the self to religion points directly to how identity and religion (and our sociological understandings of each) are connected.

Individualisation, or this idea of the unceasing construction of identity, has been proposed by a number of theorists and can be readily applied to understand the connections between religion and identity. Beyond the works of Bauman and Beck we can turn to the work of French theorist, Lipovetsky (1987, 1993), for further insights. Lipovetsky (1987, 1993), as outlined by Possamai, (2009) can be employed to better understand how the 'optional' aspect of religion and its consumption relates to identity. He argues that if roles, norms, and class were the focus of the older social world, we now live in a society in which life is organised around the individual as consumer. In this world, the individual is autonomous, seeks his or her potential, constructs who he or she is and is part of the great adventure of the self. Consumption is not solely relegated to the secular sphere. Products for sensation gathering and sensation enhancement are not restricted to commodities and services but can be, following the work of Bauman (1998), Featherstone (1991), Lyon (1994) and Possamai (2009), extended to the consumption of religious signs and texts. Bauman (1996) argues that religion has become a neatly packed consumer item – taking its place among other commodities that can be bought or bypassed according to one's consumption whims.

The focus, according to Lipovetsky (1993), is now on constructing our own identity, our own personality, and on generating our own narcissistic knowledge. If before we inherited our cultural predispositions from our family and kept them as part of our identity for the rest of our life, today, it can be argued that we make ourselves who we want to be. For example, in the sphere of religion, we can explore different religions and pick and mix various parts electively and make of it a personal spirituality. Peter Berger (1983 cited in Beck, 2012) demonstrates this with his illustration of the Japanese who he argues display the outcomes of plurality through a syncretistic toleration. For instance, you can find religiosity expressed by visiting a Shinto shrine, celebrating a marriage with Christian rites and making use of a Buddhist monk presiding over burials. Berger reflects on why this may be the case in Japanese culture and, by way of explanation, quotes the Japanese philosopher, Hajime Nakamura, who argues:

> The West is responsible for two fundamental errors. The first one is mono-theism – there is only One God –and the other is the Aristotelian principle of contradictions: either A or not A. Every intelligent person in Asia knows that there are many gods and that things can be both A as well as not A. (Berger, 1983 cited in Beck, 2012, p. 100)

It is important to note that the works of theorists such as Bauman and Lipovetsky present individuals as living in an 'unfettered logic of action, juggling in a virtually empty space' (Beck and Beck-Gernsheim, 2009, p. 14). The works of theorists such as Beck and Giddens make us question, how-ever, 'which new modes of life are coming into being where the old ones, ordained by religion, tradition or the state are breaking down?' (Beck and Beck-Gernsheim, 2009, p. 14). This question taps into the three components of individualisation. I have already outlined the first component – 'disembed-ding'. Disembedding is the breakdown of traditional norms, beliefs and expec-tations that, in turn, frees the individual from these forms of constraints and allows flexibility in our life biography. The second component of 'disenchant-ment' signifies the loss of security in practical knowledge and guiding norms. It is reflected in the lack of trust that individuals in contemporary society feel towards expert systems. The third component, 're-embedding', presents a new type of social commitment. The re-embedding dimension presents an often neglected area when discussing the concept of individualisation – the ques-tion of reintegration. If we have been freed from the chains of our constraints Beck and Beck-Gernsheim (2002, p. 203) ask the question – 'what has taken their place?'. The stage of re-embedding argues that the marketplace has taken the place of tradition. As Beck argues (2009, p. 14):

> in modern societies new demands, controls and constraints are being imposed on individuals. Through the job market, the welfare state and insti-tutions, people are tied into a network of regulations, conditions, provisos. From pension rights to insurance protection, from educational grants to tax rates, all these are institutional reference points marking out the horizon within which modern thinking, planning and action must take place.

In contemporary society, individuals, by necessity, must make an active effort; our biographies have therefore become what he terms the 'do it yourself biography'. It is this re-embedding component that can allow us to further understand how consumption of religion, or the religion a la carte made reference to above, relates to identity. Individuals exposed to this 'elective biography', and construction of self through the hyper-consumption of religion would seem to pick and choose ad infinitum. However, a high degree of standardisation is found within this group. The free-floating identity that Lipovetsky argues for does not appear to eventuate in the manner he describes. Rather, we find, through the re-embedding dimension that Beck speaks of, constraints of choice. What of the alternative then? Previous research carried out by Possamai-Inesedy (2002), and discussed in the case study below, indicates that individuals confronted by the insecurities and anxieties of the freedoms presented by high modernity can turn towards a form of hypo-consumption by aligning themselves with religions that can be termed 'fundamentalisms'. It is within these forms of religiosity that we find a seeking out of the identity as a given that we found in first modernity. Here we find a reassertion of the ties that have become increasingly lost in high modernity.

Case study: the achieved religious identity

Much of the research dedicated to understanding the intersections between religious institutions and religious identity focuses on the maintenance of religious identity in the face of the mass migration that is an aspect of globalisation (see Chapter 10 for further discussion). How do individuals maintain religious identities when faced with a new culture which exposes them to new beliefs and practices that can leave them questioning their taken-for-granted assumptions about their own? Research points to the use of religious spaces and gatherings not only to sustain older cultural ways, but also to provide a space for potential transition to the new culture (Warner and Wittner, 1998). Further to this is the emphasis on the increased decentralisation, plurality and voluntarism with regard to religious life. Within this context, religious groups that are part of new immigrant and ethnic communities are landing in a pluralistic social context and very often take on new forms of identity in order to develop the capacity to survive in the new land. They are thus reaching beyond traditional ethnic and religious identity boundaries (Possamai and Possamai-Inesedy, 2007).

Following from this, the case study presented here emphasises the choice inherent in the forms of religious identity that we find in contemporary Western society. Our religious affiliation as well as the centrality of the belief system in our life can be seen to change over our lifetimes. At one point the religious identity can be seen as a master or primary role; at another point in our life it can become secondary (Hammond, 1988). Further, in the presence of multiple belief systems, the individual is able to choose whether to be religious and, if so, to what extent. Subsequently, Bauman points to the prevalence and robustness of both forms of religious fundamentalisms and consumer religions in liquid modernity.

Consumer religions, or those forms of belief that are characterised as containing both individuation and syncretic and organisational openness, are a reflection of contemporary fluidity. On the other hand, the growth in forms of fundamentalism can represent a reaction against this defining feature of liquid modernity. The self, no longer seen as a homogenous, stable core which resides within the individual but as routinely created and sustained in the reflexive activities of the individual, may seek out a more stable sense of identity through an all-encompassing framework of fundamentalist religious groups.

In a 2001 study, Possamai-Inesedy (2002) examined responses to the parameters of the 'risk society' across belief systems. Interviews were carried out with three groups: a new religious movement, those who identify as atheist and finally a fundamentalist group. The then Assemblies of God, now known as Australian Christian Churches (ACC), was studied as it represented a Christian literalist form of fundamentalism. Hillsong, the megachurch of the ACC, with over twenty thousand people attending its services every week, is identified as Australia's largest religious congregation. These numbers are staggering, particularly in a country that is often characterised as secular. With such a large community it was surprising to find that those individuals who belonged to the ACC presented with a stronger sense of a unified self. The respondents of the study argued that their Christian self was represented in every sphere of their life, as such they presented an identity largely organised around a core religious belief that was associated with one community.

This could be further explained by the research carried out by Maddox (2012, 2013) who investigated this church in relation to its consumer aspects and gender relations. Maddox (2013) highlights the traditional gender roles that are reasserted within the ACC through material on headship, authority, relationships, the wealth and prosperity gospel, Christian living and end of times. Maddox's study shows that for some, the disembedding of traditions and norms is not emancipatory but anxiety-producing. The ACC's guidelines create the stability of self that is lost within wider society.

Risk, consumer religions and fundamentalisms

An awareness of the risks and anxieties of contemporary society is among other factors, part of a new type of psychological pressure. If we work on a crude continuum, which can illustrate the reaction of social actors to our contemporary social malaise, we find at one extreme a person who faces constant existential anxiety in their everyday life. This person would be an ontologically insecure individual and would be characterised by an obsessive exaggeration of risks to personal existence, extreme introspection and moral vacuity. On the other end of the spectrum we might find a person who experiences ontological security; that is, a sense of reliability towards persons and things, aided and abetted by the predictability of the apparently minor routines of day-to-day life. He or she is not troubled by, or may even be oblivious to, existential questions. Faced with a predictable routine, they are able to cope effectively with risk situations, personal tensions and anxiety (Giddens, 1990). This state incorporates trust in the reliability of persons and things. Trust, therefore, may be regarded as a means of dealing psychologically with risks that would otherwise paralyse action or lead to feelings of engulfment, dread and anxiety. Only a small part of the Western population is close to these ideal-type extremes. The large part of the population is moving back and forth between the two extremes depending on the life they are experiencing at a specific moment.

As people experience existential anxiety, it is not a surprise if many of them wish to re-affirm a threatened self-identity. Any collective identity that can offer a way out from this anxiety has the potential to attract these individuals. Harskamp (2008) argues that as religions are attempting to eliminate angst, or to create systems to cope with it, the rise of existential insecurities (as created in the risk society) thus facilitates new religiosities. According to Kinnvall (2004, p. 742), nationalism and religion are two 'identity-signifiers' that are strong in providing this source of security in the risk society context because they 'convey a picture of security, stability, and simple answers'. If these levels of ontological insecurity increase, it is likely that the search for securitised subjectivity will also rise (Kinnvall, 2004, p. 757).

> Institutionalized religion often concurs with the nation as being territorially defined, as it refers to bounded entities such as churches, organizations, or political parties. In this form, religion, like nationalism, supplies existential answers to individual's quests for security by essentializing the product and providing a picture of totality, unity and wholeness. The fact that God has set the rules and made them difficult to contest relieves the individual psychologically from the responsibility of having to choose. (Kinnvall, 2004, p. 759)

Not only are institutionalised religions found to provide a source of security in risk society, but new forms of religions such as the consumer religions or New Religious Movements (Possamai-Inesedy, 2002; Dawson, 2006) appear to provide some form of help as well.

While mainstream religions and inner-worldly new religious movements might offer parts of an island of security in the adversity of ontological insecurity, fundamentalism appears to be better equipped to offer a whole island of security. There is therefore a type of religious market available and fundamentalism is situated within this market. And it is the argument of this chapter that if individuals choose a religion in terms of what it can offer to alleviate ontological insecurity, fundamentalism appears to be the 'best product' on the market.

The term 'fundamentalism' refers to religious groups that claim their religious system is the most true – if not absolutely and exclusively true – and that no other religious system can compete with its sole true way of life. It is a term that includes an array of religious groups. It is also a negative label applied by some religious groups to point out groups more conservative than them. It also can be used to silence and marginalise some religious groups by labelling them as anti-intellectual, bigoted and intolerant. As terms evolve in the use and misuse of language and appellation, a new appellation has even come out to distance ultra-conservative groups even further from lesser ones – 'fundagelism'. This term comes from a Christian context and is a compound of 'fundamentalist evangelism'. It embraces people who believe in the future as foretold by the book of Revelation; that is, the destruction of Babylon (Iraq) and the immanent mass conversion of Jews.

Fundamentalism can be found in all religions and has different characteristics according to the faith where it is situated. In Christianity, for example, fundamentalism can be equated to Christian literalists who believe that the Bible contains the actual words of God and directly apply it entirely to contemporary life. People who join these fundamentalist groups tend to not find answers in mainstream churches and seek more 'engaged' forms of religions (for example, certain forms of Pentecostalism) by looking for a stability of commitment in a community which would give a stronger sense of identity, authority and tighter system of beliefs and practices, that is, a more structured world/spiritual view. Tamney (2002) equates fundamentalism to traditionalist religions. These are groups that are trying to regenerate religious tradition and make it socially significant which is quite different from traditional religions. Tamney discovered that what these groups try to preserve above all is the group above the individual. Collectivity and belonging is valued above individual life and viewed as superior to all other institutions in society. As Bauman (1998, p. 74) states:

> On a world in which all ways of life are allowed, yet none is safe, they muster enough courage to tell those who are eager to listen what to decide so that the decision can remain safe and stand up in all courts that matter. In this respect, religious fundamentalism belongs to a wider family of totalitarian or proto-totalitarian offered to all those who find the burden of individual freedom excessive and unbearable.

Conclusion

As stated above, early theorists of risk society, such as Beck and Giddens, saw religion as withdrawing from the front stage of Western societies and as having less importance in people's lives, yet religion is alive, and rather than disappearing, it is changing in adaptive and reactive ways. Religion is no longer part of the public sphere the way it used to be in yesteryear. In Western societies especially, it no longer provides a close-knitted system of beliefs united with specific social and cultural collectivities, for example, a nation – leaving the ascribed, collectively based religious identity largely a product of the past. As religion is metamorphosing into new, renewed and different forms at various levels, it is also part of, as outlined above, consumer culture. In current Western societies, there is an increase of freedom in which the individual makes his or her own sense of his or her life, identity and rapid social and cultural changes. More people claim to have no religious affiliation, but they are not necessarily atheists; they believe without belonging and might see themselves as more spiritual than religious. One of the many reasons for this gain in freedom of faith is the development of consumer culture which affects, whether we like it or not, religion as well. In this consuming world, the individual becomes his or her own authority. People are now 'free' to choose; and these choices impact on the saliency of the religious identity. Consumer choice, it must be said, is not limited to shopping but is extended to education, health, politics *and* religion. Our identity as a worker, a family member, a partner, a follower of a party and a believer of one religion is in constant flux. The religious person is now faced with a proliferation of spiritual/religious/philosophical knowledges in our pluralist western societies. What to choose? What to be?

Questions for students

- How has the study of secularisation impacted on the study of identity and its connection to religion?
- By way of contrast, how is religious identity impacted on by the increase of religiously plural societies?
- What connections do you see between Beck's concept of risk and individualisation and the rise of fundamentalisms?
- Lipovetsky argues that individuals within contemporary society can be characterised as free floating. How does the concept of individualisation challenge this argument?
- How does consumer society impact on religious identity?

Recommended reading

Beckford, Sage James A. and N.J. Demarath III (eds.). (2007) *Handbook of the Sociology of Religion.* (London: Sage).

Castells, M. (2010) *The Power of Identity* (Second Edition) (Oxford: John Wiley & Sons).

Giddens, A. (2013) *Modernity and Self-Identity: Self and Society in the Late Modern Age* (Oxford: John Wiley & Sons).

Lyons, D. (2000) *Jesus in Disneyland* (Cambridge: John Wiley & Sons).

CHAPTER 10

Migration

Mary Hawkins

Introduction

The Swedish film *The Emigrants* was released in 1971 to general acclaim and went on to win Best Foreign Language Film at both the Golden Globe and the Academy Awards of 1972. Directed by Jan Troell, *The Emigrants* tells the story of the migration of one couple, Karl Oskar and Kristina, from Sweden to North America in the nineteenth century, a time when more than one million Swedes left their homeland for Canada, New Zealand, Australia and South America, but overwhelmingly for the United States (Martenius, 2014, p. 1). *The Emigrants* explores themes that are purportedly common, in both the popular and the scholarly imagination, to the migrant experience: Karl Oskar and Kristina, a farming couple, leave home following poor harvests and the death of their child (push factors); they choose the United Sates as their destination because they have heard of the prosperity to be found there and because friends and neighbours have already made the journey (pull factors); and on their arrival and for some time after they experience a sense of loss, dislocation and alienation (assimilation barriers). But this is their chance at a new life, and they firmly intend to stay, and to belong. Migration, then, entails permanent relocation, and the creation of a new identity, and a new, albeit problematic, sense of belonging to a new home.

If a permanent relocation was ever true of nineteenth-century migrants (of the more than one million Swedish emigrants about 200,000 returned to Sweden (Martenius, 2014, p. 1)), it is certainly the case that *The Emigrants* narrative strains to capture the contemporary migrant experience. Today, migration need not mean a total removal from the homeland. For many, the migratory movement is a circular one; a young Indonesian man, for example, may spend some part of each year working on construction projects in Singapore and the remainder of each year at home in his village in Java. Email, Skype, text messaging, Facebook and other similar globally ubiquitous communication platforms mean that all migrants can easily, and relatively cheaply, remain in close contact with friends and family at home. More than that, they can read their home town newspapers, watch sporting events and even vote in 'home' elections. Globalisation, or the 'process whereby hitherto bounded societies are experiencing increasing cross-border flows of people, goods, services, ideas, information, money, images, knowledge and culture' (Hawkins, 2014, p. 9) allows migrants, and many others as well, to experience what Robertson (1992) has called the sense of the world as a single place. Migrants today are not necessarily suspended between two worlds; rather, as transnationals, they may simultaneously occupy, be it virtually or in person, multiple places. While this experience is not entirely new – there is an entire literary genre, in many languages, of 'letters home' – the speed, volume and accessibility of contact are new (Vertovec, 2004). In such a globalised world, identity and belonging are problematised. Perhaps some individuals do think of themselves as citizens of the world, but the majority of people look first to the local and second to the nation (see Chapter 8) for their sense of them-selves. How, then, do migrants today construct their identity, and to what do they think of themselves belonging?

This chapter commences with a brief account of the global history of migration and of types of migratory movements. It then explores the forces for international migration, including neo-classical models, the new econom-ics of migration and world systems approaches. Finally, the chapter returns to the questions of identity and belonging posed above, in the context of a discussion of transnationalism.

A brief global history of migration

People have always been on the move. The development of agriculture some 10,000 years ago was accompanied by the growth of population centres and the introduction of a more sedentary life for many, but even so, travel, some-times over long distances, was common, motivated by a host of factors: reli-gion (pilgrimage and holy wars such as the crusades); trade (from individual explorers to the British empire) and the search for knowledge (Darwin's voy-ages to the Galapagos). Today, everyone seems to be travelling, as workers, as tourists, as backpackers or as students, but most travellers are not migrants. 'Migrant' is conventionally restricted to those who emigrate from a home-land with the intention of settling, for a longer or shorter period of time, in another nation-state. For some, emigration is a choice, but for others migra-tion may be forced – refugees for example, or those fleeing natural disasters or chronic warfare. We can also include in the 'migrant' category people who are displaced and compelled to take up residence within their nation-state but often far removed from their original home, in a region where the local people speak another language and practise another culture. Chinese people displaced by the construction of the Three Gorges Dam, completed in

2012, are one example of this type of migration; indigenous Dayak groups of Sarawak displaced by the Bakun dam, where flooding commenced in 2010, are another. Indeed, the relocation of populations has often accompanied development in many parts of the developing world; see the case study on Javanese migrants in this chapter.

Finally, 'circular migration' and 'labour migration' should be included as common types of migration. 'Circular migration' can be represented by the example of *merantau,* whereby a young Malay man leaves his village home and seeks work, life experience and hopefully wealth in a big city before returning home. Culturally this is a rite of passage, a transition to manhood, and has been practised by many Malay groups, including the Minangkabau of west Sumatra and the Acehnese of north Sumatra (Siegel, 1969; Wang Gungwu, 1985). 'Labour migration' on the other hand refers to the movement of people from one country to another for the purposes of employment. Labour migration has become a key feature of the globalised economy, and according to the United Nation's International Organisation for Migration, it now includes over 100 million people (www.imo.int), who work in all sectors of the economy, from construction and banking to domestic services and transport.

Globally, while there is a long history of, for example, Chinese migration to Southeast Asia, mass migration dates to the 1820s, when long-distance and trans-oceanic migration began to rapidly increase (Mckeown, 2004, p. 167). Western historians have tended to focus on the movements of people from Europe to the Americas, a migratory flow that comprised some 55–58 million people between 1846 and 1940. Many, like our Swedish couple Karl Oskar and Kristina, left behind famine and sought new and more productive farmland. Others fled religious persecution, political upheaval and disease. Migration in the global south, however, was on an equally massive scale. Between 1846 and 1940 some 48–52 million people from India and southern China migrated to Southeast Asia and the South Pacific, while 46–51 million left Northeast Asia and Russia for Siberia, Japan and Manchuria (Mckeown, 2004, p. 156).

There has been a tendency to view Asian migration as a product of European colonialism, in particular the colonial plantation systems' voracious demand for labour. Certainly nineteenth-century Malay rubber, tea and coffee plantations, Fijian sugar plantations, and Indonesian sugar, rubber, coffee and tea plantations required more labour than could locally be sourced, but this demand was met in a variety of ways. In Fiji, the British colonial government brought in indentured labourers (*girmityas*), typically poor Indian men who had contracted to work for 5 years for a set, low, payment. At the end of their indenture they were given the choice to remain or return to India, but as the latter choice was at their own expense, and their wages were insufficient to allow them to save for a passage home, most stayed, either renewing their contract, renting a small plot of cane land, or setting up small businesses in the emerging townships. Over time these labourers were supplemented by free Indian migrants from Gujarat and the Punjab, many of whom went into trade and business. Today, Fiji's Indo-Fijians account for more than one third of the total Fijian population. In Malaysia, indentured labourers from India arrived to work on the plantations under a similar scheme to that pertaining in Fiji, but in contrast to Fiji, where the British held the primary financial interest in the plantation sector, in colonial Malaya wealthy Chinese businessmen, who were third and fourth generation descendants of long-settled Chinese traders, also established plantations, as did wealthy Indian businessmen (Boon, 2014). Indentured labour continued, but it was supplemented by an alternative *kangany* (Tamil for 'overseer' or 'superior') system, whereby entire families rather than single men were recruited from India as labourers (Periasamy, 2007). Assisted emigration was banned by the Indian government in 1938, but free labourers continued to arrive. By the time of Malaya's independence from Britain in 1957 the Indian population numbered nearly one million, from a total population of about six and a quarter million.

The Dutch colonial government's 'solution' to labour demand in Indonesia differed markedly from that of the British in Fiji and Malaya. The Netherlands did not count among its imperial possessions a labour source like India, and it was in any case hampered by its desire to 'keep the natives native' (Geertz, 1963a), that is, not introduce to Indonesia, or the Dutch East Indies as the archipelago was then known, foreign groups that might provoke cultural disruption. Hence, while Chinese peoples, who had been migrating to Indonesia for centuries, were not banned from entry, they were restricted to residences and businesses in towns and could not buy village land. Instead of importing workers, the Dutch compelled all Indonesians to either work on Dutch-controlled plantations or give some of their own land to the cultivation of crops for the colonial government (Hawkins, 2014, pp. 43–44). This cultivation system brought great wealth to Holland and kept Indian workers out. To this day, Indonesia's marked ethnic diversity is due to indigenous, rather than migratory, factors.

From the 1920s, global migration flows have been sparked and sustained by many of the same factors that were evident in the nineteenth century. The desire for a better life, the need to escape persecution, war and natural disaster, has prompted a continued movement, particularly to the new settler states such as the United States, Canada, Australia and New Zealand. At the same time, de-colonisation has seen a movement of people from former colonies to former imperial powers, for example, from North Africa to France, from Pakistan and India to Britain and from Indonesia to Holland. Further, the creation of new polities like the European Union has provided opportunities for people to move from one European nation-state to another, in search of work, education and greater life opportunities. Sociologists, historians and economists have developed several theoretical models to assist in understanding these movements.

Case study 1: Javanese transmigrants in Kalimantan, Indonesia

Transmigrasi is the name of an Indonesian programme of state-sponsored population movement, whereby poor and landless Javanese and Balinese are assisted to move from Java and Bali to the outer Indonesian islands, where they are provided with land and housing. The first transmigration, by some 155 families from central Java to Lampung in South Sumatra, occurred in 1905, as a response by the Dutch colonial government to Java's growing population (Setiawan, 2009, p. 3). The independent Indonesian government continued the programme, sending transmigrant Javanese to all parts of the archipelago. During the mid-1970s to the mid-1980s, the 'heyday' of transmigration, some 640,000 families, or 3,200,000 individuals, were resettled out of Java. Many worked as small famers, but transmigrants were also settled as share croppers within World Bank and UNDP-funded plantation projects. While transmigration continued to be referred to as a mechanism for alleviating population pressure, other factors were prominent, including national security (Javanese settled on the border between Indonesian Kalimantan and Malaysian Sarawak, for example, were presumed to be more loyal to the national government in Jakarta than their local neighbours, who may well be of the same ethnic group as those over the border in Malaysia); national development and national integration (Hoshour, 1997). The overarching aim of transmigration, then, has been to integrate Indonesia's many ethnic groups and to produce 'the Indonesian' (discussed in Case Study 1, Chapter 2), albeit a somewhat Javanised Indonesian.

One of the first transmigration villages in Kalimantan was Gunung Makmur, settled in 1953 by 500 East and Central Javanese families. Gunung is now a relatively prosperous village, with extensive wet rice lands, two schools and a weekly market. The majority of the villagers are Javanese transmigrants and their descendants, but some 20 per cent of the villagers are local Banjar people, who make their living as traders and civil servants. Although the ethnic division has been maintained – Banjar speak their own language and marry within their own group, as do the Javanese – villagers rarely speak of 'Banjar' and 'Javanese', instead referring to individuals as either 'people of the market' (*orang pasar*), most of whom are Banjar, and 'people of the mountain' (*orang gunung*), nearly all of whom are Javanese (Hawkins, 1989, p. 4).

According to the original transmigrants, the early years in Gunung Makmur were difficult. No housing had been prepared for them, and none of the land was cultivated; indeed, most of it was a swamp. Some transmigrants simply gave up and moved on to another transmigration set-tlement or returned home; after 5 years the population had halved. Mbah (grandfather) Iman is one who remained.

Mbah Iman was 43 years old and the father of seven children when he and his family arrived in Gunung Makmur from Yogyakarta, central Java. During the next 15 years he fathered two more children and, with the assistance of his older children, acquired, either through making a small compensation payment to the owner of uncultivated land or simply staking a claim by planting vacant land, about forty-five hectares of dry fields and five hectares of wet land suitable for rice cultivation. Mbah Iman's household planted most of the dry land with clove trees and some of the wet land with rice, but they could not farm the entire area alone, so Mbah Iman became his own migrant recruiting agent. He began by persuading three of his siblings and their families to move from Yogyakarta, live in his house and help farm his land. After his first major clove harvest in 1970 Mbah Iman returned briefly to Java and during the ensuing 10 years made eight visits to his home village near Yogyakarta. On each visit he went to neighbouring villages, speaking to farmers there about the land and opportunities Gunung Makmur offered. He gathered together a group in the village square and evangelised, offering his listeners a boat passage to Kalimantan, accommodation in his house, food and eventually land in return for their assistance farming his land.

During the 10 years between 1970 and 1980 Mbah Iman persuaded thirty-four young Javanese men, most of them landless labourers, to join him in Gunung Makmur. For an average of 3 years they lived in his house and helped with the work on his land. They also sought land of their own, and now all his former clients are landowners, farming land which they claimed and began to clear while still working for Mbah Iman.

Mbah Iman did not pay a wage to the migrants who lived with him. As members of his household they were expected to assist him and in return could expect food, clothing and eventually help in setting up their own households. Help took two major forms: Mbah Iman and his wife arranged marriages for their single clients, and he also provided them with land. Although Mbah Iman has stopped recruiting clients, saying that he is too old now, and that cheap land is no longer in ready supply, he continues to benefit from his 'children'. At a three-day *slametan* (a ritual meal which in Javanese tradition is held to celebrate auspicious events, such as weddings, births and circumcisions, as well significant dates in the Islamic calendar) held by Mbah Iman for his grandson's circumcision, two cows, five hundred kilos of rice, twenty-five cartons of cigarettes, fifty-five litres of cooking oil, ten kilos of coffee, ten kilos of sugar and twenty-five packets of tea were consumed by hundreds of guests. Yet Mbah Iman himself provided only the meat, oil, cigarettes and half the rice. The rest was contributed by his many 'children', who also did most of the cooking, the serving of the food and the cleaning.

The stability of the relationship of assistance and obligation between Mbah Iman and his clients rests on the fact that Mbah Iman did not simply recruit a labour force: he recruited a family. Pak Sidi, for example, was still single when he and six friends came to Gunung Makmur in 1972. Prior to 1972 Pak Sidi had frequently considered transmigrating, but he had always hesitated. He had no family of his own and thought that Sumatra or Sulawesi might be dangerous or lonely places for a single man. When Mbah Iman came to his village, however, Mbah Iman offered both the land Pak Sidi wanted for his future children and a family to live with. The second point was the critical one in persuading Pak Sidi to leave Java. He described his arrival and first years in Gunung Makmur as great and good fun, precisely because he was part of a household, part of Mbah Iman's family, an *anak buah*. While *anak buah* is often glossed as 'staff' – a doctor may refer to nurses and public health workers as *anak buah* – it may also refer to a kin-like relationship, and it is this latter meaning which both Mbah Iman and Pak Sidi invoke when they speak of *anak buah*.

Migration theories

Migration theories have been developed in response to a number of questions, including what category of person (by occupation and socio-economic location) is most likely to emigrate and why; which countries routinely accept, or even encourage, immigration and why; which countries provide emigrants to the world and why and finally, what is the effect of migration, on both the migrant's home country and the new host country. Early twentieth-century responses to these questions were formulated as part of an attempt by neo-classical economists to understand the role of labour migration in the process of economic development. Hence the explanations were restricted largely to the economic sphere (King, 2012, p. 12) and focused on push (motivations for emigration) and pull (reasons for choosing a particular country as a destination) factors, supply and demand, and cost benefit calculations (Massey et al., 2004, p. 4). For example, migration from Ireland to North America in the late nineteenth century can be explained by low wages for labourers in Ireland, and very restricted access to capital (push factors), versus high demand for labourers in North America, higher wages and greater access to the capital necessary to build, for example, a small business (pull factors). Similarly, in the case study of the Javanese transmigrants included in this chapter, land scarcity and low wages may be posited as the primary push factors, while land supply and guaranteed sustenance, if not high wages, are the primary pull factors. Of course, in this model, if wage rates in both sending and receiving countries were to become equal, then migratory movements would cease, because the migrant is imagined as an individual rational actor solely motivated by economic considerations.

The neo-classical approach to migration has exerted a significant influence, particularly on immigration policy makers (Massey et al., 2004, p. 4), but it has also attracted extensive criticism. Importantly, it fails to explain why so few people do actually migrate and why some countries have high rates of emigration while other countries, in economically similar positions, have a very low rate (King, 2012, p. 14). Further, it neglected historic causes of mass movement such as war, disease and famine and paid little attention to global connections, initially formed by colonialism, which linked some countries to each other and not to others (for example, India to Britain and Fiji). It also failed to recognise the effect on migration patterns of the emergence of an interdependent, globalised and unequal world structure. As a response, migration theorising from the 1960s onwards sought to develop new frameworks for understanding.

An early and influential approach was offered by Wilbur Zelinsky (1971), who linked changes in migration patterns to stages of economic development, as outlined by W. W. Rostow (1960). Rostow, who assumed that economic growth was inevitable, and equated this growth with modernity and a just society, argued that there were five main stages in the movement towards modernity. In the first stage, the experience of colonisation put 'traditional' societies (or former colonies) on the modernisation track. The second stage took these societies through the pre-conditions for take-off, including the construction of infrastructure – roads, ports and markets – into self-sustaining growth. The third phase, 'take-off', was synonymous with the process of industrialisation, while the fourth phase, the 'drive to maturity', saw nations eschew their traditional, collectivist ways of thinking in favour of rational capitalist approaches. The fifth stage coincided with the arrival of these newly modern societies at the age of high mass consumption (Hawkins, 2014, p. 69). Zelinsky's contribution was to link each of Rostow's stages to a particular migration pattern, based on the historical experience of Europe. Hence in stage one, traditional societies exhibited very limited migration, restricted to local movements occasioned by marriage, or marketing. In stage two, transitional societies were characterised by mass rural-urban migration and emigration to attractive foreign destinations for settlement and colonisation. By stage three, rural-urban migration had slowed, and circular migration, for example commuting, had emerged. For advanced societies in stage four, rural-urban migration was replaced by inter-urban migration, the mass immigration of labourers from less advanced countries, an international circulation of highly skilled professionals and a high intensity of internal circulation, for both business and recreation. The fifth and final future stage would see better communications and delivery systems substitute for at least some forms of human circulation, the continued immigration of workers from low-wage countries and a possibility of strict controls over immigration (King, 2012, p. 15).

Modernisation theory as espoused by Rostow has attracted a strong critique (see Hawkins, 2014, pp. 68–69), and Zelinksky's account is undoubtedly overly descriptive and overly prescriptive, but he did foresee the potential of advances in communication technology, a factor that decades later became central to transnational approaches to migration. Central to the critique of Zelinsky, and of modernisation theory in general, was the work of dependency theorists, particularly Andre Gunder Frank (1969, 1978) and more recently Raul Delgado Wise (Castles and Delgado Wise, 2007), and world systems theorists, who drew on the work of Wallerstein (1974). Dependency theorists argued that world migration patterns were prompted by and served to reproduce global inequality; that is, the wealth of the receiving countries was dependent on the continued flow of people from the sending countries. Where the neo-classical approach posited that wages in sending and receiving countries would eventually reach equilibrium, at which point migration would cease, dependency theorists argued that the economies of the receiving societies were characterised by a dual labour market, where a stable and capital-intensive primary sector drew in native workers, and a low-wage and unstable secondary sector pulled in primarily migrant workers, to labour as cleaners, nannies and kitchen hands for those in the primary sector (Massey et al., 2004, p. 11; King, 2012, p. 17). World systems theorists took a similarly global approach but argued that the origins of international migration could be traced to the colonial period and the emergence of a world market (see the account of Malaya's and Fiji's plantation sector earlier in this chapter). First the colonial powers, and later capitalist firms from the former colonial core countries, entered poorer countries on the periphery of the world economy, in search of land, labour, raw materials and new markets. Their activities disrupted and dispossessed local peoples, generating migrant flows to urban centres of the periphery, as well as to labour markets in the core, where the migrants were incorporated in low-wage sections of the market (Massey et al., 2004). For both dependency and world systems theorists, migration was the result of greater global forces and could not be characterised, following neo-classical economists, as the choice of a rational and free agent. Indeed, dependency and world systems frameworks render migrants as passive victims of global capitalism, a depiction of the migrant experience that is no more satisfying, or persuasive, than that provided by the neo-classicists.

A new economics of migration, combined with approaches that stressed the significance of migrant networks, emerged in the 1980s as an attempt to overcome the shortcomings of previous approaches. The new economics argues that migrant decisions are not made by individual isolated actors, but by families and households, who may decide that sending one or two of their members to work in a foreign labour market is a good risk management strategy; if the harvest fails at home there will still be remittances from abroad. Migrant networks, or interpersonal ties that connect migrants, non-migrants and former migrants in webs of kinship and shared origin, further reduce risk, but in this instance risk to the migrant, who can rely on such networks for information, perhaps initial accommodation and friendship (see the case study of Javanese migrants in this chapter and its discussion of *anak buah*).

Both the new economics and the network approach allowed for a framing of migration that was structural but, in the emphasis on affective ties, was moving to an understanding of migration that focused not just on global causes and global patterns but on the experience of migration. King has termed this an 'epistemological shift' (2012, p. 25) and suggests that the theme which has dominated migration studies since the 1990s has been transnationalism.

The 'transnational turn' in migration studies can be dated to the publication of *Towards a Transnational Perspective on Migration* (Glick-Schiller et al., 1992) and the edited collection *Nations Unbound* (Basch et al., 1994). These early works argued that some migrants continue to be active in their homelands at the same time that they become part of the places where they settle, defining transnationalism as 'the processes by which migrants forge and sustain multi-stranded social relations that link together their societies of origin and settlement' (Basch et al., 1994, p. 6). Over time, a transformative emphasis was added: transmigrants do not simply link places in space, they transform these places and those already residing there. Hence 'the flow of people, money, and "social remittances" (ideas, norms, practices and identities) within these spaces is so dense, thick and widespread that nonmigrants' lives are also transformed' (Levitt and Jaworsky, 2007, p. 132), and:

> While from an individual perspective, the act of sending a remittance, buying a house in the migrant's hometown, or travelling there on occasion have purely personal consequences, in the aggregate they can modify the fortunes and the cultures of these towns and even of the countries of which they are part. (Portes, 2003, in Vertovec, 2004, p. 973)

Early studies of transnationalism were perhaps overly celebratory, depicting the transnational experience as liberating, even emancipatory (Levitt and Jaworsky, 2007; and compare with Case Study 2 in this chapter), and allocated an overly deterministic role to information and communication technology (it is unlikely that all migrants use social media all the time). They also tended to ignore the fact that migrants have historically maintained long-distance social networks (Wimmer and Glick-Schiller, 2003; Vertovec, 2004). However, a transnational perspective has allowed migration scholars to integrate studies of process, patterns and structures with those of personal migrant experience, identity and agency. In particular, attention has been paid to the manner in which migrants embed themselves in multiple places, 'embedding' referring not just to physical location but also to practices through which migrants construct a transnational identity. Vertovec has referred to this as 'bi-focality' or a dual frame of reference (2004, p. 974) and cites as an example Ruba Salih's work on Moroccan women in Italy. According to Salih, whether the women are in Italy or Morocco, they buy articles of clothing, consume specific foods and display certain items from their 'other home' in order to symbolise their ongoing sense of double belonging (in Vertovec, 2004, p. 975). Alejandro Portes provides another example of simultaneous belonging in his account of the Ticuani Potable Water Committee, a private civic group who raised funds and then purchased equipment to bring clean water to Ticuani, a small farming community in Mixteca, Mexico. The Water Committee, who had been involved in projects like the Ticuani one for 20 years, spent several weekends negotiating with contractors in Ticuani before leaving for work on Monday morning. Portes point is that the committee did not live in Ticuani, or even in Mexico, but rather all its members were resident in Brooklyn, New York. The Ticuani project marked their twentieth anniversary of transnational projects, and for it they created a new seal for the committee. The seal reads, 'For the Progress of Ticuani: the Absent Ones, Always Present' (Portes, 2004, p. 228).

Case study 2: a Bangladeshi woman in Australia: Dipti's story

The life experience of the contemporary transnational migrant, according to much of the literature on transnationalism, is a positive one, particularly when compared to the alienation and marginalisation common to historical migration experiences. To be sure, contemporary migrants may face language and cultural problems as they settle into the new country, but eventually they should be able to combine the best of both worlds. Dipti, a Bangladeshi woman who migrated to Australia in 1985, is easily characterised as transnational – she visits Bangladesh on an annual basis, she remains in close contact with her kin and she has sponsored the movement of her younger brother and his wife to Australia – but her life story cannot be characterised as one of hope and optimism. Rather, as an unmarried woman Dipti's status is low in both Bangladesh and among the Bangladeshi migrant community in Australia, and her sustained and successful efforts to financially support her family in Bangladesh has not won her their approval. Rather, the Bangladeshi cultural meaning of marriage as the single pathway to respectable adulthood, and the devaluation and denigration of unmarried women as sexually suspect, even shameful, migrated to Australia alongside Dipti. After more than twenty years as a self-supporting woman in Australia,

Dipti's identity continues to be framed by a meaning system that she ostensibly left behind in Bangladesh.

The anthropologist Santi Rozario has known Dipti for many years and has provided a compelling account of Dipti's life (2007). Dipti is the fourth in a family of seven siblings, brought up in a village near Dhaka, where she trained as a registered nurse. She came to Australia, initially as an irregular immigrant, at the age of 28, following the death of her father. According to Dipti her father had told her to look after her siblings and her poorer cousins, and the desire to provide for them, and to support them in maintaining the Bangladeshi ideal of a single extended family household, was a motivating factor in her decision to emigrate. Finding a spouse was also a consideration. Dipti was unmarried at the time of her arrival in Australia; indeed, Bangladeshi women of her generation were usually married by the age of eighteen, and as a woman in her late twenties she was considered unmarriageable by Bangladeshi standards. Dipti has not yet found a husband in Australia, but has found work.

Dipti began by working in private nursing homes as a nurse's aide, and once her resident visa was granted and she had upgraded her nursing qualifications she was employed as a registered nurse in a public hospital. For many years Dipti has been working seven days a week, in both the public and private health system, and consequently her income is quite good. The bulk of this income has gone to support her family in Bangladesh. She has bought land, built a large brick house for the family, paid for her younger brother's education, as well as that of nieces and nephews, provided funds for family weddings, bankrolled her older brother's business ventures and returned home every Christmas with a suitcase full of presents and money. But despite all her assistance, her family continued to view her not with gratitude, but as simply an unmarried woman without children, a failure in Bangladeshi eyes. As a failure, she might provide, but she did not need to be consulted; hence two of her brothers broke away from the family household to set up their own nuclear households, and the wife of one remarked, 'I will see where Aunty goes when she is old, she doesn't have any son, she will have to go back home and be at the mercy of her brother's wives' (Rozario, 2007, p. 159).

When Dipti realised that retirement to the village was an unrealistic dream, she instead focused on creating a family in Australia and to this end sponsored the migration of her youngest brother and his wife. She bought a two-bedroom apartment – with a large mortgage on it, as all her money had been going to Bangladesh – and a car and found jobs for her brother and sister-in-law. At first life with her brother and his wife was good, but in a relatively short time relations between the three of them deteriorated. Dipti's sister-in-law experienced Dipti's help as intrusive and controlling and, secure in her position as a wife, had no hesitation in voicing her opinion. Dipti, on the other hand, felt alienated in her own home, but as a single mature woman her structural position is ambiguous. For Dipti, spending her resources on her family is a reflection of her love and fealty, but her 'single status remains the overriding factor in how (her) identity is constructed by (her) family and community' (Rozario, 2007, p. 165). Not even Dipti's perhaps overly generous gifts and payments to her family could buy her a secure place in her family because, in Bangladeshi family and kin terms, Dipti does not belong in her natal family. Rather, she should belong to a husband and his family. That she does not means that she is anomalous, even sexually suspect, a liminal being.

Conclusion

Migration studies, initially an interdisciplinary field populated in the main by quantitative geographers and economists who were preoccupied with rates and statistical patterns, have in the past thirty years been transformed by sociologists, human geographers, anthropologists and social historians, who are less interested in migrant numbers and more interested in the migrant experience. These new qualitative studies have provided richly detailed accounts of the motivations for migration, and the ways in which contemporary immigrants have constructed, often via the deployment of new media, transnational fields that link the 'old country' to the new home. We now have a window on the life of the real, as distinct from the acted, Karl Oskar and Kristina.

Questions for students

- Read Dipti's story. To what extent has Dipti's experience of migration been shaped by her gender?
- Why do some people migrate and others – the majority – stay at home?
- What can a quantitative approach contribute to migration studies that a qualitative account cannot?
- Mbah Iman's story is not unique. Do you know anyone like Mbah Iman? How did your 'Mbah Iman' recruit migrants, and what obstacles did they encounter?

Recommended reading

Baldassar, L. (2001) *Visits Home: Migration Experiences between Italy and Australia* (Melbourne: Melbourne University Press).

Levitt, P., DeWind, J. and Vertovec, S. (2003) 'International Perspectives on Transnational Migration: An Introduction', *International Migration Review,* 37: 565–575.

Marchetta, M. (1992) *Looking for Alibrandi* (Penguin: Orchard Books).

CHAPTER 11

Work

Kate Huppatz

Introduction

For most of us, work is a daily occurrence. It has been estimated that workers in Organisation for Economic Co-operation and Development (OECD) countries spend 1765 hours labouring in paid employment per year and one-tenth to one-fifth of their time carrying out unpaid domestic work (OECD, 2013a). Work is therefore a common lived experience that plays a role in the production of social life, identities and experiences of belonging. The sociological significance of work has been recognised to varying degrees by social theorists of the past and present, and early sociology in particular was very concerned with the meaning of work for identities and social cohesion. This chapter very broadly, and by no means exhaustively, charts the development of social theories of work as well as the major shifts in the nature of the organisation of paid labour in the global north. The three descriptors most often used to identify these major historical shifts are 'industrialisation', 'feminisation' and 'globalisation' (although note that the wholesale use of these terms is controversial, none of these factors occurred and are occurring seamlessly, at one time, and across all nation states). Beginning with industrialisation, and paying particular attention to the relationship between gender identities and labour (gendered jobs and organisations are perhaps the sites at which identity and belonging are most obviously connected to work), this chapter examines how these historical shifts have affected workers' identities, workplace identities and experiences of belonging. The final section of the chapter will also consider the 'end of work' thesis, put forward by individualisation theorists. In recent years some scholars have claimed that work is no longer relevant for identity and belonging; leisure and consumption (discussed in Chapters 12 and 13) have been marked as more meaningful for post-industrial and late modern experiences of selfhood. This chapter will argue that while processes of globalisation may have impacted the ways in which rich nations think about and do work, this does not mean that work is irrelevant for contemporary experience.

Early industrialisation and classical theories of work

Europe's industrialisation occurred in the mid-eighteenth to early nineteenth century and featured the movement from feudal ties to the creation of employer/employee relationships in order to manufacture goods. Industrialisation at this time was therefore a radical reorganisation of labour and production that restructured social life. 'Classical' social theorists (for a problematisation of the appointment of 'classical' status to theorists see Connell (2007)) witnessed this movement and, for some, these changes produced immense anxiety. One such theorist was Karl Marx, and it is worth briefly considering his theoretical insights not only because his ideas have been foundational for work sociology, but also because he was highly preoccupied with the impact of industrial work relationships on identities and collective experiences. For Marx, the modern labour system, and therefore society at this time, became inequitably stratified into two classes: the owners of the means of production (the *bourgeoisie*) and the workers (the *proletariat*). This system was inequitable because the bourgeoisie and the proletariat existed in an exploitative relationship in which the bourgeoisie paid the workers less than their labour's worth in order to generate a surplus of wealth and elevate the bourgeoisie's own positions. An individual's location on the bourgeoisie/proletariat divide therefore informed their life chances or social class positions and identities. Worker suffering was exacerbated by the experience of *alienation*; as they had no control over their labour or the products they produced, workers increasingly experienced estrangement from the products they made, from the activities they engaged in, from what makes them human and from each other (Edgell, 2006, p. 29). However, the bourgeoisie were not immune to alienation. Marx predicted that the ruling class would also experience estrangement as a result of their role in dehumanising workers. Industrial capitalism would therefore have dire consequences for workers' experiences of both identity and belonging, for their relationships to themselves and to their community. The only solution to alienation, according to Marx, is communism. Under a communist regime, workers would come together, in communion, and experience greater levels of attachment to their labour and to each other.

Writing after Marx, but certainly within his 'evolutionary framework' (Thompson, 2003, p. 53), Emile Durkheim also considered the meaning of work for identity and belonging. However, Marx's analysis centred on social class relationships, whereas Durkheim was more interested in the individual's relationship to society. As discussed in Chapter 1, in his book, *The Division of Labour in Society* (1984), Durkheim employed a functionalist approach to examine our movement from 'primitive' to 'advanced' societies. He proposed that in primitive contexts strong moral codes and norms sustained by a 'collective conscience' produce a homogenous collective bound together by a 'mechanical solidarity'. In contrast, in advanced societies, as populations and the demand for resources grow, specialisation and a division of labour are developed so that resources may be produced to sustain a larger community. In this context the collective conscience becomes weaker and individuals experience greater freedom but social integration remains strong. This is because mechanical solidarity is replaced with organic solidarity – a belonging that is based on difference and interdependence rather than similarity. Durkheim's perspective on capitalism may therefore be differentiated from Marx's; for Marx industrialisation creates class conflict and marginalises the working class, whereas for Durkheim it does have the capacity to produce belonging.

Industrial society and Fordism

Marx's proposed revolution did not occur in the global north, but industrialisation did 'progress'. In Marx's industrial society manufacturing entailed both machine-made and hand-made products fashioned by craft workers, and this meant that many complex items were expensive and difficult to produce (Edgell, 2006, p. 73). In response to these inefficiencies, in the early twentieth century, Henry Ford (also known for his car brand) created a new production system which profoundly impacted manufacturing but also society more generally. This system contained three elements. First, Ford separated the conception of products from their execution (this is known as Taylorism) and fragmented and simplified tasks; second, he ensured greater control over production via the moving assembly line; and third, he used machines to standardise his products (Edgell, 2006, p. 74). Ford therefore made production as seamless and controlled as possible and was so effective in this task that variations of this production system were, and continue to be, adopted around the globe so that the term 'Fordism' now regularly stands in for 'standardisation'.

Ford is well known for his impact on the mode of production, and also for the ways in which he restructured working conditions and employee–employer relations, as well as for his attempts to shape workers' behaviours. Ford improved working conditions in that he increased wages and reduced working hours to eight hours per day. The relative stability of employment during this time, as well as the comparative prosperity of the manufacturing industry, meant that many workers could achieve a 'job for life' (Beck, 2000, p. 2). However, in an attempt to ensure worker productivity, Ford also expected workers to adopt clean lifestyles, devoid of addictive pursuits such as drinking and gambling, and so attempted to fashion the identities of workers. Workers were even monitored in their leisure time by Ford's 'private police' and were either punished or rewarded for their behaviours. In this way, Ford not only standardised work, but also standardised lifestyles in family and community. Any behaviours and forms of community outside of this vision, particularly unionised activities, were explicitly blocked by the Ford company (although this does not mean workers were without agency, indeed, in the 1930s, Ford lost the fight to ban workers from joining trade unions (Edgell, 2006, p. 78)).

Contemporary theorists have spent some time reflecting on the relationship between work, identity and belonging during this era. Individualisation theorists, for example, argue that this was the period in which work was most meaningful for identity. Bauman (2004, p. 27) theorises that individuals of industrial capitalism were no longer ascribed identities as they were in pre-modern society, and so work initially became the primary tool with which to construct identity: 'The fixed itinerary of work-career and the prerequisites of lifelong identity construction fit each other well'. Bauman (2004), along with Beck (2000), argues that, stable employment and strong connections between workplaces and communities resulted in employment shaping 'both individual identity as well as collective norms and values' (Strangleman, 2007, p. 83) in ways that are no longer possible in contemporary society.

While some authors positively assess the job opportunities that arose from industrialisation (see for example Kerr et al., 1960; Blauner, 1964), many more theorists have problematised the alienating and deskilling effect of industrial work and have connected industrial labour positions with social class divisions. For example, Bravermann (1974) highlights how management in industrial contexts deliberately minimised decision-making opportunities for workers and thereby reduced skills. In this way, Marx's theory continues to influence understandings of industrialisation (although note that the other 'classical' theorists were also influential. For example, Goldthorpe (1968a, 1968b, 1969) and his co-researchers drew on Max Weber to establish typologies of orientations to work). More recently, individualisation theorists also appear to echo Marx's claims, arguing that paid work during industrial capitalism was 'nothing more than degraded and alienating labour' (despite holding significance for identity) (Strangleman, 2012, p. 419). Bauman (2004) asserts that in the factory context, tasks were necessarily set and overseen by others, and so were devoid of meaning for workers; there were no opportunities for workers to express their personalities in this process.

Women and work

Ford's 'worker' was not gender neutral. In the heyday of Fordism, that is, the 1950s and 1960s, the standardised worker was a male full-time worker. While some poorer women have always worked in paid employment, women at this time were largely expected to support this standardised worker by shouldering the unpaid labour in the home. This division of labour began around the turn of the nineteenth century, when women in Western countries were separated from men in that they were confined to the home while the public sphere, including paid employment, was deemed a masculine domain, a sphere where women did not belong (for further discussion of the public/private divide, see also Chapters 4 and 8). However, during the Second World War, women were asked to take up the paid employment posts usually reserved for men as part of the 'war effort'. When the war ended, many women were unhappy with leaving the paid employment they had entered while men were deployed. From this point, women increasingly entered the paid labour market so that, in many parts of the Western world, women now attend higher education at equal rates to men and carry out many of the occupational roles that they were previously quarantined from. Yet, despite this radical reconfiguration of the labour force, if we fast-forward our discussion to the present day, women still experience hurdles (and sometimes complete roadblocks) in seeking access to masculinised jobs and senior positions (and in some cultures, it is still deemed abnormal for women to be in the workforce at all: see Case Study 2, Chapter 10). Women also continue to do most of the unpaid labour in the home, whether they are in paid employment or not. Paid and unpaid labour is therefore central to the differentiation of modern and late modern masculine and feminine identities. The next section of this chapter will consider these inequalities and what they mean for identity and belonging.

Unpaid labour: the domestic division of labour

As women traditionally carried out unpaid labour in the private sphere, they were written out of many understandings of work and employment (Marx's theory is a case in point, women were largely absent from his understanding of society). In the 1960s and 1970s feminists objected to gender-neutral theories and started to argue for women's entrance into the paid workforce but also for the acknowledgement of domestic activities (cooking, cleaning, child care, etc.) as 'labour'. In the *Sociology of Housework*, Oakley (1974), for example, argued for housework to be seen as genuine labour that is akin to unskilled and repetitive factory work rather than an essential element of feminine identities. Oakley's (1974, p. 29) conclusion from her research was that: 'The equation of femaleness with housewifery is basic to the structure of modern society'; gender difference is connected to labour activities.

More recently, feminists have further developed this argument, and suggest that the domestic division of labour *creates* gender identities; it is intimately connected to the ways in which we 'do' or 'display' gender (West and Zimmerman, 1987) (for more discussion on this approach see Chapter 4). West and Zimmerman (1987, p. 144) contend that:

> It is not simply that household labor is designated as 'women's work', but that for a woman to engage in it and a man not to engage in it is to draw on and exhibit the 'essential nature' of each. What is produced and reproduced is not merely the activity and artifact of domestic life, but the material embodiment of wifely and husbandly roles, and derivatively, of womanly and manly conduct ... What are also frequently produced and reproduced are the dominant and subordinate statuses of the sex categories.

Therefore, according to the 'gender display' perspective, the alignment that is made between household labour and femininity (via women's capacity to reproduce) has resulted in domestic activities holding significance for the differentiation of masculine and feminine identities and for the subordination of the feminine to the masculine. This process is something that individuals, particularly cohabitating heterosexual couples, continue to be invested in. As Beck and Beck-Gernsheim (2002, p. 102) argue, the allocation of unpaid household labour continues to be 'closely bound up with the self-image and the life projects of men and women'.

The gender display argument has been highly influential for research on unpaid household labour. The perspective has been supported by a number of studies (see for example Sevilla-Sanz et al., 2010) and goes some way in explaining why it is so difficult to change gendered patterns without resorting to biological understandings that essentialise and therefore dichotomise and fix masculine and feminine identities. This type of approach also helps us to understand the often minimal but also uneven changes that have taken place in heterosexual households across rich nations in recent years. In 2013a the Organisation for Economic Cooperation and Development (OECD) reported that men in OECD countries still engage in much less unpaid labour than women. Women carry out an average of 273 minutes of unpaid labour per day whereas men only complete 141 minutes. Men and women in OECD countries also continue to vary in the type of tasks they take on in households. Men spend more time on household maintenance than women and carry out more gardening and pet care than other jobs (although not at an equal rate to women) but do much less cooking and cleaning. Men therefore continue to distance themselves from 'Tasks that have traditionally been thought of as "women's work"' (Miranda, 2011, p. 25). However, attitudes to paid labour vary across social contexts. For example, while Turkish and Mexican women are occupied by roughly 4.3 hours more unpaid labour than

Turkish and Mexican men, women only spend approximately one hour more than men on unpaid domestic work in Nordic countries (OECD, 2013a). This variance may be associated with the differing attitudes to gender across these contexts. Nordic countries are very progressive when it comes to gender equality (Sweden, for example introduced paternity leave in 1974) and so may be less invested in 'displaying gender' and therefore less committed to the gendered division of household labour.

Case study 1: the gendered division of unpaid household labour for higher income earners across different cultural contexts

Further evidence for the notion that we 'do gender' identities through unpaid household labour can be drawn from Baxter and Hewitt's (2013) study on Australian heterosexual couples. Making use of the Household Income and Labour Dynamics in Australia (HILDA) Survey, Baxter and Hewitt (2013, p. 40) find that the more Australian women earn, the less time they spend on housework. However, this is only the case until women earn 66.56 per cent of the household income, after that point their contribution to household labour actually increases. These findings suggest that women may be bargaining their way out of household labour but only to a certain level of income. Once women earn 66.65 per cent of the household money the 'gender display' model becomes relevant for understanding labour arrangements as women perhaps attempt to compensate for gender inappropriate earnings. Therefore, the division of unpaid domestic labour in Australia is not necessarily the outcome of a rational choice process between partners; the data suggest that gender identities and roles play a part in the inequitable division of household tasks. Baxter and Hewitt contrast their findings with Gupta's (2007) study, which finds that the time American women spend on household labour is dependent on their own absolute earnings, rather than their earnings relative to their partner's. Baxter and Hewitt (2013, p. 29) conclude that when compared to America (which also has higher rates of full-time female employment), 'Australia has a strong male-breadwinner institutional framework that continues to hinder gender equality in paid and unpaid work'. Again, commitment to traditional gender relations in the home varies from social context to social context, which suggests that culture and socially produced identities, rather than biology, reproduce inequitable divisions.

Feminised jobs and gendered hierarchies

The gendered division of labour extends into the realm of paid employment. Although women now make up a significant proportion of the labour force, their participation does not equal men's. In 2012, 57 per cent of women were in paid employment compared to 73 per cent of men in OECD countries (although, again, the difference varies across countries and is minimal in Nordic countries) (OECD, 2013b), and due to the continuation of their unpaid domestic responsibilities, women disproportionately participate in part-time paid labour (OECD, 2012a). What is more, women and men are horizontally segregated within the workforce. This means that women tend to be concentrated in 'gender appropriate' service work that mirrors the work they carry out in the home, while men carry out rational or physical labour. In many countries, women are overpopulated in salesperson, domestic helper, cleaning, secretarial, personal care and teaching roles and men disproportionately take up driver, construction, mechanical, architectural, engineering and finance professional roles (OECD, 2002, p. 88). Paid work and unpaid work are therefore interconnected in that they are two spheres of a 'total social organisation of labour' (Glucksmann, 1995). It is very difficult to understand women's paid employment status without understanding women's relationship to unpaid domestic labour.

One way in which women's paid employment is connected to the labour they carry out in the home is that it often involves, or is seen to involve, caring or emotions in the servicing of others. Feminists have argued that this dimension of feminised work is undervalued; it is often 'hidden' and therefore not recognised as genuine labour. Ungerson (1983) and Graham (1983) for example, argue for caring to be seen as constituted by both 'love' and 'labour'. Drawing on her ground-breaking research with flight attendants, Hochschild (1983) also theorises emotion work, coining the term 'emotional labour'. Hochschild (1983, p. 7) argues that service workers must manage their own emotions as well as the emotions of their customers or clients; this kind of work requires employees to either induce or supress their own feelings and so 'calls for a coordination of mind and feeling, and it sometimes draws on a source of self that we honour as deep and integral to our individuality'. This type of labour may therefore be distinct in the ways in which it makes use of workers' identities (although it must be noted that emotional labour is now viewed as, not only a feature of feminised work, but a growing characteristic of post-industrial jobs more generally).

As connections have been made between the work that women do in the home and the labour that women carry out in the public sphere, explanations for horizontal segregation often link women's gender identities with their work activities. Gender role theory is often drawn upon to explain women's 'preference' for feminised jobs. This approach emphasises 'the culturally shaped norms, values and identities that workers exhibit, which impact their occupational pursuits' (Vallas, 2012, p. 99). However, this understanding tends to overemphasise the role of socialisation and does not allow for any movement or malleability in workers' identities and so cannot explain why men might now be taking up feminised jobs or why women might be taking up masculinised jobs (albeit slowly). Offering an alternative approach, which draws on Pierre Bourdieu's theory (outlined in Chapter 3), and empirical research with employees in the 'caring' field, Huppatz (2009, 2012) proposes that women often take up feminised jobs because 'femaleness' and femininity act as assets or 'gender capital' within feminised occupational spaces in ways that they may not in masculinised spaces (although feminine and female capital may be wielded by both men and women). Due to the connections that are commonly made between femininity, caring and the female body a (limited), gender advantage occurs in these feminised spaces when bodies are recognised as female (but not necessarily feminine), when feminine dispositions are displayed or when a worker is simply hailed as feminine (this occurs when one's body is recognised as feminine). In these ways, the nurses and social workers Huppatz interviewed communicated experiences of advantage in gaining employment, relating to female managers, patients and clients, and general job performance.

Women and men are not only separated in the types of employment they engage in but also by the status of their jobs. Women's work tends to be paid less than men's work and afforded less power and respectability (OECD, 2012a). In addition, women reach a 'glass ceiling' when it comes to promotion and career progression so that in the OECD less than one-third of managers are women (OECD, 2012a, p. 153). Women's relative isolation from senior and management positions is termed 'vertical segregation'. Explanations that focus on identity to explain women's limited progression in occupational hierarchies include Hakim's (2000) controversial 'preference theory' which proposes that women may be differentiated by their orientation to home and work. According to Hakim women exist as three identity 'types' and as such, women exhibit either home-centred, work-centred or adaptive lifestyle preferences, which means that vertical segregation is the result of women's investments in home life. The critique of this approach is, however, that it overemphasises women's freedom of choice and cannot account for workplace discrimination or why men might experience 'glass escalators' into management (Williams, 1992). Taking an alternative approach, Acker (1990, 1992) claims that organisations themselves have gendered identities and that this identity, particularly in the upper echelons, tends to be masculine, making it very difficult for women to 'belong' within prestigious organisational culture. More recently, authors have highlighted how other identities, such as social class and ethnic identities, are also disadvantaged in these hierarchies (see for example, Duffy, 2007; Wingfield, 2009; Acker 2012).

Case study 2: gendered career expectations for young people in OECD countries

The OECD's Programme for International Student Assessment (PISA) has found that young people continue to have gender-based rather than skill-based career expectations. PISAs 2006 questionnaire asked 15-year old students from 57 countries what career they expect to be taking part in, at around the age of 30. The results were remarkably gendered, despite some variations between countries. Girls were much less likely than boys to expect to work in engineering and computing jobs. On average, less than 5 per cent of girls anticipated an engineering or computing career path compared to 18 per cent of boys, and these results were consistent for both low-achieving and high-achieving students (OECD, 2012b). However, this did not mean that girls were not interested in science careers altogether. In fact, many more girls than boys indicated that they expected to achieve health science careers (even when controlling for nursing and midwifery, two jobs that often skew gendered occupations and education statistics because they are so highly feminised). 16 per cent of girls and 7 per cent of boys expected a health service career, or, as the OECD (2012b) puts it, 'a science profession with a caring component'. Nevertheless, girls did expect high achievement within their anticipated occupations; on average they were 11 per cent more likely than boys to expect to achieve legislator, senior official, managerial or professional status. This suggests that, although it seems horizontal segregation will perpetuate for this generation, girls are less likely to expect to encounter the glass ceiling than previous generations and this may have some impact on their occupational pathways.

Globalisation and labour markets

Although women continue to experience significant disadvantage in the labour market, the inroads that women have made cannot be understated. Female participation in the paid workforce is far greater than in the days of Fordism and this has dramatically altered the constitution of the labour market so that it is frequently referred to as 'feminised'. Indeed in the 1990s, McDowell (1991, p. 417) claimed that 'the feminization of the labour market is amongst the most far-reaching of the changes of the last two decades'. However, the feminisation of paid employment is not occurring in isolation. Rather, it is a significant component of a larger shift in the organisation of capitalism that has resulted in the 'global integration of financial markets' (Castells, 2010, p. 2) and feminisation is taking place alongside deindustrialisation in many parts of the world. Rich Western nations no longer feature the robust manufacturing industries of Marx's time; much of the manufacturing has moved off the shores of the global north and is carried out in poorer global south nations (although this is occurring in an uneven manner – countries like Japan and Germany still feature significant manufacturing activity (Castells, 2010, p. 245)). This means that the primary industries in rich nations are now service (although note that what is categorised as 'service' is diverse) and knowledge based and there has been a corresponding growth in professional, technical and management positions in most countries. Workers are also becoming much more transient than in the past (as evidenced by the worldwide growth in labour migration, discussed in Chapter 10), which means that they no longer remain in a single workplace for a lifetime and are much more likely to have several career changes throughout their working lives. This is, in part, due to a new demand for workplace and worker flexibility in order to cope with rapidly changing markets. Finally, society is becoming more 'informational' and this means that societies 'organize their production system around the principles of maximizing knowledge-based productivity through the development and diffusion of information technologies' (Castells, 2010, p. 219–220). The next section of this chapter will discuss the ramifications of these changes for workers' identities and experiences as well as workers' collective identities and movements.

Precarious employment

Castells (2010) has much to say about the impact of globalisation on the organisation of work and work identities. In particular, Castells asserts that, even though not all work is organised in response to a global economy, globalisation has affected the ways in which work activities are organised in space and time. Castells (2010) emphasises (along with Beck, 2000) that adaptability and flexibility are key to successful global workplaces and this has led to the proliferation of non-standard forms of work. However, while an increase in flexibility may enable businesses to become more competitive, as outlined in Chapter 3 (with reference to the 'precariat'), it is also resulting in a growth in part-time, temporary and irregular work. This means that, although there has been an expansion of professional, technical and managerial jobs, many people are becoming increasingly work-poor. Beck (2000, p. 1) proposes that if neo-liberal free-markets continue unchecked we will see the 'Brazilianisation of the West'; the structure of employment in the global north will mirror the structure of employment in semi-industrialised countries like Brazil where 'those who depend on a wage or salary in full-time work represent only a minority of the economically active population; the majority earn their living in more precarious conditions'. The relatively stable working conditions observed during the Fordist era are therefore diminishing and individuals are increasingly engaging in, what was once predominantly a characteristic of women's labour, that is, multiple activities of training and employment (Beck, 2000, p. 2).

Edgell (2006) notes that Beck and Castells agree that work has transformed because of the relationship of capital to labour. These theorists argue that capital tends to be organised on a global scale whereas labour is organised on a national scale and this impacts the efficacy of collective action. Other factors that contribute to the increase in capital power and decrease in labour power include: (1) government incentives to transnational corporations (intended to encourage transnational corporations to locate their business within national boundaries and create jobs. These incentives can include adjusting or ending labour legislation); (2) the capacity for transnational corporations to relocate to where labour is less expensive and less regulated; (3) capital is increasingly located in a smaller number of companies and this has consolidated power in relation to employees and governments. This means that in contemporary society, Marx's revolution based on worker experiences of collectivism and communion seems unlikely. However, workers are not completely disempowered. Unions are increasingly organising themselves so that they are also global entities; although governments offer incentives they also place some limits on transnational corporations, and pay and conditions are not deteriorating at equal rates across all contexts (Edgell, 2006, p. 192).

Case study 3: fixed-term contracts in academia in the United Kingdom

As Beck (2000, p. 82) points out, insecurity is occurring at all levels of the skills hierarchy, including academia. In the United Kingdom, the number of tenured teaching and research lecturing positions have declined while the number of fixed-term positions have increased 'from a small base to 16,000, about 21 per cent of the total' (Bryson, 2004, p. 194). In his study, which draws upon data from the Working in Higher Education (WiHE) Survey, Bryson (2004, p. 202) discovers that workers on fixed-term contracts find it very difficult to achieve full-time employment and that 'fixed term contracts lead to a deterioration in employment and career structures'. While both men and women are impacted by this precarity, women are more disadvantaged by this phenomenon as it has coincided with women's increased representation in academia (and Bryson's data shows that this has nothing to do with women's 'preferences'). Bryson therefore suggests that the divide between fixed-term and permanent employment may be viewed as a third form of gendered segregation (after vertical and horizontal segregation) operating within academia. While the recent changes in the organisation of capitalism have impacted many, if not all, types of work in rich nations, including high-status professions, women continue to bear the brunt of inequalities in workplaces.

Work and identity in the new capitalism

What do the changes in the organisation of capitalism mean for the relationship between work and identity? Theorists like Castells argue that this means that work is no longer as relevant for our identities. Castells states (2000, p. 3) that while, 'in a world of global flows of wealth, power, and images' both collective and individual identities may be more important to us than ever, the 'widespread destructuring of organizations, delegitimation of institutions, fading away of major social movements, and ephemeral cultural expressions' have meant that 'people increasingly organize their meaning not around what they do but on the basis of what they are, or believe they are'. Similarly, Beck (2000, p. 75) argues that the flexibilisation of work has led to increasing individualisation; in this context 'the standard biography becomes an elective 'do it yourself biography, a risk biography" and is no longer informed by tradition or 'a job for life'. In the same vein, Bauman (2004, p. 27) claims:

> A steady, durable and continuous, logically coherent and tightly structured working career is however no longer a widely viable option. Only in relatively rare cases can a permanent identity be defined, let alone secured, through the job performed.

As we no longer experience the conditions for forging lifelong identities in late modernity, identity is experienced as temporary, incomplete, conditional and plural, and so the desire of identity is better fulfilled by impermanent consumer goods, the antithesis of 'jobs for life' (Bauman, 2004, pp. 28–29). For Bauman, we have entered a new era, where we are now a 'society of consumers' rather than a 'society of producers' (see also Chapters 10 and 13) and where the aesthetic of consumption is more important for our identities than a work ethic:

> In the industrial phase of modernity one fact was beyond all questioning: that everyone must be a producer first, before being anything else. In 'modernity mark two', the consumers' modernity, the brute unquestionable act is that one needs to be a consumer first, before one can think of becoming anything in particular (Bauman, 2004, p. 23).

Many contemporary sociologists, particularly individualisation theorists, therefore question the relevance of work for late modern identities. As Strangleman (2012, p. 412) states: 'Whereas sociologists in the 1960s and 1970s lined up to explore the way employment shaped identity, latterly debate has been marked by a series of claims which suggest the detachment of meaning from work.'

However, there is also much evidence to show that work is not obsolete. To start with, consumption demands income. There is no way individuals can fashion identities unless they have the capital to purchase products (and the more well-paid an individual is, the more they may buy). Employment therefore directly impacts our capacity to consume identities and by extension construct social class positionings (see Chapter 3). Moreover, Bauman (2004, p. 35) comments that there are new divisions in labour between those who engage in self-fulfilling or honourable labour (the elite) and those who do not. Elite occupations, as with most other jobs, may not last for life, but they do convey status and position; they create distance between those who 'have' and those who 'have not' and so play a significant role in identity building. Strangleman (2007) points out that work continues to hold meaning for the working classes as well. Strangleman (2007, p. 100) argues that the literature that proclaims the end of work 'does violence to the experience of work in the past and present' and that the working classes are not simply passive victims of global capital, rather, work continues to provide 'structure and meaning' in peoples' lives. Finally, if we return to gender, it is very clear from the data that has been collected on unpaid household labour and gendered occupational segregation that work still holds significance for displaying gender identity. As workforces become more feminised, paid employment is arguably becoming increasingly significant for women's identities.

Conclusion

This chapter has focused on labour force patterns, working conditions, labour divisions and work experiences and has broadly considered the impact of industrialisation, feminisation and globalisation on identities and experiences of belonging. In doing so, it has considered a number of conceptual approaches to the relationship between identity, belonging and work, paying particular attention to theories of gender and work. While work has long been an object of study for sociology, and while from early sociology, labour has been considered significant for identity formation, recently an argument for the 'end of work' in global economies has held sway. In response to this proposition, this chapter has asserted that work continues to be meaningful for both the affluent and the poor and that it holds particular significance for gender identities. Labour activities intersect with gender identities and work is one arena in which women continue to experience profound inequality.

Questions for students

- In what ways can work activities be connected to gender identities?
- Describe the ways in which globalisation has impacted contemporary work experience, as outlined in the chapter. Can you provide evidence for this from your own working life or the working lives of your friends and family?
- What does Marx mean by 'alienation'? In your opinion, is alienation only an experience of the past?
- Why is unpaid household labour an important issue for feminists? How is domestic labour divided in your family home?

Recommended reading

Crompton, R. (1999) *Restructuring Gender Relations and Employment: The Decline of the Male Breadwinner* (Oxford: Oxford University Press).

Echrenreich, B. and Hochschild, A.R. (eds.). (2002) *Global Woman: Nannies, Maids and Sex Workers in the New Economy* (New York: Holt).

Grint, K. (2005) *The Sociology of Work*, (Cambridge: Polity Press).

Strangleman, T. and Warren, T. (2008) *Work and Society: Sociological Approaches, Themes and Methods* (London: Routledge).

CHAPTER 12

Leisure

Amie Matthews

Introduction

In 2009 Tourism Australia, the national government agency responsible for international and domestic tourism, launched their *No Leave, No Life* marketing campaign (Tourism Australia, 2013a). Aimed at encouraging Australians to take more holidays, the campaign consisted of print, radio, online and television advertisements, a website, employer-delivered leave programmes and an associated television series (also entitled *No Leave, No Life*). In the context of the 2009 Global Financial Crisis, the most obvious objective of the campaign was to lift the domestic tourism profile for Australia and thereby boost the tourism industry and local economy. A second objective, of relevance to this chapter, was to address the fact that Australians were stockpiling a substantial amount of annual leave, a situation that was deemed indicative of contemporary struggles to maintain work-life balance.

According to Tourism Australia, the accrual of leave by full-time employees had grown by 11 per cent between 2006 and 2008 and, as of 2011, had resulted in Australians having stockpiled '129 million days' of leave or '$33.3 billion in wages' (Tourism Australia, 2013b). The campaign argued that this stockpiled leave was detrimental to employers and employees, pointing to the fact that stockpiled leave posed a substantial financial liability for businesses on the one hand and that employees who do not take leave are likely to be more stressed, less motivated and less fulfilled, on the other. *No Leave, No Life* also argued that stockpiled leave had the potential to decrease staff productivity and lower workplace morale (for further discussion see Tourism Australia, 2013a and 2013b). What is of particular interest though as we consider the relationship between leisure, identity and belonging is how 'taking a break' from work is deemed to be crucial to maintaining physical, mental and social well-being. This message was reinforced in the *No Leave, No Life* television series (2009–2012), which showed self-defined 'workaholic' protagonists enjoying surprise holidays with friends and family. In each episode as participants in the *No Leave, No Life* programme were exposed to new and exotic travel destinations and various leisure experiences, they would reflect on the fact that time away from work had given them opportunity to relax, pursue new interests or learn new skills, reprioritise their commitments and reconnect with loved ones. Many of the participants in the programme also seemed to give voice to a dominant discourse of being 'more oneself' while on holiday. They spoke of returning to or developing authentic or more genuine selves and, in some cases, of developing improved social relationships, away from work. The *No Leave, No Life* campaign sheds light then not only on the significance of tourism and travel for individual and social health and well-being, but the significance of leisure time more generally to personal development and social relationships. Indeed, on the basis of what we know about the role of leisure in contemporary society and the significance it has for identity and belonging, we could perhaps supplement the slogan 'no leave, no life' with the phrase 'no *leisure*, no life'.

While not as useful for Tourism Australia's purposes of increasing domestic tourism yield, the latter declaration does capture what appears to be a reasonably common sentiment in many contemporary Western societies: that without leisure, one is not *truly* living. While this is not an entirely new attitude (consider for instance the old adage that 'all work and no play makes Jack a dull boy'), concerns with leisure, and more specifically, work-life balance, do seem to have amplified in recent decades. One of the concerns of this chapter then is to examine why it is that leisure is deemed so significant in contemporary society and what influence it wields with respect to identity and belonging. More specifically, and drawing on case studies from tourism (a specific form of leisure), this chapter will examine how leisure is conceptualised, how it is experienced by individuals and how it in turn comes to mediate social relationships. Before turning to these issues though it is necessary to first identify what exactly is meant by the term 'leisure'.

What is leisure?

While there is much debate about how best to define leisure, it has been argued that it can be understood on the basis of the interplay between such things as time (specifically free time), activity, and personal orientation or attitude towards that activity (for further discussion of this interplay, see Kelly, 2012; McLean and Hurd, 2012; Veal et al., 2013). McLean and Hurd (2012, p. 24) summarise as follows:

> Leisure is that portion of an individual's time that is not directly devoted to work or work-connected responsibilities or to other obligated forms of maintenance or self-care. Leisure implies freedom and choice and is

customarily used in a variety of ways, including to meet one's personal needs for reflection, self-enrichment, relaxation, pleasure, and affiliation. Although it usually involves some form of participation in a voluntarily chosen activity, it may also be regarded as a holistic state of being or even a spiritual experience.

It is obvious from this definition that a number of benefits are commonly associated with leisure. Leisure has frequently been positioned (socio-historically and academically) as a source of pleasure and skill development, as a tool to social and psychological health and well-being and as a means to self-improvement, personal growth and/or self-actualisation (for further discussion of this history see Harrington, 2006; Cohen, 2013; Veal et al., 2013). More broadly, leisure has also been idealised as a common good and lauded at various points in history as a mechanism for social reform. Additionally, it has operated to reinforce dominant social norms and traditions and has been conceived as an endeavour that assists with the maintenance of social institutions (such as the family) and subsequently, as a practice that fosters social cohesion (see Harrington, 2006; Roberts, 2013; Veal et al., 2013). Such outcomes contribute to the valorisation of leisure, both at an individual and socio-cultural level. They also go some way towards explaining the power that leisure wields with respect to identity and belonging. While I will turn to this issue momentarily, in unpacking the above definition that McLean and Hurd (2012) provide, what also becomes clear is that leisure is perceived as being intimately connected with work (which, we know from Chapter 11 also has great influence on our identities and social relationships). In saying that, it should be noted that leisure is a predominantly Western concept, one that does not necessarily translate to other cultures, where the work and non-work demarcation is either not so clearly made or not (particularly in the case of many poorer countries) available (for cross-cultural perspectives on leisure, see Veal et al., 2013).

Despite the fact that leisure is positioned in many societies as something that occurs outside of or separate to work, many leisure practices rely upon the disposable income that employment generates. This is especially so in an increasingly consumer-driven society (see Chapter 13) and illustrates why leisure may be so closely tied to social class (though of course, as discussed in Chapter 3, the leisure activities that different groups pursue are shaped not just by economic capital but also by taste and cultural capital). Interestingly though, it is the double-bind of the over-worked and time-poor, as well as the underworked or unemployed that neither time alone, nor money, is enough for leisure (for further discussion, see Critcher and Bramham, 2004; Rojek, 2004). Thus, while work can at times inhibit leisure, it also enables it and gives it some of its subjective or experiential qualities. For whether we talk of paid or unpaid work, leisure is commonly perceived as compensation for, a release from, or an antidote to such pursuits (see Veal, 2004; Zuzanek, 2006; Veal et al., 2013). As opposed to work, leisure is frequently characterised as being self-directed, freely chosen, unobligated, unfettered, relaxing and entirely pleasurable, and again these are the reasons (as I will discuss below) why many deem their leisured selves to be their 'true' selves. However, this divide between work and leisure (and by extension work and leisure identities) is not as absolute as it might seem at first glance.

For starters, there are many who take a great deal of satisfaction and enjoyment from their work. Indeed, in their ground-breaking comparative study of individual's work and leisure experiences, Csikszentmihalyi and LeFevre (1989, p. 821) identified that those they studied had 'more positive feelings in work than in leisure', but that it was the assumed 'obligatory nature of work' that made participants feel that they would rather be somewhere else and that masked 'the positive experience' that work provided. Also challenging a clear work-leisure divide is the fact that there are many who undertake what might typically be understood as leisure activities in their work time and whose work spaces may be dedicated to leisure (this is particularly so with the growth in the service industries, documented in the previous chapter). Veal et al., (2013, p. 17) point, for instance, to the professional sportsperson, for whom sport may be more work than play. In a similar vein, I would argue that the divide between work and leisure may become blurred for hospitality and tourism workers, who work in leisure spaces and also frequently carry out leisure in their work spaces, with many bar staff for instance socialising over after-work drinks. Speaking from experience, even leisure and tourism academics, who may carry out their work in leisure zones, may find it difficult to truly switch off in these same places when at leisure or on holiday! There are also those who engage in activities that might be considered domestic or 'self-care' duties (unpaid work) as leisure, and some who might 'work at' or apply themselves quite 'seriously' to otherwise leisurely activities (Stebbins, 2004). For example, there are many who swear by gardening as a means of unwinding at the end of the working week, and it seems that the popularity of celebrity chefs and reality television shows focused on cooking have contributed to a growing number of individuals viewing meal preparation less as a daily chore and more as a relaxing pursuit or pleasure. As with these individuals, for the would-be musician who dedicates all of his or her spare time to writing and playing music, to band rehearsals and shows, the distinction between leisure and work may have all but disappeared.

Thus, just as free time and money are not likely to result, on their own, in leisure, the absence of work or presence of certain types of activity (such as sport, or music, or hobbies like cooking and gardening) cannot automatically be assumed to denote leisure either. This is why leisure is defined on the basis of the interplay between each of these elements and why attitude in particular, or the meaning that individuals give to their leisure, is deemed to be of paramount importance. As Kelly (2012, p. 9, original emphasis) observes:

> Leisure is done in a leisurely or relatively unconstrained and uncoerced manner. It is *done freely*. Leisure is freely chosen because the activity or the companions, or some combination of the two, promises personal satisfaction. It is the personal and social orientation of the participant that makes an activity leisure – or something else. Leisure is defined by the use of time, not the time itself. It is distinguished by the meaning of the activity, not its form.

I emphasise this because it is the freely chosen, or intrinsically motivated, nature of leisure that many authors point to when examining the significance of leisure to identity and belonging.

Leisure as an exercise in agency

In recent decades, there have been growing arguments that where work may have once been the key defining aspect of one's lifestyle, identity and social networks, leisure has increasingly taken centre stage. Proponents of the so-called 'leisure society thesis' have pointed to rapid changes in work (including casualisation, greater work mobility and the decrease in 'jobs for life' that was discussed in Chapter 11) as key factors in this shift. Others have disputed such arguments, contending instead that many people's lives are becoming *more* rather than less work-centric and that individuals (like those featured in *No Leave, No Life*) are facing increased challenges when it comes to maintaining work-life balance (for an overview of these debates, see Veal, 2011, 2012). Indeed, as outlined in Chapter 11, there is still ample empirical evidence that work influences our experiences of identity and belonging. However, what is also clear is that whether one feels that leisure exists in abundance, or simply longs for it in its absence, it is a valuable commodity in contemporary society. In addition, because it is deemed to be freely chosen, it is often understood as an uninhibited (and therefore, perhaps) truer or more authentic response to the questions of '*who am I?*' and '*who do I want to be?*'.

Central to this conceptualisation of leisure as free choice is its oppositional positioning to work and its connection with consumerism and the experiential. Gammon (2013, p. 237), drawing on a vast body of leisure studies literature, argues that leisure has the 'ability to encourage action and behaviour that is driven by perceptions of choice and intrinsic interest' and that as a result it is through leisure that individuals can 'realise' who they are, communicate that realisation to others and perhaps escape some of the roles that they are forced to perform in other life domains. On the same basis, he argues that leisure is 'an opportunity to work out identities' and 'a relatively self-contained practice that potentially enables individuals to (re)invent and concoct idealised versions of themselves' (Gammon, 2013, p. 242). This is something that has frequently emerged in my own research on young backpackers (see for example, Matthews, 2008, 2009), many of whom talked of international travel as an escape from their everyday 'home' lives and as a means (as also discussed in Chapter 6) of accumulating experience. Crucially, as discussed in Case Study 1 (below) it was that accumulated experience that many of them in turn associated with heightened self-knowledge and/or a more authentic existence.

Case study 1: young backpackers, travel and the freedom to be

In contemporary society much tourism advertising and indeed tourist discourse oscillates around the idea that when undertaken for the purposes of leisure, travel away from one's home – away from a physical and social environment that is familiar and where one is known, to a place of difference and anonymity – is freeing. Countless tourism promotions, magazine and newspaper articles, films and stories promulgate the idea that leisure travel (particularly international leisure travel) is escape – a means of bypassing that which is mundane, everyday, and ordinary in exchange for that which is exciting and new. This discourse is especially strong amongst young backpackers or independent travellers, for whom travel is conceived as a means of moving beyond routine to a realm where one is surrounded by choice: where to go, what to see, where to stay, where to eat, who to spend time with and even who to be! In fact, over the last ten years conducting ethnographic research into the global backpacking culture, I have frequently come across individuals who had embraced the experiential opportunities afforded by international mobility to create new or different lifestyles, and in some cases, relationships, identities and careers, for themselves. The following reflections from young Australian backpacker, Danielle, about her experiences travelling, living and working in the United Kingdom are exemplary:

> [I] definitely try new things overseas because it isn't a dress rehearsal. There is no second chance to do things that I have only one opportunity to do. But this has now adapted to my outlook on life regardless of where I am geographically. I definitely picked up this outlook from travelling and I guess in essence it was because there are fewer inhibitions when

travelling. [Travel has made me] more sociable, push boundaries more frequently, go outside my comfort zone regularly, stubborn and independent. [It's also made me] more motivated and spiritual.

While Danielle talked of travel as being freeing and of that freedom having an impact on her attitudes (and by extension, how she saw herself), others like Jessica (a young Australian traveller, interviewed in Guatemala) talked about her around-the-world trip as providing opportunity for abandoning 'old' social behaviours and relationship patterns, observing that:

When I went away I decided that 'I don't want to hang around people that I don't want to be around... maybe it's because at home there was a lot of people I'd spend time with but that I really didn't like... And one of my things for when I went away was that I wanted to meet so many different people and I wanted them to be people I could learn from.

What unites both of these narratives then is, firstly, the idea that there is a freedom in leisure travel and that individuals are less constrained by personal or social inhibitions when far from home. Secondly, these narratives also make clear that experiences in the globalised space of travel can have an impact on individuals' identities and social relationships: relationships with those at home, as well as, importantly, relationships with those dispersed around the world. Indeed, the backpacking scene is experienced by many travellers as a simultaneously local (confined to the city, hostel or tour bus that one inhabits) and transnational community. Aided by the various forms of digital media and communication technologies discussed in Chapter 14, many of my research participants spoke of feeling more globally interconnected as a result of their journeys and the friendships they made along the way.

So whether we look at tourism, the arts, entertainment and cultural industries, or even outdoor recreation and adventure sports, many leisure activities are intertwined with the experience economy, and in contemporary society, experience is *everything*. Nearly thirty years ago Roger Abrahams (1986, p. 46) observed that experience had been elevated to society's 'new holy word', arguing that individuals were increasingly concerned with accumulating experience in efforts to 'enhance' their lives and achieve some kind of personal development or self-realisation. It is an argument that seems to sit well with Bauman's (1996) equally enduring assertion that consumerism has fast become a means by which individuals are defining and constructing themselves and that consumer choices (many of which are also leisure choices) are perceived as integral steps to '*become* what one *is*' (Bauman, 2000, p. 32, original emphasis. For further discussion, see also Chapters 10, 11 and 13).

Becoming what one is: the transformative possibilities of leisure

To put it another way then, in contemporary society, leisure is a means by which individuals are understood as being able to pursue new and different experiences, marking themselves in the process as 'unique'. In leisure we have opportunities to purposefully construct our identities in specific ways, to play with who we are and to 'express and affirm the self' (Jun and Kyle, 2012, p. 354). Certainly this is apparent in the travel discourses that feature in Case Study 1. It is also apparent in other leisure domains, such as sport.

In their study of male and female golfers, Jun and Kyle examine the extent to which men and women engaged in the sport of golf may adopt this as part of their identity. They argue that high rates of participation in a particular leisure activity like golf can be linked to individuals incorporating that activity 'into their self-definitions' (Jun and Kyle, 2012, p. 369) – a trend that can also be seen quite clearly when it comes to many leisure-based youth subcultures (discussed in Chapter 6). Interestingly, Jun and Kyle (2012) also point to the fact that for women, participation in certain sports or outdoor activities may also be a way of constructing an identity which resists dominant gender norms (see also Case Study 2, Chapter 4). Similarly, Dionigi et al. (2013) have argued that sports participation may enable older people to resist dominant discourses that associate ageing with decline and to adopt instead more self-empowered images that invariably resist, redefine or accept ageing. To this end, the authors observe that the participants in their research:

> were redefining ageing in terms of physical competency, resilience, social engagement and mental stimulation. They showed that older bodies can be competitive and athletic and that sport is not only the domain of youth. Being older and highly physically active allowed older people to *become* athletes in later life or maintain their identity as a sportsperson. In other words, they were redefining themselves and providing alternative meanings of what it is to be an older athlete (specially) and an older, western adult more generally. (Dionigi et al., 2013, p. 385)

Moving away from the specifics of sport, Fullager (2008) has shown how a variety of leisure pursuits (for instance, arts and crafts, socialising with friends and family, gardening, writing, yoga and swimming) have enabled women with depression to recover, recreate and redefine themselves in resistance to their illness, as well as restrictive gender norms. In reflecting on the experiences of the women in her study, she notes that 'leisure was a practice that constituted and transformed self in subtle ways' and that 'as a site of playful relations leisure enabled a different performance of identity' (Fullager, 2008, p. 47–48). Indeed, it seems for some of the women in Fullager's (2008) study, one of the crucial aspects of leisure was the fact that it provided time away from duty or obligation to pursue enjoyment, relaxation, reflection, fun and pleasure and opportunity to be someone else (if only momentarily).

In keeping with this, it is not just the activities that leisure enables that make it significant for identity. As a specific time and space separate from obligation and the routines of work and domestic care, leisure also provides 'opportunity for contemplation and self-examination, for the wistful wanderings of imagination' (Kleiber, 1999, p. 94). It is the contemplative possibilities fostered in leisure that are, according to Kleiber (1999, p. 94), so crucial to the 'discovery or creation of alternative "possible selves"'. On this basis, there is often a transformative potential that is associated with leisure – a transformative potential that Victor Turner (1982, p. 37) recognised when, in his study of ritual and play, he argued that:

> Leisure is ... (1) *freedom* to enter, even to generate new symbolic worlds of entertainment, sports, games, diversions of all kinds. It is furthermore, (2) *freedom* to transcend social structural limitations, freedom to *play* ... with ideas, with fantasies, with words ... with paint ... and with social relationships.

For Turner (1982), the power of leisure – individual leisure in particular – lay in the fact that it was predominantly a matter of choice or 'optation', rather than obligation. While he was quick to acknowledge that certain leisure activities were governed by rules and thus not entirely free (noting for instance the structured nature of sports and games like chess), he also argued that where leisure was freely chosen, without a sense of obligation to one's social networks, it was likely to have a strong ludic or experimental quality. Such freely chosen leisure activities had the potential to challenge social structures and were regarded by Turner (1982, p. 37) as 'part of an individual's freedom, of his [sic] growing self-mastery, even self-transcendence'.

In making these reflections, Turner (1982) also drew on the notion of flow, a concept which was first put forward in the 1970s by Mihalyi Csikszentmihalyi and which remains influential in leisure studies (and, incidentally in studies of work) to this day. According to Csikszentmihalyi (1988, 1990) the 'optimal experience' of 'flow' is what contributes to enjoyment and by extension personal growth and happiness. Flow comprises a transcendental moment (or series of moments) and most likely occurs when individuals engage in activities that are intrinsically motivated, intrinsically rewarding and which carefully balance skill and challenge. The results are flow moments where the individual is so caught up in his or her pursuits, so absorbed in meeting the challenges at hand, that he or she loses the self-consciousness that ordinarily accompanies individual activity. Freed from distraction, Csikszentmihalyi (1988, 1990) argues that under conditions of flow individuals achieve a rare sense of clarity, purpose and self-assurance: a wholeness that is not commonly found amidst the fast-paced and complex nature of everyday life. The experience is deemed to be pleasurable and as having a regenerative potential, the potency of which, it seems, rests in comparison. Flow is only extraordinary when held against the ordinariness of mundane activity, and because it generates feelings of pleasure and happiness individuals are likely to continue seeking out the conditions that make it manifest. By so doing they extend their 'capabilities with the likelihood of learning new skills and increasing self-esteem and personal complexity' (Csikszentmihalyi and LeFevre, 1989, p. 816).

While it would be hard to envision an entire travel experience comprised of flow, my own research with young backpackers has identified that those engaged in relatively long periods of travel do experience liminal and flow-like moments during their journeys. These can have transformative effects (see Matthews, 2014), and as Case Study 2 (below) attests, part of that transformation stems from the contrast and challenge that this form of leisure provides.

Case study 2: older travellers navigating life transitions through leisure

In their study of mid-life and older long-term travellers touring the Australian outback, White and White (2004) noted that many of them had chosen to travel to the outback in particular because of the challenges (physical and cultural) that it posed. Certainly the fact that it was 'different' from home was a significant drawcard (as it is for many tourists – difference being one of the key motivations for travel (see Cohen, 2004)). However, what White and White (2004) noted was the extent to which that difference was positioned as a means by which individuals could 'test themselves'. Thus in ways similar to the young backpackers discussed in Case Study 1, the mid-life and older travellers in White and White's (2004) study conceived of the newness and challenge of travel as a means by which they could re-define themselves and establish new ways of being. This was enabled by their distance from social networks at home and encouraged by their already transitional life stages.

Many of the participants in White and White's (2004) study had been motivated to travel by significant life changes. These included the death of a spouse and other changed family circumstances (such as divorce or children having moved out of home), as well as retirement or increased dissatisfaction with work, and shifting social networks (including a lack of community ties after moving to a new home and neighbourhood). Interestingly, these same motivations appeared also in Desforges (2000) study of British travellers to Peru. Concerned that their old identities (as for example, housewife or mother) no longer served them, some of the older women in his study embarked on international travel as a means to redefine and reconstruct their sense of self. Such purposeful identity (re)constructions are also apparent in Holloway's (2007) study into discourses about 'grey nomads', which she argues challenge dominant narratives about ageing, providing instead positive images for entering a new life stage.

Leisure and structure: reinforcing communal bonds and identities

It stands to reason that people undertake leisure pursuits that are congruent with their sense of self and that help them, by extension, to perform or enact who it is that they think they are or who it is that they want to be in the future. However, it is easy to forget that leisure choices and leisure performances are also contextual: they are the product of one's environments, both socio-cultural and geographic. For instance, one is unlikely to take up the sport of surfing if one lives a long distance from the ocean. Therefore, one is also unlikely to be able to take up the identity of being a *surfer*. Just as geography might influence one's leisure choices and identity, so too may other variables, like gender. It is well documented that gender may significantly influence leisure. This occurs both at the level of access to leisure time and also in terms of chosen leisure activity (see for example, Wearing, 1998; Burgess et al., 2003; Fullager, 2008). Further, social class, ethnicity and age, as well as the social institutions that one belongs to (such as the family, school, religion or workplace) may serve to structure individuals' leisure experiences.

This is clearly evident in Spaaij's (2012) study of Somali people with refugee backgrounds in Australia and their involvement in football (soccer). Spaaij (2012) notes both the opportunity for sport to serve as a site for socialisation and community, but simultaneously as a site of exclusion. He writes as a preface to his study that:

> As sites for socialization experiences, sports activities may help cultivate a sense of belonging and reduce social isolation, especially when they are connected positively within the social fabric of local communities. (Spaaij, 2012, p. 1520)

This claim is realised in his research, with many of the Somali people interviewed indicating that they felt social networks within the Somali community in Melbourne (the site of the study) were strengthened through sport. However, what Spaaij's (2012, p. 1520) research also revealed is that the capacity for sport to operate 'as a significant site for civic participation, potentially enabling resettled refugees to foster social relationships with, and cultural knowledge of, the host community' should not be assumed. While ethno-cultural belonging appeared to have been enhanced by football, sports participation didn't necessarily translate into experiences of belonging in the broader soccer-playing Melbourne community. Further, Spaaij (2012) noted that sport could also be a leisure space where racism and exclusion, on the basis of ethnicity and gender, were experienced.

The tendency for sport to operate as both a site of inclusion and exclusion is also apparent in Burgess et al's (2003) study of football culture in an Australian school. In their study the authors make clear how hegemonic masculinity (defined in Chapter 4) may be reinforced through sport and how this can result in strong or weak social bonds with one's peers, depending on whether or not one is able to live up to the hyper-masculinised and in some cases violent performances that are assumed to be part of the dominant sporting culture.

Leisure may serve then to reinforce social bonds and social divisions – the two being largely inextricable. While this can mean exclusion for some, for others it means strengthened social networks, feelings of community and in some cases, subsequent strengthening of identity and improved well-being. Fullager's (2008) study into the role of leisure in the lives of women recovering from depression (discussed above) identifies that the social connections that leisure provides can be highly significant to recovery and to the assertion of identity. She notes that friends were often the motivation for some women to take up particular leisure pursuits in the first place or to continue with them once already involved. In a similar vein, there is also a growing body of research that has identified that leisure in the family can have positive effects with respect to socialisation, family bonding and social cohesion (see Case Study 3, for further discussion).

Case study 3: the family that plays together stays together

According to Harrington (2006), there is a long history that underpins the assumption that leisure can contribute to family cohesion. She argues that although leisure studies have tended to focus more on the individual than the family, early research in the field took as its starting point the idea that 'family leisure was good for both individual and family development' and 'that shared leisure experiences [would] have positive benefits for the quality of family relationships, in terms of family stability, family interaction and family satisfaction' (Harrington, 2006, pp. 422–423. See also Lehto et al., 2009).

While family leisure does not always result in such idyllic outcomes – Harrington (2006) notes for instance that family leisure can in fact be imbued with tension and conflict, inequity and feelings of obligation, guilt and disillusionment – these positive benefits are apparent in the findings of recent studies into family tourism.

In their research on social tourism in the United Kingdom (defined as tourism that derives 'from the participation of disadvantaged groups in tourism activity, facilitated by financial and social measures') McCabe and Johnson (2013, p. 43) identify 'a positive link between "family life, social life, family time and well-being"' (2013, p. 55). In examining the connections between social tourism and well-being, they note that over two-thirds of their respondents reported an improvement in 'family bonds' after a vacation together and nearly half indicated they had experienced improvements in the quality of the time spent with family (that is, that they found it to be more enjoyable). Similarly, Lehto et al. (2009, p. 43) found in their study of American families on vacation that family travel provided 'unique opportunities for interaction among family members', prompting increased communication and greater levels of bonding and feelings of solidarity. While there is insufficient scope in this chapter to discuss these two studies (and others like them) in detail, what they demonstrate is that leisure can play an important role not only in our individual lives, but also in our social interactions and communities.

Conclusion

As a socio-cultural and temporal space, which is at least partially (if not completely) removed from other more obligatory spheres of social life (such as work and domestic responsibility), leisure may encourage increased experimentation, agency, experiential accumulation and reflection. Subsequently, leisure is central to processes of individuation (for further discussion, see Kleiber, 1999). That is, by providing the space whereby individuals can construct themselves (on the basis of their interests, passions and hobbies) as unique and different, leisure encourages an active construction of identity. In some cases, this construction will involve distinguishing oneself from groups or identities that one might otherwise be seen as belonging to. Empirical studies of leisure discussed in this chapter have shown, for instance, how young people might embrace global mobility and embark on an extended period of overseas travel in order to experiment with and construct new identities for themselves, far from the constraints of home life. Similarly, older travellers may embrace tourism or sport as a means of transitioning from one life stage to the next, developing more life stage appropriate or personally meaningful identities and positive images of ageing, as a result.

At the same time, though leisure may be considered a largely individual affair, this chapter has also demonstrated that it can be structured by our socio-cultural contexts and that it mediates our social relationships. Thus gender, social class and ethnicity may influence the leisure activities we engage in and also the way that we experience them. Leisure pursuits are also the basis for identification with others and it is on the basis of leisure that some of our social bonds are formed, developed and reinforced. Individuals may take up particular leisure activities out of interest and then form social relationships with those with whom they share this interest. Alternatively, they may use leisure as a means of constructing an identity and social membership that they aspire to or, in the case of family travel, may experience increased social solidarity and feelings of belonging and community as a result of shared experience. Ultimately then, irrespective of the type of activities that individuals engage in during their non-work time, or who they engage in those activities with, leisure is intrinsically connected to our experiences of identity and belonging. This – more than the pleasurable feelings that leisure generates or the relaxation that a break from work engenders – may well be why it is deemed so central to contemporary life.

Questions for students

- What leisure activities do you engage in? How significant are these to your identity? Are some more important than others? If so, why do you think that is?
- To what extent do you think your own leisure choices are influenced by agency and to what extent do you think they are the product of your social structures?
- Can you think of a time where you might have experienced flow? If so, did it occur in work or in leisure, or somewhere else entirely? What do you think contributed to this optimal experience and how did it make you feel?

Recommended reading

Csikszentmihalyi, M. (1990) *Flow: The Psychology of Optimal Experience* (New York: Harper Perennial).

Elkington, S. and Gammon, S. (2013) *Contemporary Perspectives in Leisure: Meanings, Motives and Lifelong Learning* (Hoboken: Taylor and Francis).

Veal, A.J., Darcy, S. and Lynch, R. (2013) *Australian Leisure* (Frenchs Forest: Pearson Australia).

CHAPTER 13

Consumption

Joanne Finkelstein and Melissa Johnson Morgan

Introduction

In a consumer society, cyclical change is constant whether it is driven by the seasons or by events such as world music festivals, sporting fixtures like the Olympics and celebrity events such as Royal weddings and births or high-profile deaths (e.g. Michael Jackson, Amy Winehouse). Consumption promotes the value of material possessions and the pursuit of fashion. It associates objects with desirable qualities. Being fashionable creates a sense of immediacy as we respond to the constant pull of the latest fashion and consumer novelty. Inherent in this position is the idea that the fashioned and adorned body has greater stature and that we are automatically enlarged, our identity and personality are made more expressive through our adoption and display of fashionable goods.

While the emergence of consumption as a dominant ideology and social practice is commonly associated with the industrial age of the nineteenth century, asserting identity and social position through the consumption of goods has been a common motif in most societies and is not confined to any specific moment in history. For instance, the Renaissance scholar, Stephen Greenblatt (2004), has described the emphasis on self-fashioning that marked the Shakespearean age. The Globe Theatre, like contemporary television, film and YouTube, functioned to display the latest ideas. It was hugely popular, playing to audiences of thousands of people on a daily basis. This audience witnessed narratives in which invention and persuasion were on display. Actors manipulated situations; they reversed the social order, impersonated one another, ridiculed the customs of the day, breached the rules and suggested endless possibilities for everyday amusement. The theatre made the social world less stable and demonstrated that strategic reasoning and thinking about how to manipulate others were clever ways for gaining social advantage. The theatre demonstrated how the manners of the day including styles of self-presentation could be adopted for personal use. The impact of The Globe has reverberated through centuries of Western culture as a significant turning point where individuals, en masse, began thinking about personal identity as a plaything. The popularity of the theatre supported a growing general acceptance of the malleability of the social world. Importantly, it marked a moment in the sixteenth century when audiences learned the value and pleasures of dissemblance, a pleasure which remains to this day.

Whenever material goods and possessions become symbols of valued human sentiments they influence our subjectivity. Bauman (2001) has argued that a singularly important driving force in contemporary human society is the desire for the unobtainable; we are impelled more by hope and desire than their opposites – attainment and satisfaction. The consumer society sustains desire by constantly asserting the value of distraction and of avoiding a sense of completion and surfeit. The essence of the consumer ethic is to live in a state of desire; this emotion or sensation makes us feel as if we can defy entropy, the inevitable running down of energy. Thus, we can see how consumption and the pursuit of material pleasure become a form of escape from the banal occupations of daily life, and as such they offer a future of endless entertainment (Bauman, 2001, p. 2004).

In this chapter, we begin with a review of early theories and practices associated with consumer trends and then lift them into a discussion about the formation of identity. This approach aims to show how identity shifts with its context and not vice versa. That is, how we think of ourselves is more often associated with our particular material situation. It is not a causal relationship but a complicated interplay between fashion, social status, circumstances and individual aspirations.

Early theories on consumption

In the centuries before industrialism, goods of most kinds were expensive and scarce, and this curtailed the possibilities for the majority of individuals to use such items to present or re-fashion themselves. Wealth from colonial empires supported a market in luxury goods that were used to bolster claims for social identity and the superiority of an elite. However, with the mass production of cheaper items in the nineteenth century goods became more readily available and this fuelled the rapid expansion of the consumer ethic. The industrialisation (discussed in Chapters 3 and 11) of the economy radically changed the status of goods so that, in a short time, they became encoded as symbols of personal identity.

In a period where social mobility was increasingly available, where new wealth was creating different social classes and rankings, the concern with knowing the pedigree and moral position of the stranger became increasingly important. It was accepted that a great deal could be deduced from appearances, from the cut and style of clothing. 'People took each other's appearances in the street immensely seriously', reports Sennett (1976, pp. 165–166); clothing and mannerisms were taken as evidence of psychological and emotional properties. The attention paid to details of dress and manners of speech rested on the assumption that character was immanent in appearance. Industrialism and consumption had produced the tools for inventing oneself and in this fusion of identity with materialism is the origin of contemporary fashion.

An early commentator on consumption, Thorstein Veblen (1899), produced *A Theory of the Leisure Classes* in which he described the lifestyle of the new rich in the growing economy of nineteenth-century America. He noted the importance given to conspicuous display. Those individuals made rich through the rapid expansion of industry appeared to be highly concerned with the need to gain prestige and social status, and used conspicuous displays of wealth in order to assert social superiority. He understood that in a society where the traditional social hierarchies had collapsed and where new opportunities for social mobility were available, there was a constant shifting of status and this, in turn, supported an underlying sense of social rivalry, competition and conflict.

Most aspiring individuals were engaged in a continual exchange of imitation and differentiation. The so-called 'trickle-down effect' (a term not used by Veblen) supported the constant consumption of new types of material goods. The trickle-down effect assumed that the practices of the elite would be observed by others outside that circle and would be imitated as a form of social mobility. This concentration on appearances and following fashionable practices created a culture in which the various social segments were preoccupied with one another, always engaged in constant, mutual scrutiny. This in turn engendered an ethic of contingency in which fashionability and consumption thrived. These competitive tensions between social groups were not expressed through physical violence and bloody class war but were, instead, symbolically enacted through displays of wealth and status (or, as discussed in Chapter 3, cultural capital). The upper classes would engage in a leisure activity, say, driving cars, playing tennis and dining a la carte, and the lower classes would imitate them. The effect was to destabilise the upper classes and drive them towards new acts of consumption in order to ensure they were always different and distinctive. This circularity of inventing new pleasures, imitating lifestyles and constantly creating social distinctions had the effect of transforming every experience into a commodity and every individual into a calculating actor who constantly evaluated the worth of their own activities and social practices.

Case study 1: men well suited

Towards the end of the eighteenth century male fashion began a period of previously uncharacteristic austerity, dubbed by the early psychoanalyst Johan Flugel as 'The Great Masculine Renunciation'. This change in fashion emphasised the issue of gender as more important than social class. Previous fashion trends revolved around fabrics, styles and adornments that staked the wearer firmly to a particular social class and hierarchical position. Whether male or female, a person who appeared 'beautiful' with excellent hygiene, grooming and sense of style was easily recognisable as a member of the social elite. During the so-called *masculine renunciation*, however, men appeared to abandon their claims on physical beauty in order to pursue the opportunity to gain great wealth. The modern male business suit emerges during this period. Its unadorned plainness and uniformity reflected military order and organisation and a sense of economic rationality and sensibility.

Fashion and identity

Veblen (1899) described fashion as an irrational yet defining force in the shaping of modern society. Being fashionable often meant wearing clothes that were more for display than comfort. The thriving economy of the industrial age generated a desire to display status through conspicuous consumption and waste. Fashionability was a symbol of social superiority as it required a great deal of leisure – time to shop, to acquire goods and then to display them in a wide range of different activities such as walking in the park, attending the opera and hunting on horseback. Personal grooming became a tool for displaying wealth: elaborate hairstyles, heavy jewellery, crisp linen shirts and cuffs and fine leather shoes were all signs that the individual did not engage in manual work. Fashionable appearance became an assertion of class position; it was a sign of location on the social hierarchy. For the next century, fashions in appearance would continue to be relied upon as indications of social position, personal identity and even moral values.

A century later, however, this reliance was no longer effective. The swinging Sixties in London saw the opening of World's End on the King's Road, a fashion shop designed by Malcolm McLaren and Vivienne Westwood that displayed post-modern punk aesthetics. The style (discussed also in Case Study 2, Chapter 6) was sensational, drawing on the look of Sid Vicious and the Sex Pistols. The clothes were ripped, the jewellery was made from motorbike chains, razor blades and strips of black leather. The contrast with the suburban Fifties style of polished cotton frocks and grey flannel suits could not have been greater. The ascendance of street-style with World's End marked the collapse of fashion as a reliable sign of subjective human qualities. Instead, it became a signature of shifting social values that constantly challenged established hierarchies. Exterior rebellion expressed through fashion and a sense of dandyism gave legitimacy to new social ideologies including gay liberation, identity politics and diversity in artistic expression.

In the next decades, the fashion catwalks of *haute couture* slowly adopted the sensational styles set in motion by rock n' roll and the punk era. The orderly values of the establishment were overturned not through the historic method of class revolt but through the circulation of ideas and fashions in music and entertainment. Following the Second World War, the industrial machinery was producing a new entrepreneurial wealth and the abundance of material goods from domestic appliances like vacuum cleaners and washing machines to shark-finned twenty-foot-long motorcars was echoed in artistic and cultural production. The music and film industries changed the kinds of entertainment on offer; advertising and retail flooded the market with new ideas and desires. Fashion magazines and *haute couture* became big business. Department stores were refurbished into elegant arenas of opulence, and gigantic shopping malls were built across the ever-expanding suburbs.

Towards the close of the twentieth century, the signs of aesthetic exhaustion were apparent in attempts to re-ignite the consumer exuberance of the post-war era. The fashion house Comme des Garcons grabbed headlines in the mid-1990s with its neo-Nazi iconography; Madonna outraged the public with her exo-costumes that displayed suspender belts, brassieres and the blatantly sexualised body; and then there was Lady Gaga who ambiguously promoted animal rights by wearing a costume with matching hat and handbag that appeared to be made of marbled red meat (Clott, 2010). Pop culture and celebrity artists formed part of the production of new cultural styles in a rapid cycle of continuous novelty.

Consumption and pop culture

While conspicuous consumption is harnessed to social class and position (see Chapter 3), it also supports a massive economy through which style and aesthetics are constantly being re-invented and circulated. Fashionable appearance may identify a certain style such as Goth, Sloane Ranger, Punk, Chav, Establishment, Preppie and so on; however, the reliability of this to define position, wealth and personal power is relatively short-lived as social class insignia are constantly adopted, modified, circulated and re-shaped in ways that continually undercut their reliability. The Beatles effectively changed the meaning of clothes and personal appearance by adopting the mainstream trademarks of the social order with their modified business suits and vibrantly coloured military uniforms. Andy Warhol transformed soup cans into art, Hollywood and Madison Avenue created supernumeraries like James Dean, Elvis Presley, Marilyn Monroe and the Marlboro Man. Every conceivable object and surface became a site of fashionable expression including T-shirts, coffee mugs, toys and car bumper stickers. The roiling fashions of the twentieth century have provided a kaleidoscope of examples where fashion and consumerism overlap (see Hebdige, 1993; Lipovetsky, 1994; Inglis, 2010; Kemp, 2012).

Some distinctive fashions have been regarded as expressions of resistance to mainstream values. Zoot suits, blue jeans, dyed hair, athletes' trainers, drag fashions and body tattoos all appear, at one time or another, to repudiate the conventions. This resistance to the mainstream ironically catalogues a form of belonging, albeit to new and evolving subcultures (such as those discussions in Chapter 6). For a time, they succeed in challenging the prevailing aesthetic forms, but then they are regularly plundered for novelties that are modified and incorporated into the dominant aesthetic. While such expressions blur gender distinctions and subvert the conventions they are soon drawn out from their distinctive enclaves and subsumed into new markets. In effect they create cross-over styling and new advertising targets that are then marketed to an ever wider audience of global consumers.

While adherence to an aesthetic style can be a declaration of a kind, an allegiance to a particular group or social order, it is, at the same time, an expression of social inclusion and belonging. It signals a desire to be recognised as a member of a tribe, community, gender and religion; in this way it indicates conformity to certain rules of appearance and re-asserts the value of appearance. As a consequence, fashion does not remain in the economic realm of consumption but expands to influence 'theoretical convictions' and even 'the moral foundations of life' (Simmel, 1904, p. 304). Thus, fashion is an important element in the shaping of individual sensibilities and tastes. It speaks of personal values, character and social values and, in an ironic gesture, locates the *fashionista* in an inherently conservative space. While fashion can structure the physical world through architectural styles, the design of cars and the value of art, it also influences subjectivity by defining thresholds of sentiments – what we find pleasing, repugnant, desirable and abhorrent. In this way, fashion makes everything contingent, subject to the influences of more remote circumstances such as political and economic events.

To take two contemporary examples, the Che Guevara T-shirt was a symbol of resistance during the 1970s to the Vietnam War as well as the Americanisation of a certain type of democracy. It continues to circulate heavily as a countercultural and pop cultural fashion item today. Likewise, the Guy Fawkes masks associated with the anonymous organisation occupying Wall Street are currently used to protest the Global Financial Crisis. These visual symbols have become effective messages in these examples of highly complex and debateable world events. However, their meaning can be ambiguous and unreliable. Such symbols can be worn in protest as well as in support of their representative causes. Fashion then becomes less personal and more commonly a vehicle for expressing a variety of cultural conventions.

Thus consumer decisions in regards to fashion could inherently be simplified to a dyadic choice between associative or dissociative referents: to supporting or (as with Case Study 2, below) challenging, the dominant paradigm.

Case study 2: boy beauty

Australian model Andrej Pejic is known as the 'androgynous' model and has pushed the boundaries of previously gender-specific high fashion. Pejic is a male who has been signed by the haute couture house of Jean Paul Gaultier, the department store Myer, and Vogue magazine, and many others to model both men's *and* women's clothing and perfume. Gaultier has adopted this androgynous image in recent campaigns and used Pejic in all the traditional female platforms: boudoir, wedding dress, evening gown and so on.

Pejic's effeminate look is the opposite of the lean, handsome, buff male models favoured by fashion houses since the 1980s. He has been recognised by agents and designers as jarringly feminine and shockingly beautiful and the irony of this is irresistible to high fashion houses and photographers. The fashion world has long amplified the importance of gender identity (discussed in Chapter 4) in the marketplace by creating male and female versions of everything from handkerchiefs to T-shirts. The 'femiman' form is certainly challenging to the gendered realm of fashion.

Appearance matters

Body awareness has penetrated deep into Western culture making physical appearance seem important. The desire to control the opinion of others by managing appearance characterises much of our interpersonal commerce. This was the astute observation of the American sociologist Erving Goffman (1961) whose writings in the mid-twentieth century were framed by a renewed period of socio-economic growth and cultural re-definition. He described the social practice of 'impression management' as the desire to control others by manipulating our own demeanour. He identified the discredited and discreditable body as an important key to social success; if we failed to convince others that we meet the expectations of convention, if we appear to them as discreditable in some way, then social exchange will be difficult, even impossible. Goffman's (1961) concentration on physical appearance and demeanour drew on a long history of the body as a site of social categorisation (highlighted, for instance, in arguments about race and ethnicity, discussed in Chapter 2, and the distinction between sex and gender, discussed in Chapter 3).

The growing cosmopolitanism of the West, with its increasing numbers of strangers in the public domain, created an atmosphere in which appearances and manners of conduct became the means for deciphering identity and social position. So reliable did this concentration seem to be that a regime of professional scrutiny developed in which individuals could locate their opinions and assumptions within a quasi-scientific and verifiable framework. Michel Foucault (1977, 1980) identified this new approach to reading physical appearances as a form of social engineering. Foucault (1977) used the term 'carceral' to define the social milieu in which dire consequences could result from being outside the notional boundaries of the normal. Where there were instances of irregularity, Foucault noted, there were professional agencies that policed the aberrant in an attempt to re-assert prevailing conventions. Physical and emotional anomalies could be defined as instances of illness that potentially represented a danger to society that needed to be controlled. This was the signature of the scientisation of appearances as exercised through the emerging medical, health and psychiatric professions. These new moral entrepreneurs (to use Goffman's phrase) became the authorities whose task it was (even today) to guide us towards normalcy through various procedures – some benign such as diets, exercise and some dangerously interventionist such as electric shock treatment and pharmacological medication.

Reading human appearance in order to understand the nature of others has a long history. Lavater (1885), and after him, Samuel Smiles, Dale Carnegie, John Molloy and Paul Ekman have been popular authorities on how to read appearances and use fashion to uncover other more submerged human qualities. This degree of attention paid to the human body has heightened consciousness of its malleability. Our willingness to shape and cultivate appearance is a characteristic of contemporary fashions that may well be supported by the specious beliefs of the past several centuries during which physiognomic ideas have been promulgated. Underlying this perspective is an enduring belief that appearances matter, that character is immanent in appearance and that social success can be augmented when we look and act in accord with prevailing styles and fashions. As discussed above, the social manners and literary fashions of the late eighteenth and early nineteenth centuries in the West are particularly illustrative of the emphasis given to physical appearances. The scrutiny given to dress and mannerisms signalled the firm belief that character and moral fibre could be deduced from outward appearance. However, we see this scrutiny continue today.

As we have become increasingly socially mobile, with greater opportunities to change lifestyles, travel widely, pursue different careers, create a variety of social networks, extend and blend families and friends, we have increased the value we accord to the control of our own identity and reputation. We tacitly support a belief system in which we assume we can reach our goals, achieve our desires and become what we want. Underlying this confidence in self-determination is the axiom that physiognomy matters that we can read the other from appearance and influence their opinion of us by shaping our own appearance.

Such an emphasis on appearance and fashionability has created opportunities for new services and commercial products that modify physical appearance. Without much effort now we can correct and reshape the body to approximate prevailing views of attractiveness. Hair transplants, hair colouring, developing musculature, dieting, tanning, straightening and whitening teeth, dermabrasion for smoothing the skin and prosthetic implants are all instances of accepted practices designed to homogenise appearance. This appetite for controlling appearance is sustained by a variety of uncoordinated influences – from competitive sociality and displays of luxury consumption to popular media entertainments (for example, The Biggest Loser and Embarrassing Bodies) in which physical appearance is emphasised.

Life at the surface

The changes in cultural habits across the centuries of social and commercial development are not linear or logical, and it is difficult to itemise all the links that chain together meanings from one set of actions to another. With identity and consumption, for instance, it is possible to describe trends and tastes, say, for a cup of coffee bought from a global outlet such as Starbucks or from a local espresso bar or for shopping at a farmers' market in preference to a chain supermarket. Tastes are closely associated for a while with external circumstances and with social status and self-identification as illustrated by Bourdieu's (1984) study of the French middle classes (discussed also in Chapter 3). He identified certain patterns of consumption with levels of income and education: women eat more fish than men; office managers eat more vegetables than construction workers. These associations, however, are not static but need to be constantly reinforced. Advertising and the mass media create patterns of consumption and this regularity makes certain patterns seem natural. In many ways this is how a disciplined society, as described by Foucault (1980), works; it advertises patterns of conduct that by repetition are made to seem commonplace and taken-for-granted. Consumption itself gives entrée to belonging in an ever-changing landscape of groups and subcultures.

Everyday pursuits are embedded in the wider world of socio-economic circumstances even though they often seem much more personal and intimate. The everyday social world is not a private universe even though it is represented as such. As we purchase entertainments from a wide array of goods and services, we think of ourselves as free, autonomous beings but our daily transactions are constrained within a grid of more remote circumstances.

For instance, the emotional investments we make in ordinary practices are linked to commercial factors such as advertising, fashion and popular entertainments. In effect, as we become increasingly interested in fashions and trends we become more deeply and complacently inserted into recognisable patterns and practices – as a result it becomes harder to see any reason to challenge or change them. In this way, the consumerist culture, with its comprehensive network of communications and promotion of the illusory world of advertising images, has come to prefabricate much of our everyday social life. Cultural values become embedded in goods and are sold to us at every opportunity. The fashionability of goods and the popularity of the celebrity (film stars, musicians and artists) who use endorsed products are mechanisms that reinforce and transmit mainstream cultural values. Cars, for instance, are not simply modes of transportation, they are (as evidenced in Case Study 3, below) symbols of freedom; houses are not physical shelters but domains of domestic happiness; wrist watches are scientific tools in the calculation of speed and location.

Case study 3: romance on wheels

In a current car advertisement (the badge is not important) the female's ruminations about her lover and his car reveal the collapse of the animate into the inanimate:

Champagne from my slipper? He begs for it.
The pearls I admired in Cartier's on the Rue de la Paix? Mine without a murmur. But when he is driving (name of car) – suddenly I am nothing. How can a car mean so much to a man when it cannot even kiss?

The globalisation of consumerism bears witness to the power of consumption in driving and defining economic and social well-being. The thriving popularity of consumer goods in non-Western countries has seen brands like Rolex, Coca Cola, Audi and Apple become symbols of modernity and have ushered countries like China into the world of branding and service delivery where previously the culture did not exist. This phenomenon is not new with Chinoiserie for example being a recurring theme in European artistic style and design since the seventeenth century. The favoured blending of Chinoiserie with the rococo style made it a favourite amongst various European monarchs and ensured its popularity among aristocratic households keen to advertise their nobility and belonging by association of their preferred style.

In various accounts of contemporary emotions, Fred Inglis (2010), Norbert Elias (1978), Foucault, Illouz, Goffman and others have argued that certain historical epochs cultivate specific emotional responses that in turn influence how we think of identity and ourselves. Certain cultures and social groupings promote specific feelings and rank these in a hierarchical system of order. As a result, some emotions become entangled with other values; thus we learn to 'love' chocolate as well as money, physical beauty and individual freedom. Reality television programmes are highly effective in promoting the cult of celebrity and give emphasis to certain types of behaviours. Popular television and film provide persuasive examples of how specific ideas and fashions percolate across different corners of the globe and come to form connecting discourses that promote particular values. It is a point made by Eco (1986) in his arguments about the dominance of hyper-reality, that is, the heightened value given to the image over that of the actual.

Visual culture

We live in an era of dense visuality in which we have become accustomed to connecting what we see with what we get. Brand images of top-end goods and the logos of international companies supposedly guarantee the quality of products. The *Nike* whoosh, *McDonald's* Golden Arches, the *Dior* initials and *Ferrari* red are shortcut claims of quality, identity, belonging and status. The almost universal recognition of product logos demonstrates the power of the symbol to express highly regarded social values.

Displaying these superior qualities and making them seem real is essential to the reputation of the goods themselves. Accordingly, any claims for elite superiority must include qualities that are widely valued – such as happiness, love, power and privilege. The circularity of this process is immediately apparent; Boorstin (1962) described how the communications industries were (and remain) knowing merchants of illusions. Their stock-in-trade is persuading vast numbers of people that certain events, people and products are important, necessary and valuable when, indeed, it may not be so.

On the surface, this viewpoint depicts us as gullible and naïve, but that is not all that Boorstin argues. There is a complicity at work between the grand claims of the image-makers and our willingness to accept the rhetoric. In that exchange lies an essential feature of the modern consumer experience. Goffman (1961) refers to the dramaturgy of everyday life, de Certeau (1984) to ordinary practices and Eva Illouz (2007) to the cold intimacies of emotional capitalism. In their various ways, these theorists are emphasising the adoption of certain beliefs that occur at the individual level; Zygmunt Bauman (2001) also describes it through the idea of liquid sociability – of being able to extract an understanding from the flow of social life by adopting recognisable symbols of communication as a means of identifying oneself and locating a community. At this point, the convergence of consumption and identity is illuminated.

Conclusion

As it became more acceptable to mingle the social ranks of the privileged high with the canny low, it became more obvious that there was no logic to social position; instead, there was a growing recognition that arbitrary circumstances played a part. Our emotions, needs, sensibility and appetites seem to be arbitrarily acquired and thus we are free to explore their variation and limits. The displacement of a received social order strengthens the belief that we are 'perverse by definition, sexually ambidextrous, and potentially unlimited in the range of (our) desires' (Castle, 1987, p. 158). With such an understanding, there can be an absence of constraint and that, in turn, provides the opportunity to escape 'into new realms of voluptuous disorder' (Castle, 1987, p. 161). The *mentalité* of the early modern period was fuelled by material abundance and an explicit erotic charge (Hunt, 1993).

In the modern era the producing and consuming of images coupled with rampant consumerism has given rise to an identifiable personality type. Hebdige (1993) has described this type as the modern consumer who is obsessively self-conscious, chronically uneasy about his or her health, afraid of ageing and death, constantly searching for flaws and signs of decay, hungry for emotional experiences and haunted by a sense of failure. It is a description that resonates in the works of Sennett (1976), Lasch (1982) and Illouz (1997, 2007). The ubiquity of rampant narcissism focused on self-presentation provides a platform for sustaining a consumer culture where appearance, display, performance and personal impressions have become dominating elements of everyday life. Our cultural heritage illuminates the importance that appearances have assumed, especially so when we also know, ironically, that appearances are plastic and that the person on the high street, in military garb, wearing the camouflage outfit of the combat soldier, is probably not a soldier and the figure wearing a frock may not be female (Butler 1990).

Questions for students

- What influences an individual's investment (economic and social) in their physical appearance?
- Do you think modern fashion is grounded in gender or social class or something else?
- What role does the male business suit and necktie play in modern society?

- Why would Gaultier (as discussed in Case Study 2) use a male model to represent his female creations?
- How do you think Pejic's image would fit with a female's self-concept? How would it fit with a male's?
- In Case Study 3, what meaning(s) do you think the male attaches to the car?
- Why does the female interpret the male's attention to the car as having romantic qualities?
- Explain why the male and the female might interpret this situation differently.

Recommended reading

Bauman, Z. (2001) *The Individualized Society* (Oxford: Polity).

Finkelstein, J. (2007) *The Art of Self Invention* (London: IBTauris).

Simmel, G. (1904) 'Fashion' in *The Sociology of Georg Simmel* (Chicago, IL: University of Chicago Press).

CHAPTER 14

Digital media

Philippa Collin

Introduction

Millions of babies being born into the world today will come to quickly recognise the rectangular-shaped devices so often put in front of their faces. (They will do this, perhaps, as technologies such as print newspapers, fixed-line telephones and analogue radio and television fade to the register of historical artefact.) From conception their progress through life will be captured, edited, shared and replayed through digital media devices with relatives, friends and wider social networks. The quantum and role of media in the exploration and documentation of their 'lives' will far exceed that of any generation that has come before them. Platforms for the production, storage and sharing of texts that articulate their activities, relationships, curiosities and the banal punctuations of their everyday lives will seem commonplace and obligatory. But how will this pervasive digital mediation of the everyday shape their sense of self, their sense of belonging and the ways in which they distinguish themselves and identify with others?

As media and communication technologies have evolved, there has been much interest in the relationship between identity formation and media (Livingstone, 2002; Gitelman, 2006). The study of the relationship between new technologies and social change is highly contested. It is often conceptualised as *determined by technology* (technological determinism) – the view that technology produces change in individuals and societies (eg. Turkle, 1995, 2011; Tapscott, 1998). This position asserts a neutral logic to technological advances that is outside of human or social influence and tends to focus on the effects of technology *on* users. Critics of this view point out it fails to sufficiently acknowledge the role of social, political, economic and cultural forces that shape how technology develops and how it is deployed (Buckingham, 2008a). Others argue it is *socially determined* (social determinism) – the view that technology is the outcome of social processes. For example, in her book *Technoculture*, Lelia Green argues 'social processes determine technology for social purposes' (Green, 2002). She argues that every technological development throughout history was born of a social need, be this need economic, political or military. However, this insufficiently accounts for the inherent potentialities or 'affordances' that make it much easier to use some technologies for some purposes than others. This chapter takes a third position: a dialectical, or radical, position which argues that there is a more complex relationship between the two. As David Buckingham suggests, the role and impact of information and communication technologies ('ICT') is 'partly determined by the uses to which it is put, but it also contains inherent constraints and possibilities which limit the ways in which it can be used, and which are in turn largely shaped by the social interests of those who control its production, circulation, and distribution' (Buckingham, 2008a, p. 12). For example, the role and impact of a mobile phone in a rural village in Indonesia will be a complex combination of the functionality, connectivity and age of the device, as much as it is by who it is owned by and paid for (the head of a family, a village chief or a community organisation), the local customs and views on gender and education and the village's place within a local and global economy.

In recognising the interplay between the social and the technological, this chapter highlights the ways in which digital media, identity and belonging can all be understood as *social processes*. It will discuss how recent developments in digital media are associated with diversifying and complicating ways of thinking about and practising identity. It will also consider how digital media is shaping the ways in which we feel a sense of belonging and connectedness to others and the ways we articulate these connections and relationships. It begins by outlining a conception of digital media that enables thinking about the subjective, structural, material and relational dynamics of technology. This chapter then examines the opportunities that these developments have provided for new modes of self-expression, identity construction, communication, belonging and social activism and highlights how these developments intersect with gender, class, disability and ethnicity, further complicating identity formation and ways of belonging.

Globalisation and digital media

The emergence of ICT – integrated systems and devices that transfer huge amounts of compressed digital data – has dramatically accelerated and shaped processes of globalisation, altering the ways we identify ourselves and connect with others. Cable and satellite technology has become more efficient and less expensive enabling the establishment of vast technology networks to carry information from one place to another. As these communications systems have rolled out, access to the data these networks carry has extended, via the Internet, into the workplace, public facilities (such as libraries), commercial zones (such as shopping malls), educational institutions and homes of an estimated 2.7 billion people worldwide (Union, 2013, p. 1). People access the Internet and other digital resources via a range of devices such as personal and laptop computers, tablets, mobile and smart phones, gaming consoles, digital television and media players, diversifying interactions with information, individuals and groups. These technologies make possible many kinds of media practices including consumption, production, sharing and mixing of text-based, photographic, video and audio content (via websites, social network and content-sharing platforms), role-playing (via virtual worlds and online communities), gaming, video and Internet phone and video communications. Lievrouw and Livingstone (2006) provide a useful way to frame and analyse the social impacts of digital media. They suggest these forms of 'digital media' are enabled by ICT that can best be understood as 'infrastructures':

> Infrastructures with three key components: *artefacts or devices* used to communicate or convey information; the *activities or practices* in which people engage to communicate or share information; and the *social arrangements or organizational forms* that develop around those devices and practices (drawing on Star and Boweker, Lievrouw and Livingstone, 2006, p. 2).

It is through ICT that digital media becomes possible and has both material and relational dimensions that are significant for the ways in which we explore and express our identities and connections to others. While all media has been 'new', at one time or another (Gitelman, 2006), ICT has enabled both a convergence in the production, distribution and consumption of 'traditional media' and the expansion of platforms and practices in 'citizen', or social, media (sometimes referred to as 'new' media). As Henry Jenkins puts it:

> Media convergence refers to a situation in which multiple media systems coexist and where media content flows fluidly across them. Convergence is understood here as an ongoing process or series of intersections between different media systems, not a fixed relationship. (Jenkins, 2006, p. 282)

Therefore, 'new' or 'digital media' must be understood, not as separate to, but as increasingly synonymous with 'old media'. For example, globally franchised reality television shows, such as *The X Factor*, incorporate social media such as Twitter feeds, Facebook pages and 'fango' fan communities into the overall 'show'. Similarly, news and current affairs programmes use Twitter feeds and Skype calls in live broadcasts and are re-broadcasting news stories on video-sharing platforms such as YouTube. As such, digital media, like globalisation, can be understood as a process that is constantly changing.

ICT and digital media practices are particularly associated with dynamics of mobility in late modern societies. In sociology 'mobility' often refers to 'social mobility' and the ability of individuals to move within class categories. However, the recent emergence of a field of mobilities research is concerned with how humans, non-humans, objects and information 'travel', as well as the physical and informational infrastructures for spatial movement (and inertia). John Urry (2003, 2007) argues that in a world increasingly shaped by the dynamics of travel, physical (and mediated) co-presence is a central feature of the networked society. Digital media practices are inherently mobile – decoupled from place by increasingly mobile populations powered by mobile devices, mobile relationships and mobile practices (Urry, 2003, 2007). In contrast with theories of globalisation, emphasising movement and flow, mobilities theory contends there is a persistent relationship between social life and 'place', stillness and immobility.

Considering the role of mobility for identity and belonging calls into question the ways in which particular identity practices or forms of belonging are privileged over others. For example, are practices such as VoiP or videoconferencing, blogging, gaming or brief micro-communications, such as Tweets, favoured over other forms of inter-personal communication such as 'face-to-face' and deep conversations (Turkle, 2011) or forms of self-exploration and expression such as non-digital drawing, painting and music-making (See Elliot and Urry, 2010)? Following Goffman (1963), Urry has argued that in an increasingly mobile and mediated society, face-to-face or, rather, eye-to-eye contact – what he calls 'meetingness' – is still necessary for people to feel properly connected to others within their social network (Urry, 2003). However, as digital media has become more sophisticated, immersive and participatory, it is able to facilitate both actual and simulated co-presence 'at-a-distance' and while on the move (via, for instance, iPhone 'face time' or video Skype calls via tablet or laptop). This renders new possibilities for expressing oneself and connecting with others. Nevertheless, physical co-presence remains a crucial function of network sociality by holding together the weak ties of broad and disembedded network relations (Urry, 2003). These networked relations, enabled by digital media, can be extensive in number, diversity and geography and are associated with the blurring of a number of dichotomies including work/leisure, friends/family and public/private (Urry, 2003, p. 168). To identify and understand the impact of digital media for identity and belonging, we must therefore take into account how people make meaning through technology as they negotiate and shape social structures and processes.

The information, associations and forms of expression that people can engage in have moved beyond the geographies, relationships and values of the local and national and are increasingly global in their potential. However, like many of the processes of globalisation, ICT access and usage is highly uneven around the globe. More than half the world's population is not yet online (Union, 2013, p. 1) and the cost of access to fixed line and mobile broadband remains highly unaffordable for people in developing countries (Union, 2013). Mobile-cellular penetration is much more even in the most populous and poorest regions of the world (Africa and South Asia), though mobile-broadband remains low and unaffordable (see Union, 2013, p. 42). The level of access (quality of Internet connection and digital media infrastructures including devices and software) and capacity for use (including knowledge and digital literacy) varies enormously according to location (Union, 2013) and intersects with other social structures including class, gender, cultural background and disability (see for example, Mossberger, 2003; Dobransky and Hargittai, 2006). Furthermore, claims of a 'digital generation' – implying that technology has produced 'naturally technologically enabled' children (Tapscott, 1998) – have been fiercely disputed. While acknowledging that developments in digital media do reshape the experience of childhood and youth, David Buckingham has argued that technologically determinist positions such as Tapscott's fail to account for a range of other issues and phenomena generally associated with late modernity, as well as those specific to the experience of childhood and youth (see Case Study 1 in Chapter 6 for further discussion). Even in parts of the world with high Internet penetration, studies have shown that the consequences of digital media depend on what it is used for and that there is a significant degree of variation between, and among, different age groups. Buckingham and others remind us that it is necessary to view the role of digital media as intersecting with other social structures (such as class, gender and ethnicity) and social change (for example, the massive commercialisation and marketing focus on children and young people) (Buckingham and Willett, 2006). Nevertheless, there are some broad implications of digital media for the ways in which we explore and make sense of who we are and how we relate to others.

Digital media, social change and identity

Manuel Castells has theorised that, powered by ICT, networks have become the defining organisational structures of society where traditional boundaries between individuals, groups or countries can be overcome with relative ease (Castells, 2000). He argues that ICT is facilitating new forms of social identities and communities (Castells, 1996). He claims that ICT enables social relations to be drawn beyond geographical place, to be embedded in networks and increasingly associated with processes of globalisation such as social and geographical mobility, rapid economic change, breakdown of traditional social ties such as family and the general fragmentation of human association. According to this view, the increasing prominence of 'networked individualism' is reshaping the ways in which people identify and relate to others (Chambers, 2006). Digital networks enable access to information and opportunities to explore and express one's point of view, make connections and organise in new ways beyond the immediate personal connections of family, friends, neighbourhoods and work. For example, using websites, social networks, blogging and instant message services and email, global activist networks highlight the ways in which people are able to identify with global issues, join with like-minded people from different parts of the world and organise and influence decision-makers at an intra-state level while deepening connections to local community. The information, interactions and actions enabled by digital media provide ways to evade or resist forms of authority, social and cultural expectations.

Case study 1: digital media and political identity

The rise of global activism has been closely attributed to the emergence of the Internet and the formation of wide, shallow networks through which information, values and shared goals are created and mobilised (Bennett, 2003). In recent years two common forms have emerged. Firstly, there are issues-based movements such as the Zapatista movement in Mexico, the 'Arab Spring' protests, G20 protests following the 2008 global economic crisis and Occupy Wall Street 2011 which utilised digital media, particularly mobile phone, SMS and video in addition to offline strategies. Secondly, platforms for national and global networks for social activism have been developed. For example, YouthActionNet, Taking it Global, change.org and avaaz.org combine community features including forums, profiles and social media integration for commenting and status updates with campaigning tools including information, polling facilities and digital media artefacts (photos, posters and video) that can be shared via social media. Furthermore, governments, non-government organisations and grass-roots community organisations use digital media to engage individuals in identifying and making decisions about issues of concern. One of the theorised consequences of the coupling of digital media and participation is that new forms of political identity are emerging. Several studies of the views and actions of young people have demonstrated an increasing orientation towards issues-based and project-based identities whereby 'everyday' and individualised modes of expression are seen as more attractive and relevant than traditional, institutional forms of participation (Bang, 2005; Marsh et al., 2007; Collin, 2008). In a study of young people in Australia and the United Kingdom, Collin found that digital media enabled a merging and overlapping of various dimensions of social life such as work, study, health, relationships and family. Young people associated accessing information, connecting with communities of interest and taking action on issues they care about with their new media capabilities. Similarly, in a mixed-methods study on youth civic and political engagement, Harris and colleagues found that digital media was significant for exploration and expression of social and political views that were often informal and mundane in nature (Harris et al., 2010, p. 27). They highlight the ways in which, outside of formal strategies for mobilising youth participation in institutions and networks, digital media is valued as a site for unregulated, intimate and social forms of self-expression and belonging for young people (Harris et al., 2010, p. 27).

Using digital media, people can also explore different aspects of their identities (such as disability, gender, sexuality, ethnicity and religion) and form online communities based on shared interests and experiences.

Case study 2: online communities, chronic illness and disability

People living with a chronic illness or disability often have restricted social opportunities due to ill health, limited mobility and inaccessible environments. Critical studies highlight the ways in which digital media technologies can be enabling or disabling depending on the norms that are built into technology systems. Furthermore, many people living with a disability or chronic illness experience economic barriers to good access to digital media (Dobransky and Hargittai, 2006). The population of people living with disability or illness is diverse and problems associated with access to digital media are substantial and varied (Eardley et al., 2009, pp. 28–29). Studies highlight the importance of a nuanced approach to account for diversity and specificity of use and the implications for selfhood and community (Dobransky and Hargittai, 2006).

Third and Richardson have taken up this challenge in their study of the use of an online platform for young people aged 10–21 years living with a serious illness, chronic condition or disability (Third and Richardson, 2009). Run by the Starlight Foundation, Livewire (www.livewire.org.au) is a customised, safe and secure online community featuring social networking tools and relevant content, including online chat, blogging, member profiles, games, music, articles, community forums and competitions. The study used an online user survey, online content analysis and focus groups to examine the use and attitudes of community members. Ethnography was also used to examine the relationship of users to technology in their own environments through home visits where researchers conducted interviews and technology walk-throughs. This methodology allowed the researchers to consider socio-cultural, technological, embodiment and material-cultural factors for young people's digital practices. Third and Richardson (2009) found that members used Livewire to engage in chat, games and competitions, to share their creativity and help others by offering empathy and advice (for instance regarding everyday issues as well as treatments and recovery). Most importantly, site users emphasised that Livewire is not about being ill or disabled. Rather, members articulated a sense of self and community where they could 'just be a kid like other kids' in an environment where there was acceptance and 'normalisation' of illness and disability (Third et al., 2009, pp. 29–31). They conclude that use of the Livewire platform enables a sense of identity and embodiment for these young people by providing a safe and reliable environment for acceptance, self-expression and social connection.

It is argued that digital media practices, along with other processes of globalisation (for example, the decline of the welfare state, increased transnationalism of markets and production and increased mobilisation of workforces) are associated with the decline of traditional social structures and processes, where once powerful sources for identity formation, such as the family, organised religion, nation-states, are now less significant (Giddens, 1991. See also Chapters 10 and 11). This includes a decline in formal membership of social, cultural and political groups (Putnam, 2000; Norris, 2002). Individuals are now thought to be required to make more choices and be more 'self-reflexive'. They are more likely to associate with broad, shallow, dense networks and to participate in individualised collective communication practices that narrate both individual and group identity (Bennett, 2012). Digital media plays an important role in identity work by facilitating access to all kinds of information, sites for experimental self-expression (virtual worlds), communities of interest (climate change, gaming and knitting!) and broad, shallow social and political networks (such as Facebook or avaaz.org) that often operate outside of (although not necessarily free of) traditional institutions and social structures. This approach broadly views the role of digital media as a positive force for change and an enabling resource for 'self-actualisation', often emphasising the ways in which new forms of expression, belonging and connectedness are made possible via digital media.

However, digital media might also be interpreted as forms of what Foucault has described as 'governmentality' (Foucault, 1979). That is, digital media acts to further diffuse power through social relationships. Individual use of digital media becomes a form of self-monitoring and surveillance. This approach to the analysis of digital media for identity and belonging questions the ways in which use of digital media for self-expression and the formation of community is 'free' of oppressive discourses. For example, to what extent do blogs on mothering and childrearing reassert binary notions of gender in the form of traditional female roles as mothers and care-givers? Similarly, what is the role of commercial interests and marketing in digital media and the ways in which 'big data' and increasingly 'intelligent' forms of computing shape what we experience in our online lives (boyd and Crawford, 2012)? Networks enable new channels of influence by commercial forces raising important questions about the ways in which people are being encouraged to form identities and social relations that are conducive to consumerism (Buckingham, 2008b, p. 5). Furthermore, new mobile digital devices contain surveillance and tracking systems (such as Global Positioning Systems) which can be integrated with institutional and social media platforms identifying the physical locality of users.

While differently conceptualising power, these two theoretical approaches emphasise that digital media is relational and deeply social and that neither the technology nor the associated practices or social relations are 'neutral'. They remind us of the importance of questioning the way in which digital media challenges, reinforces or transforms social structures and dominant discourses.

There is a wide range of questions emanating from a consideration of the relationship between digital media and identity. The interdisciplinary and rapidly evolving nature of digital media means there is an almost inexhaustible range of ways to examine how social identity and ways of belonging are being transformed. The remainder of the chapter will briefly consider two key questions: does digital media strengthen or weaken identity and social ties and how does the changing nature of public and private in the context of digital media shape processes of identity and belonging?

Strengthening or weakening identity and social ties

Early studies of digital sociality enthusiastically claimed to identify new forms of identity and communities of belonging that were independent or disassociated with 'offline' lives. These early approaches tended to conceptualise 'cyberspace' as dis-embodied. That is, the virtual world was separate, and the emphasis was often on how people used the Internet to connect with individuals not known offline and play out aspects of identity they would not perform in 'real life' (Turkle, 1995). However, more recent research on how online practices fit with offline relationships and activities indicates that digital media largely supports existing social ties (Boase et al., 2006) while providing opportunities for new associations and forms of self-expression. In this way, digital media blurs or collapses the distinction between 'real' and 'virtual' life (Poster, 1995 cited in Chambers, 2006), particularly as digital media has become increasingly personalisable, interactive and mobile and, therefore, increasingly embedded in everyday life. This shift is illustrated by considering research on migrant and transnational communities' use of the Internet to reassert, rearticulate and regenerate forms of identity and belonging despite physical and geographical distance.

Case study 3: transnational virtual communities

Studies of migrant use of new media have problematised the relationship between geographical place and self by demonstrating the ways in which communities form and function. These include the creation of virtual spaces for political, social and cultural practices. For example, Victoria Bernal has conducted extensive studies of the Eritrean diaspora to show the ways in which new media has been used to generate, share and debate information, perspectives and stories and to organise and mobilise actions and resources associated with the nationalist movement in Eritrea throughout the 1990s and 2000s (Bernal, 2006). Drawing on a range of evidence including online textual analysis, participant observation and interviews, Bernal demonstrates how Eritreans in diaspora have utilised new media to explore cultural, social and political ways of being that challenge – indeed transcend – traditional physical boundaries, place and official narratives and norms of nationalism.

Other research on migrant digital practices has examined how new media contributes to the embodiment of 'home' in 'host' countries in everyday life through the transmission of the artefacts, practices and relationships of geographical place into the everyday living environments of the receiver country (Kang, 2009). Studying Chinese migrants in London, Kang identified the ways in which offline social, cultural and spatial activities are transformed and shaped by Internet use. Kang finds that ICT transforms Chinese migrants' experiences of place by helping to 'recreate the visual, audio, physical and social contexts of their homelands in both personal and public spaces' (Kang, 2009, p. 339). This takes place via a range of devices and consumptive and productive media practices (such as listening to radio and sharing video online). ICT are also used to transform public places in urban areas (including but not only Chinatown) to involve larger numbers of members of the 'Chinese diaspora'. In this way, argues Kang, Chinese in London feel able to 'safely' practise culture and community in new public spaces. Furthermore, the ways in which new media shapes the 'narrative space' (Pertierra, 2012) of migrants may not only pertain to the geographies of 'home' and 'host' but to a 'set of significant places' enabling multiple orientations and interests – from ethnic heritage to pop music, and familial and peer networks – both local and global (Wilding, 2012).

Notwithstanding the evidence that digital media can enable self-expression and maintain existing social ties despite physical and geographical distance, there are concerns that digital media leads to the fragmentation of identity and the weakening of social ties. In her book, *Life on Screen*, examining identities in the digital age, Sherry Turkle (1995) argued that identities had become incomplete, ever-changing and fragmented. In contrast, in their discussion of youth digital media practices and identity, and Weber and Mitchell (2008) have argued that the fluid, fragmented nature of identity in the context of digital media can still be understood as forming part of a single 'work in progress' – a unified, if not always coherent, whole. Creative production required in digital media practices highlights the ways in which identities are 'assembled'. Weber and Mitchell argue that youth digital media practices demonstrate the ways in which digital production entails individual and collective negotiation, subversion and adaptation of the technology, the setting and the relationships at play (Weber and Mitchell, 2008, p. 39). They argue the 'constructedness' that characterises identity processes in digital media highlights the contingent and changing nature of identity as 'work-in-progress'. They argue for the notion of 'Identities-in-Action' to highlight the ways in which digital media is part of the social and cultural material drawn upon as people and communities construct identity through action, in a form of 'personal and social bricolage' (Weber and Mitchell, 2008, p. 43). The 'components' of identity in a digital society can be augmented, renovated or discarded but will always retain some features – 'shadows' or 'traces' – of past assemblages. As such, 'Identities-in-Action' are inherently more public than ever before. The ways in which digital media practices are associated with a blurring of public and private have significant implications for identity and belonging.

Rethinking public and private lives

As digital media has become increasingly mobile, participatory and social, scholars argue that the Internet is making people's private lives increasingly public (Harris, 2004; Livingstone, 2006). The focus is now on understanding how this occurs and what effects this might have. In her study of girls' use of digital media, Anita Harris argues that authoring oneself online is manifest in 'confessional styles' that transform 'intimate details and experience into material for popular consumption' such that what is private and public converge (Harris, 2004, p. 128). By 'living large' through membership of online communities and the authoring and publication of online content, Harris suggests young people construct and claim new, legitimate spaces in the public sphere (Harris, 2004, p. 128).

These public acts and conversations are increasingly undertaken via social network services and content-sharing platforms which constitute and are deployed in new forms of public-ness. danah boyd has argued for social network services (or sites) to be conceptualised (along with other sites of online interaction) as 'networked publics'. She argues that networked publics are those social formations and spaces enabled by technological networks such as the Internet (boyd, 2008). She argues that the emergence of networked publics signals a new kind of public (social formation) and space (locality). These networked publics are distinguished from other kinds of mediated and non-mediated publics by being persistent (permanent), searchable (individuals and their personal information can easily be located), replicable (information, comments and multimedia can be copied and disseminated) and scalable (extending beyond immediate or physical connections) (boyd, 2011, pp. 46–48). They are also potentially populated by 'invisible audiences' (boyd, 2008, p. 126). These 'affordances' shape the way identities, relationships and practices are performed in networked publics. Affordances are part of the architecture of online and networked environments (boyd, 2011) and it is the architecture, boyd argues, that plays an increasingly important role in the structuring of social life – the ways in which we act, communicate, represent ourselves and make sense of others. Information in these new 'publics' is both knowingly shared by individuals and unknowingly collected by third parties (companies and governments). The information we share through our digital media activities can also be used by others, including corporations and governments, to make assumptions about the 'kind' of person we might be: our beliefs, our preferences and our actions. This can shape the kind of information (and advertising) delivered to us online via search engines, social network services, government and community sites. The digital media content and connections that we share and have recommended to us, in turn, inform decisions on the development of policies and products as analysts read and interpret user data. The blurring of public and private is also a blurring of the control and use of information – information that is used to represent, interpret and shape who we are and how we relate to others.

Conclusion

Social life is more complex and communicative in a digital society raising important questions about how digital media is implicated in reshaping identity and the ways in which people identify with others. Digital media makes possible practices, spaces and relationships for the exploration and expression of identity and belonging. This chapter highlights that this is a highly uneven and diverse process that is shaped by social structures including nationality, age, gender and disability. And yet digital media disrupts the spatial and temporal dimensions of sociality offering new ways for embodying the communicative practices that constitute our identity work and relationships. In doing so, individual and collective practices have emerged to evade or resist forms of authority, social and cultural expectations. In this way, digital media is associated with changing understandings, relationships and negotiations of many aspects of the social world: politics, community, nationhood, culture, ethnicity, the public and the private. As such, there are important questions about the ways in which digital media opens up and expands our possibilities for identity and belonging. At the same time, the ways in which digital information is generated, viewed, shared, captured, aggregated and used by individuals, communities, corporations and governments to shape our own understandings of who we are and our place in the world requires ongoing critical attention.

Questions for students

- In what ways does digital media feature in everyday practices of self-expression and belonging?
- How do digital media practices enhance or constrain our ability to express ourselves and relate to others? (Are we more or less 'free' to be ourselves online?) How might this differ depending on who we are, where we live in the world, our gender and our physical or intellectual abilities?
- How does the increasingly mobile and participatory nature of digital media influence who we communicate with (e.g. friends, family, work colleagues or strangers) and how (e.g. SMS, blogging, in person or video face-to-face conversations)?

Recommended reading

boyd, d. (2014) *It's Complicated: The Social Lives of Networked Teens* (New Haven, CT: Yale University Press).

Buckingham, D. (ed.). (2008) *Youth, Identity, and Digital Media* (Boston, MA: MIT Press). (Particularly the Introduction.)

Chambers, D. (2006) *New Social Ties: Contemprary Connections in a Fragmented Society* (Houndsmills: Palgrave Macmillan). (Particularly Chapter 6, 'Network Society'.)

Howard, P.N. (2011) *Castells and the Media* (Cambridge: Polity Press).

Papacharissi, Z. (ed.). (2011) *A Networked Self : Identity, Community, and Culture on Social Network Sites* (First Edition) (New York: Routledge).

Epilogue

As we were collating the chapters for this book, in October 2014, Australian not-for-profit organisation Welcome to Australia was launching (in conjunction with other community groups) their third annual series of 'Walk Together' marches and events around the country. Operating under the tagline of 'Common people, Common dreams', Walk Together was designed to promote ideas of shared or common humanity and to celebrate Australia's cultural diversity. According to Welcome to Australia, it is a campaign that strives to foster positive images of multiculturalism and opportunities for intercultural exchange, at the same time as raising awareness of the issues facing migrants, refugees and asylum seekers in Australia (see Welcome to Australia, n.d. for more information). It seems that in a socio-political climate where debates over migration and refugee and asylum seeker policy are intensifying, such campaigns, which seek to include rather than exclude, are on the increase. Certainly inclusive campaigns have much to resist: 'stop the boats' rhetoric was at an all-time high during the 2013 Australian Federal election, and 2014 saw both praise for, and scrutiny of, the coalition governments' 'Operation Sovereign Borders' as well as their decisions to continue with the mandatory detention of asylum seekers, extension of offshore processing, repeated attempts to change migration legislation and development of the so-called 'Cambodia solution' (for a timeline of these events, see Asylum Seeker Resource Centre, n.d.).

Irrespective of which side of the debate one sits, in this socio-political climate we can see the Walk Together campaign and the beliefs, behaviours and policies that it challenges, as involving clear statements about identity and belonging: about who Australians are (as individuals and as a group) and who they want to be. So when politicians claim that 'This is our country and we determine who comes here' (ABC News, 2013) or that 'boatpeople' are not acting in a 'Christian' manner arriving 'by the back door rather than the front door' (Nicholson, 2012), we see clear barriers to group belonging being drawn. Such boundaries (between 'us and them' and 'ours and theirs') are further demarcated when the same politicians resist United Nations criticism on the basis that 'Australia's border protection policies are made in Australia, nowhere else' (The Australian, 2014). Similarly, but on the other side of the political spectrum, when Walk Together Australia is promoted by community groups as 'the event for you' if 'you believe that Australians are welcoming, generous and compassionate', if 'you believe in an Australia that recognises the equality and dignity of all people' and if 'you believe in an Australia where prejudice is unpopular and cruelty actually hurts at the polls' (Amnesty International Australia, 2014), we see a collective identity being formed. One that individuals can connect with if they also see their own individual identities (as compassionate, generous, welcoming and concerned citizens) reflected in these descriptions.

More recently, and as we were making final edits to the collection, world-wide attention was drawn to the 'Charlie Hebdo' terror attacks in Paris, France, where ten staff at the office of the controversial satirical magazine *Charlie Hebdo*, and a police officer who was first on the scene, were murdered by Islamic extremists. This incident, while seemingly far removed from Australia and its debates about migration, refugees and asylum seekers, is more closely connected than we may think. Indeed, the Charlie Hebdo attack raised similar questions about migration, nationality, religion and ethnicity – in short, about identity and belonging. Even a superficial analysis of the events that unfolded in France reveals, on the one hand, expressions of religious fundamentalism (which we know from Chapter 9 is one means by which some in contemporary society have sought security and belonging in a destabilised and uncertain world). On the other, it reveals expressions of nationalist defiance and solidarity. The first, 'Je suis Charlie' (I am Charlie) slogans that circulated at vigils in Paris and then across France, can be read as communal outpourings of grief and as demonstrations of solidarity and empathy with the victims. As they spread across the world, taken up by members of the French diaspora scattered globally, they became expressions of French national identity (closely connected to the tightly held ideals of 'liberty, equality and fraternity') and imagined community. Spread further still, adopted for instance by politicians, journalists, artists and those on social media (for example, as Facebook profile photos), they came to represent a broader, Western democratic ideal of freedom of speech. These slogans are, simultaneously then, expressions of identity, of personal values and ethics and of unity. But they are also expressions of inclusion and exclusion and of barrier and boundary drawing around who one is (who and what they support) and who one is not.

What Welcome to Australia and the Charlie Hebdo case also make clear is that in contemporary globalised society, identity and belonging are inevitably complex and inherently messy. Categories or modes of identity, and the sites in which they are expressed and where experiences of belonging play out, clamour for our attention. They intersect, overlap, change, adapt, evolve and in some cases even compete as priorities, and they do this across our micro and macro social worlds. Thus in this collection, we see interconnections between discussions of ethnicity, the home and neighbourhood, migration and nationality; we see social class and gender playing out with respect to leisure, home, work and consumption; we see consumption being connected to religion and religion to nationality, ethnicity and gender; and we see many of these aspects of identity and belonging being given new vitality or extended and challenged in different ways through digital media and information and communication technologies. We also see that these are issues not just experienced in Australia, or Britain, Europe or North America (where many of the contributors to this volume are based or focus their research). Rather, they are also experienced and given unique expression in Indonesia, Bangladesh, Mongolia, Singapore, Sri Lanka, China, Uganda, the Cayman Islands, Mexico and Colombia, to name but a few of the countries where empirical examples in this collection are taken from.

Finally, what these events from Australia and France also reveal is how quickly identity and belonging can become political and how when group identity becomes politicised, it can also be connected to social change. In turn social change movements can quickly be adopted as platforms for belonging and as means of articulating certain types of identity and identity politics (at the same time as resisting others). These two examples and the chapters in this volume draw attention then to the interconnections between identity and belonging, power, politics, social division and social inequality. While globalisation may be a force for cultural homogeneity, and new communication technologies may allow geographically dispersed individuals and communities to be immediately connected in ways never before possible, the chapters in this collection also point, ultimately, to the persistence of difference. It remains the case that difference and, on the basis of that differentiation, issues of identity and belonging are as central to twenty-first-century societies as they were to those that came before. Given that there are now more nations in the world than there were in 1945, when the United Nations was formed; that there are more recognised ethnic groupings; and that there are new, rapidly globalising identities – 'LGBTI', for example – it might be argued that the identity repertoire has never been greater and that there have never been more potential loci of belonging.

References

ABC News. (2013) 'Refugees to be Denied Permanent Residency under Coalition Plan to "Determine Who Comes Here"', *ABC News*, 16 August 2013. http://www.abc.net.au/news/2013-08-16/asylum-seekers-to-be-denied-residency-under-coalition/4890968 (Accessed 28 January 2015).

Abrahams, R.D. (1986) 'Ordinary and Extraordinary Experience', in Turner, V.W. and Bruner, E.M. (eds.) *The Anthropology of Experience* (Urbana and Chicago, IL: University of Illinois Press).

Acker, J. (1990) 'Hierarchies, Jobs, Bodies: A Theory of Gendered Organisations', *Gender & Society*, 4(2): 139–158.

Acker, J. (1992) 'From Sex Roles to Gendered Institutions', *Contemporary Sociology*, 21(5): 565–569.

Acker, J. (2012) 'Gendered Organisations and Intersectionality: Problems and Possibilities', *Equality, Diversity and Inclusion: An International Journal*, 31(3): 214–224.

Aldrich, R. (2010) *Gay Life and Culture: A World History* (London: Thames and Hudson).

Allison, S. (1999) 'How Young and Old Are Youth?' *Australian Clearinghouse for Youth Studies*. http://www.acys.info/__data/assets/pdf_file/0008/62297/Editorial_-_September_1999.pdf (Accessed 29 October 2014).

Allon, F. (2002) 'Translated Spaces/Translated Identities: The Production of Place, Culture and Memory in an Australian Suburb', *Journal of Australian Studies*, 26: 99–110.

Altman, D. (1996) 'Global Gaze/Global Gays', *GLQ*, 3: 417–436.

Amnesty International Australia. (2014) 'Let's Walk Together', 17 September 2014. http://www.amnesty.org.au/refugees/comments/35562/ (Accessed 20 January 2015).

Anderson, B. (1983) Imagined Communities: Reflections on the Origin and Spread of Nationalism (London, New York: Verso).

Andersen, C. (2008) 'From Nation to Population: The Racialisation of "Métis" in the Canadian Census', *Nations and Nationalism*, 14(2): 347–368.

Ariely, G. (2012) 'Globalisation and the Decline of National Identity? An Exploration across Sixty-Three Countries', *Nations and Nationalism*, 18 (3): 461–482.

Armitage, D. (2013) *Foundations of Modern International Thought* (Cambridge: Cambridge University Press).

Asylum Seeker Resource Centre. (n.d.) http://www.asrc.org.au/resources/fact-sheet/timeline-of-events/ (Accessed 22 January 2014).

Australian Bureau of Statistics. (2007) 'Using Children and Youth Statistics', (Updated 25 June 2013). http://www.abs.gov.au/websitedbs/c311215.nsf/web/Children+and+Youth+Statistics+-+Using+Children+and+Youth+Statistics (Accessed 29 October 2014).

Australian Bureau of Statistics. (2012) 'Year Book Australia, 1985: International Year of Youth', Updated 23 November 2012. http://www.abs.gov.au/ausstats/abs@.nsf/Previousproducts/1301.0Feature%20Article21985?opendocument&tabname=Summary&prodno=1301.0&issue=1985&num=&view= (Accessed 29 October 2014).

Baert, P. (1998) *Social Theory in the Twentieth Century* (Oxford: Policy Press).

Bang, H. (2005) 'Among Everyday Makers and Expert Citizens', in Newman, J. (ed.) *Remaking Governance* (Bristol: The Policy Press).

Barth, F. (ed.). (1969) *Ethnic Groups and Boundaries: The Social Organisation of Cultural Difference* (London: Allen & Unwin).

Basch, L., Glick Schiller, N., Szanton-Blanc, C. (eds.). (1994) *Nations Unbound: Transnational Projects, Post-Colonial Predicaments and Deterritorialized Nation-States* (Amsterdam: Gordon and Breach).

Bates, D. (1938) *The Passing of the Aborigines: A Lifetime Spent Among the Natives of Australia* (London: Murray).

Bauman, Z. (1996) 'From Pilgrim to Tourist – Or a Short History of Identity', in Hall, S. and du Gay, P. (eds.) *Questions of Cultural Identity* (London, California and New Delhi: Sage).

Bauman, Z. (1998) 'Postmodern Religion?', in Heelas, P. (ed.) *Religion, Modernity and Postmodernity* (London: Wiley Blackwell), pp. 55–78.

Bauman, Z. (2000) *Liquid Modernity* (Cambridge: Polity Press).

Bauman, Z. (2001) *The Individualised Society* (Cambridge: Polity Press).

Bauman, Z. (2003) *Liquid Love: On the Frailty of Human Bonds* (Cambridge: Polity Press).

Bauman, Z. (2004) *Work, Consumerism and the New Poor* (Second Edition) (Berkshire: McGraw-Hill Education).

Bauman, Z. (2009) 'Identity in a Globalizing World', in Elliott, A. and du Gay, P. (ed.) *Identity in Question* (Los Angeles, CA: Sage), pp. 13–36.

Baxter, J. and Hewitt, B. (2013) 'Negotiating Domestic Labour: Women's Earnings and Housework Time in Australia', *Feminist Economics*, 19(1): 29–53.

Bayly, C. (2004) *The Birth of the Modern World 1780–1914* (Maiden and Oxford: Blackwell).

Beck, U. (1992) *Risk Society: Towards a New Modernity* (London: Sage).

Beck, U. (2000) *The Brave New World of Work* (Malden: Polity).

Beck, U. (2010) *A God of One's Own: Religion's Capacity for Peace and Potential for Violence* (Cambridge: Polity).

Beck, U. (2012) *Twenty Observations on a World in Turmoil* (Cambridge: Polity Press).

Beck, U. and Beck-Gernsheim, E. (2002) *"Division of Labour, Self-Image and Life Projects: New Conflicts in the Family"* in their *Individualization: Institutionalized Individualism and its Social and Political Consequences* (London: Sage).

Beck, U. and Beck-Gernsheim, E. (2009) 'Losing the Traditional: Individualization and 'Precarious Freedoms'' in Elliot, A. and du Gay, P. (eds.) *Identity in Question* (Los Angeles, CA: Sage), pp. 13–36.

Beck-Gernsheim, E. (1996) 'Life as a Planning Project', in Lash, S., Szerszynski, B. and Wynne, B. (eds.) *Risk, Environment and Modernity: Towards a New Ecology* (London: Sage).

Benedict, R. (1940) *Race, Science and Politics* (New York: Viking Press).

Bennett, A. (2011) 'The Post-Subcultural Turn: Some Reflections 10 Years On', *Journal of Youth Studies*, 14(5): 493–506.

Bennett, A. and Kahn-Harris, K. (eds.). (2004) *After Subculture: Critical Studies in Contemporary Youth Culture* (Basingstoke and New York: Palgrave Macmillan).

Bennett, S., Maton, K. and Kervin, L. (2008) 'The "Digital Natives" Debate: A Critical Review of the Evidence', *British Journal of Educational Technology*, 39(5): 775–786.

Bennett, W.L. (2003) 'Communicating Global Activism. Information', *Communication and Society*, 6: 143–168.

Bennett, W.L. (2012). 'The Personalization of Politics: Political Identity, Social Media, and Changing Patterns of Participation', *The ANNALS of the American Academy of Political and Social Science*, 644: 20–39.

Berger, Peter L. (1967) *The Sacred Canopy: Elements of a Sociological Theory of Religion* (New York: Doubleday).

Berger, Peter L. (1974) 'Modern Identity: Crisis and Continuity', in Dillon, W.S. (ed.) *The Cultural Drama: Modern Identities and Social Ferment* (Washington, DC: Smithsonian Institution Press), pp. 159–181.

Bernal, V. (2006) 'Diaspora, Cyberspace and Political Imagination: The Eritrean Diaspora Online', *Global Networks*, 6: 161–179.

Billig, M. (1995) *Banal Nationalism* (London, Thousand Oaks, New Delhi: Sage Publications).

Binnie, J. (2004) *The Globalisation of Sexuality* (London: Sage Publications).

Binnie, J. and Klesse, C. (2012). 'Solidarities and Tensions: Feminism and Transnational LGBTQ Politics in Poland', *European Journal of Women's Studies*, 19: 444–459.

Biressi, A. and Nunn, H. (2013) *Class and Contemporary British Culture* (London: Palgrave Macmillan).

Blauner, R. (1964) *Alienation and Freedom: The Factory Worker and His Industry* (Chicago, IL: University of Chicago Press).

Blunt, A. and Dowling, R. (2006) *Home* (London: Routledge).

Boas, F. (1983 [1911]) *The Mind of Primitive Man* (Westport, CN: Greenwood Press).

Boase, J., Horrigan, J.B., Wellman, B. and Rainie, L. (2006) *The Strength of Internet Ties: The Internet and e-mail Aid Users in Maintaining Their Social Networks and Provide Pathways to Help When People Face Big Decisions* (Washington, DC: Pew Internet and American Life Project).

Boon, Weng Siew (2014) 'The Malaysian Plantation Industry, 1880–1921'. www.mpoa.org.my.

Boorstin, D. (1962) *The Image: A Guide to Pseudo-Events in America* (New York: Vintage).

Booth, C. (1889) *Life and Labour of the People in London* (London). Volume 1: East London (London: Macmillan, 1889).

Bottomore, T. and Nisbet, R. (eds.). (1979) *A History of Sociological Analysis* (London: Heinemann Educational).

Bouma, G. (2006) *Australian Soul: Religion and Spirituality in the Twenty-First Century* (Melbourne: Cambridge University Press).

Bouma, G., Cahill, D., Dellal, H. and Athalia, Zwartz (2011) 'Freedom of Religion and Belief in 21st Century Australia, A Research Report Prepared for the Australian Human Rights Commission'. (Sydney: Australian Human Rights Commission).

Bourdieu, P. (1977) *Outline of a Field of Practice* (Cambridge: Cambridge University Press).

Bourdieu, P. (1984) *Distinction: A Social Critique of the Judgement of Taste* (London: Routledge).

boyd, d. (2008) 'Why Youth ♥ Social Network Sites: The Role of Networked Publics in Teenage Social Life', in Buckingham, D. (ed.) *Youth, Identity, and Digital Media* (Boston, MA: MIT Press).

boyd, d. (2011) 'Social Network Sites as Networked Publics: Affordances, Dynamics, and Implications', in Papacharissi, Z. (ed.) *A Networked Self: Identity, Community, and Culture on Social Network Sites* (First Edition) (New York: Routledge).

boyd, d. and Crawford, K. (2012) 'Critical Questions for Big Data', *Information, Communication & Society*, 15(5): 662–679.

Bradley, H. (2013) *Gender* (Second Edition) (Malden and Cambridge: Polity Press).

Bravermann, H. (1974) *Labour and Monopoly Capital: The Degradation of Work in the Twentieth Century* (New York: Monthly Review Press).

Bridge, G. and Dowling, R. (2001) 'Microgeographies of Retailing and Gentrification', *Australian Geographer*, 32: 93–107.

Brill, D. (2007) 'Gender, Status and Subcultural Capital in the Goth Scene', in Hodkinson, P. and Deicke, W. (eds.) *Youth Cultures: Scenes, Subcultures and Tribes* (New York and London: Taylor and Francis Group, Routledge).

Brook, I. (2003) 'Making Here like There: Place, Attachment, Displacement and the Urge to Garden', *Ethics, Place and Environment*, 6: 227–234.

Brooke, S. (2001) 'Gender and Working Class Identity in Britain during the 1950s', *Journal of Social History*, 34(4) (Summer, 2001): 773–795.

Brown, M. (2013) 'Gender and Sexuality II: There goes the Gayborhood?', *Progress in Human Geography*, in press. doi:10.1177/0309132513484215.

Browne, K., Brown, G. and Lim, J. (2007) *Geographies of Sexualities* (Ashgate: Farnham).

Bryson, C. (2004) 'The Consequences for Women in the Academic Profession of the Widespread Use of Fixed-Term Contracts', *Gender, Work and Organisation*, 11(2), March 2004: 187–206.

Buckingham, D. (2008a). 'Introducing Identity', in Buckingham, D. (ed.) *Youth, Identity and Digital Media* (Cambridge, MA: Massachusetts Institute of Technology).

Buckingham, D. (ed.). (2008b) *Youth, Identity, and Digital Media* (Cambridge, MA: Massachusetts Institute of Technology).

Buckingham, D. and Willett, R. (eds.). (2006) *Digital Generations: Children, Young People, and the Digital Media* (Mahwah, NJ: Lawrence Erlbaum Associates).

Burbank, J. and Cooper, F. (2010) *Empires in World History: Power and the Politics of Difference* (Princeton, NJ and Oxford: Princeton University Press).

Burgess, I., Edwards, A. and Skinner, J. (2003) 'Football Culture in an Australian School Setting: The Construction of Masculine Identity', *Sport, Education and Society*, 8(2): 199–212.

Butcher, M. and Thomas, M. (2006) 'Ingenious: Emerging Hybrid Youth Cultures in Western Sydney', in Nilan, P. and Feixa, C. (eds.) *Global Youth?: Hybrid Identities, Plural Worlds* (New York: Routledge).

Butler, J. (1990) *Gender Trouble* (New York: Routledge).

Butler, J. (1999) *Gender Trouble: Feminism and the Subversion of Identity* (London: Routledge).

Butler, T. (2007) 'For gentrification?', *Environment and Planning A*, 39: 162–181.

Castells, M. (1996). *The Rise of the Network Society: The Information Age: Economy, Society and Culture Volume I* (Oxford: Blackwell Publishers).

Castells, M. (2000) *The Rise of the Network Society* (Oxford: Blackwell).

Castells, M. (2010) *The Rise of the Network Society: The Information Age: Economy, Society and Culture Volume I* (Second Edition) (Oxford: Wiley-Blackwell).

Castle, T. (1987) *Masquerade and Civilisation* (Redwood City, CA: Stanford University Press).

Castles, S. and Delgado Wise, R. (2007) *Migration and Development: Perspectives from the South* (Geneva: International Organization for Migration).

Chambers, D. (2006) *New Social Ties: Contemporary Connections in a Fragmented Society* (Houndsmills: Palgrave Macmillan).

Clark, A. (2009) 'From Neighbourhood to Network: A Review of the Significance of Neighbourhood in Studies of Social Relations', *Geography Compass*, 3: 1559–1578.

Clarke, A.J. (2002) 'Taste Wars and Design Dilemmas: Aesthetic Practice in the Home', in Painter, C. (ed.) *Contemporary Art and the Home* (Oxford and New York: Berg).

Clarke, J., Hall, S., Jefferson, T. and Roberts, B. (1993) 'Subcultures, Cultures and Class', in Hall, S. and Jefferson, T. (eds.) *Resistance Through Rituals: Youth Subcultures in Post-War Britain* (London: Routledge).

Clott, S. (2010) 'Everything You Wanted to Know about Lady Gagas VMA Meat Dress!. http://style.mtv.com/2010/09/13/2010-vmas-lady-gaga-meat-dress-real/ (Accessed 13 September, 2013).

Cohen, E. (2004) *Contemporary Tourism: Diversity and Change* (Amsterdam, San Diego, Oxford and London: Elsevier).

Cohen, S. (2013) 'Leisure, Identities and Personal Growth', in Elkington, S. and Gammon, S. (eds.) *Contemporary Perspectives in Leisure: Meanings, Motives and Lifelong Learning* (Hoboken, NJ: Taylor and Francis).

Collin, P. (2008) The Internet, Youth Participation Policies, and the Development of Young People's Political Identities in Australia', *Journal of Youth Studies*, 11: 527–542.

Collins, A. (2004) 'Sexual Dissidence, Enterprise and Assimilation: Bedfellows in Urban Regeneration', *Urban Studies*, 41(9): 1789–1806.

Collins, J. (2013) 'Multiculturalism and Immigrant Integration in Australia', *Canadian Ethnic Studies*, 45(3): 133–149.

Collins, J., Noble, G., Poynting, S. and Tabar, P. (2000) *Kebabs, Kids, Cops and Crime: Youth Ethnicity and Crime* (Annandale, NSW: Pluto Press).

Connell, R. (1997) Why is Classical Theory Classical?, *American Journal of Sociology*, 102(6): 1511.

Connell, R. (1998) 'Masculinities and Globalization', *Men and Masculinities*, 1(1): 3–23.

Connell, R. (2002) *Gender* (Cambridge, Oxford and Malden: Polity).

Connell, R. (2003) 'Masculinities, Change, and Conflict in Global Society: Thinking about the Future of Men's Studies', *The Journal of Men's Studies*, 11(3): 249–266 (Spring 2003).

Connell, R (2005) 'Globalization, Imperialism, and Masculinities', in Kimmel, M., Hearn, J. and Connell, R.W. (eds.) *Handbook of Studies on Men and Masculinities* (Thousand Oaks, CA: Sage Publications), http://dx.doi.org/10.4135/9781452233833.n5.

Connell, R (2007) 'Empire and the Creation of Social Science' in her *Southern Theory: The Global Dynamics of Knowledge in Social Science* (Crows Nest: Allen and Unwin), pp. 3–25.

Connell, R. and Messerschmidt, J. (2005) 'Hegemonic Masculinity: Rethinking the Concept', *Gender and Society*, 19: 829–859.

Connell, R. and Messerschmidt, J. (2012) 'Hegemonic Masculinity', in Lorber, J. (ed.) *Gender Inequality* (Fifth Edition) (New York and Oxford: Oxford University Press).

Cooper, F. (2003) 'Conflict and Connection: Rethinking Colonial African History', in Le Sueur, J.D. (ed.) *The Decolonisation Reader* (London: Routledge), pp. 23–44.

Cowan, D. and Marsh, A. (2004) 'Community, Neighbourhood and Responsibility: Contemporary Currents in Housing Studies', *Housing Studies*, 19: 845–853.

Cressey, P.G. (2008) *The Taxi-Dance Hall: A Sociological Study in Commercialized Recreation and City Life* (Chicago, IL: University of Chicago Press).

Critcher, C. and Bramham, P. (2004) 'The Devil Still Makes Work', in Haworth, J.T. and Veal, A.J. (eds.) *Work and Leisure* (London and New York: Routledge).

Csikszentmihalyi, M. (1988) 'The Flow Experience and its Significance for Human Psychology', in Csikszentmihalyi, M. and Csikszentmihalyi, I.S. (eds.) *Optimal Experience: Psychological Studies of Flow in Consciousness* (New York: Cambridge University Press).

Csikszentmihalyi, M. (1990) *Flow: The Psychology of Optimal Experience* (New York: Harper Perennial).

Csikszentmihalyi, M. and LeFevre, J. (1989) 'Optimal Experience in Work and Leisure', *Journal of Personality and Social Psychology*, 56(5): 815–822.

Cusack, T. (2000) 'Janus and Gender: Women and the Nation's Backward Look', *Nations and Nationalism* 6(4): 541–561.

Davidson, M. (2010) 'Love Thy Neighbour? Social Mixing in London's Gentrification Frontiers', *Environment and Planning A*, 42: 524–544.

Dawson, L. (2006) 'Privatisation, Globalisation, and Religious Innovation: Giddens' Theory of Modernity and the Refutation of Secularisation Theory', in Beckford, J. and Walliss, J. (eds.) *Theorising Religion. Classical and Contemporary Debates* (Aldershot: Ashgate), pp. 105–199.

de Certeau, M., Giard, L. and Mayol, P. (1998) *The Practice of Everyday Life, Volume 2, Living and Cooking* (Minneapolis, MN: University of Minnesota Press).

de Certeau, M. (1984) *The Practice of Everyday Life* (Oakland: University of California Press).

de Gobineau, A. (1915 [1853]) *The Inequality of Human Races*, translated by A. Collins (London: William Heinemann).

DeHaan, S., Kuper, L.E., Magee, J.C., Bigelow, L. and Mustanski, B.S. (2013) 'The Interplay between Online and Offline Explorations of Identity, Relationships, and Sex: A Mixed-Methods Study of LGBT Youth', *Journal of Sex Research*, 50(5): 421–434.

D'Emilio, J. (1989) 'Gay Politics and Community in San Francisco Since World War II', in Duberman, M.B., Vicinus, M. and Chauncey, G. (eds.) *Hidden from History: Reclaiming the Gay and Lesbian Past* (London: Penguin).

Desforges, L. (2000) 'Traveling the World: Identity and Travel Biography', *Annals Of Tourism Research*, 27: 926–945.

Devine, F. and Savage, M. (2005) 'The Cultural Turn, Sociology and Class Analysis', in Devine, F., Savage, M., Scott, J. and Crompton, R. (eds.) *Rethinking Class: Culture, Identities and Lifestyle* (London: Palgrave Macmillan).

Dionigi, R.A., Horton, S. and Baker, J. (2013) 'Negotiations of the Ageing Process: Older Adults' Stories of Sports Participation', *Sport, Education and Society*, 18(3): 370–387.

Dobransky, K. and Hargittai, E. (2006). 'The Disability Divide in Internet Access and Use', *Information, Communication & Society*, 9: 313–334.

Dowling, R. and Power, E. (2012) 'Sizing Home, Doing Family in Sydney, Australia', *Housing Studies*, 27: 605–619.

Duffy, M. (2007) 'Doing the Dirty Work: Gender, Race and Reproductive Labour in Historical Perspective', *Gender & Society*, 21(3): 313–336.

Duggan, L. (2002) *The Twilight of Equality? Neoliberalism, Cultural Politics and the Attack on Democracy* (Boston, MA: Beacon Press).

Durkheim, E. ([1915] 2001). *The Elementary Forms of Religious Life* (Oxford: Oxford University Press).

Durkheim, E. (1984 [1893]) *The Division of Labour in Society (The Study of the Organization of Advanced Societies)* (Basingstoke: Macmillan).

Eardley, T., Bruce, J. and Goggin, G. (2009) *Telecommunications and Community Wellbeing: A Review of the Literature on Access and Affordability for Low-Income and Disadvantaged Groups* (Sydney: Social Policy Research Centre; Journalism and Media Research Centre, University of New South Wales).

Eco, U. (1986) *Travels in Hyper Reality: Essays* (San Diego, CA: Harcourt Brace Jovanovich).

Edgell, S. (2006) *The Sociology of Work: Continuity and Change in Paid and Unpaid Work* (London: Sage).

Elias, N. (1978) *The Civilising Process* (New York: Urizen).

Elliott, A. and Urry, J. (2010) *Mobile Lives.* (New York and London: Routledge).

Eriksen, T.H. (1993) *Ethnicity and Nationalism* (London and New York: Pluto Press).

Erikson, E. (1994) *Identity, Youth and Crisis* (New York: Norton).

Featherstone, M. (1991) *Consumer Culture and Postmodernity* (London: Sage Publications).

Feixa, C. (2006) 'Tribus Urbanas and Chavos Banda: Being a Punk in Catalonia and Mexico', in Nilan, P. and Feixa, C. (eds.) *Global Youth?: Hybrid Identities, Plural Worlds* (New York: Routledge).

Finch, L. (1993) *The Classing Gaze: Sexuality, Class and Surveillance* (St Leonards: Allen and Unwin).

Flint, J. and Nixon, J. (2006) 'Governing Neighbours: Anti-Social Behaviour Orders and New Forms of Regulating Conduct in the UK', *Urban Studies*, 43: 939–955.

Foucault, M. (1976) *The History of Sexuality: 1: The Will to Knowledge* (London: Penguin).

Foucault, M. (1977) *Discipline and Punish* (New York: Vintage).

Foucault, M. (1980) *The History of Sexuality* (New York: Vintage).

Foucault, M. (1979). *The History of Sexuality: Volume 1* (Harmondsworth: Penguin).

Fozdar, F., Wilding, R. and Hawkins, M. (2009) *Race and Ethnic Relations* (Melbourne: Oxford University Press).

Frank, A.G. (1969) *Capitalism and Underdevelopment in Latin America* (New York: Monthly Review Press).

Frank, A.G. (1978) *Dependent Accumulation and Underdevelopment* (London: Macmillan).

Freeman, C. (2001) 'Is Local: Global as Feminine: Masculine? Rethinking the Gender of Globalisation', *Signs*, 26(4): 1007–1037.

Fullager, S. (2008) 'Leisure Practices as Counter-Depressants: Emotion-Work and Emotion-Play within Women's Recovery from Depression', *Leisure Sciences*, 30: 35–52.

Furlong, A., Woodman, D. and Wyn, J. (2011) 'Changing Times, Changing Perspectives: Reconciling "Transition" and "Cultural" Perspectives on Youth and Young Adulthood', *Journal of Sociology*, 47(4): 355–370.

Gammon, S.J. (2013) 'I am What I Pretend to Be: Performance and Deception in Leisure', in Elkington, S. and Gammon, S. (eds.) *Contemporary Perspectives in Leisure: Meanings, Motives and Lifelong Learning* (Hoboken, NJ: Taylor and Francis).

Gatens, M. (1983) 'A Critique of the Sex/Gender Distinction', in Allen, J. and Patton, P. (eds.) *Beyond Marxism? Interventions After Marx* (Sydney: Intervention Publications), pp. 143–160.

Geertz, C. (1963a) *Agricultural Involution: The Process of Ecological Change in Indonesia* (Berkeley: University of California Press).

Geertz, C. (ed.). (1963b) *Old Societies and New States: The Quest for Modernity in Asia and Africa* (New York: The Free Press of Glencoe).

Gellner, E. (1983) *Nations and Nationalism* (Oxford: Basil Blackwell).

Gellner, E. (1996) 'The Coming of Nationalism and its Interpretation: The Myths of Nation and Class', in Balakrishnan, G. (ed.) *Mapping the Nation* (London and New York: Verso), pp. 98–145.

Giddens, A. (1990) *The Consequences of Modernity* (London: Polity Press).

Giddens, A. (1991) *Modernity and Self-Identity. Self and Society in the Late Modern Age.* (Cambridge: Polity).

Giddens, A. (1994) 'Living in a Post-Traditional Society', in Beck, U., Giddens, A. and Lash, S. (eds.) *Reflexive Modernization: Politics, Tradition and Aesthetics in the Modern Social Order* (Cambridge: Polity Press).

Gidley, B. (1997) '*The Proletarian Other: Charles Booth and the Politics of Representation*', (Goldsmiths: Critical Urban Studies, Occasional Papers).

Gillies, V. (2005) 'Meeting Parents' Needs? Discourses of "Support" and "Inclusion" in Family Policy', *Critical Social Policy*, 25(1): 70–90.

Gillies, V. (2007) *Marginalised Mothers: Exploring Working-Class Experiences of Parenting* (Oxford: Routledge).

Gil-White, F. (1999) 'How Thick is Blood? The Plot Thickens…: If Ethnic Actors are Primordialists, What Remains of the Circumstantialist/Primordialist Controversy', *Ethnic and Racial Studies*, 22(5): 789–820.

Gitelman, L. (2006) *Always Already New: Media, History and the Data of Culture* (Cambridge, MA: Massachusetts Institute of Technology).

Glazer, N. and Moynihan, D.P. (1963) *Beyond the Melting Pot: The Negroes, Puerto Ricans, Jews, Italians and Irish of New York City* (Cambridge, MA: Harvard University Press).

Glazer, H. and Moynihan, D. (eds.). (1975) *Ethnicity: Theory and Experience* (Cambridge, MA: Harvard University Press).

Glick Schiller, N., Basch, L. and Szanton-Blanc, C. (1992) *Towards a Transnational Perspective on Migration: Race, Class, Ethnicity and Nationalism Reconsidered*, Volume 645 (New York: Annals of the New York Academy of Science).

Glucksmann, M. (1995) 'Why "Work"? Gender and the "Total Social Organisation of Labour", *Gender, Work and Organization*, 2(2): 63–75.

Goffman, E. (1961) *The Presentation of Self in Everyday Life* (New York: Doubleday).

Goffman, E. (1963) *Behaviour in Public Places* (New York: Free Press).

Goldthorpe, J.H., Lockwood, D., Bechhofer, F. and Platt, J. (1968a) *The Affluent Worker: Industrial Attitudes and Behaviour* (Cambridge: Cambridge University Press).

Goldthorpe, J.H., Lockwood, D., Bechhofer, F. and Platt, J. (1968b) *The Affluent Worker: Political Attitudes and Behaviour* (Cambridge: Cambridge University Press).

Goldthorpe, J.H., Lockwood, D., Bechhofer, F. and Platt, J. (1969) *The Affluent Worker in the Class Structure* (Cambridge: Cambridge University Press).

Google (2012) 'Legalise Love: LGBT Rights Are Human Rights'. http://www.google.com.au/diversity/legalise-love.html (Accessed 25 July 2013).

Gorman-Murray, A. (2006) 'Gay and Lesbian Couples at Home: Identity Work in Domestic Space', *Home Cultures*, 3: 145–168.

Gorman-Murray, A. (2007) 'Rethinking Queer Migration through the Body', *Social and Cultural Geography*, 8(1): 105–121.

Gorman-Murray, A. (2009) 'Intimate Mobilities: Emotional Embodiment and Queer Migration', *Social and Cultural Geography*, 10(4): 441–460.

Graham, H. (1983) 'Caring: A Labour of Love', in Finch, J. and Groves, D. (eds.) *A Labour of Love: Women, Work and Caring* (London: Routledge and K Paul).

Graham, S. and Connell, J. (2006) 'Nurturing Relationships: The Gardens of Greek and Vietnamese Migrants in Marrickville, Sydney', *Australian Geographer*, 37: 375–393.

Green, L.R. (2002) *Technoculture: From Alphabet to Cybersex* (Sydney: Allen and Unwin).

Greenblatt, S. (2004) *Will in the World: How Shakespeare Became Shakespeare* (New York: Norton).

Greil, A.L and Davidman, L. (2007) 'Religion and Identity', in Beckford, J.A. and Demerath III, N.J. (eds.) *The Sage Handbook of the Sociology of Religion* (London: Sage), pp. 549–565.

Grillo, R.D. (2003) 'Cultural Essentialism and Cultural Anxiety', *Anthropological Theory*, 3(2): 157–173.

Grosby, S. (1994) 'The Verdict of History: The Unexpungeable Tie of Primordality – A Response to Eller and Coughlan', *Ethnic and Racial Studies*, 17(1): 164–175.

Gupta, S. (2007) 'Autonomy, Dependence, or Display? The Relationship between Married Women's Earnings and Housework', *Journal of Marriage and Family*, 69(2), 399–417.

Habermas, J. (1996) 'The European Nation-State – Its Achievements and Its Limits. On the Past and Future of Sovereignty and Citizenship', in Balakrishnan, G. (ed.) *Mapping the Nation* (London and New York: Verso), pp. 281–294.

Hage, G. (2000) *White Nation: Fantasies of White Supremacy in a Multicultural Society* (Sydney: Pluto Press).

Hage, G. (2003) *Against Paranoid Nationalism: Searching for Hope in a Shrinking Society* (Annandale, NSW: Pluto Press).

Hakim, C. (2000) *Work Lifestyle Choices in the 21st Century: Preference Theory* (Oxford and New York: Oxford University Press).

Hall, S. (1996) 'Introduction: Who Needs "Identity"?' in Hall, S. and Gay, P.D. (eds.) *Questions of Cultural Identity* (London, California and New Delhi: Sage).

Hall, S. (1997) 'Race, the Floating Signifier', www.mediaed.org.

Hall, S. (1998) *Representation: Cultural Representations and Signifying Practices* (London: Sage).

Hall, S. and Jefferson, T. (1976) *Resistance Through Rituals: Youth Subcultures in Post-War Britain* (London: Psychology Press).

Hall, S. and Jefferson, T. (eds.) (1993) *Resistance Through Rituals: Youth Subcultures in Post-War Britain* (London: Routledge).

Hall, S. and Jefferson, T. (2006) 'Once More around Resistance through Rituals', in Hall, S. and Jefferson, T. (eds.) *Resistance through Rituals: Youth Subcultures in Post-War Britain* (Second Edition) (London and New York: Routledge).

Hammack, P. and Cohler, B. (2011) 'Narrative, Identity, and the Politics of Exclusion: Social Change and the Gay and Lesbian Life Course', *Sexuality Research and Social Policy*, 8: 162–182.

Hammond, P.E. (1988) 'Religion and the Persistence of Identity', *Journal for the Scientific Study of Religion*, 27: 1–11.

Harrington, M. (2006) 'Family Leisure', in Rojek, C., Shaw, S.M. and Veal, A.J. (eds.) *A Handbook of Leisure Studies* (Basingstoke: Palgrave Macmillan).

Harris, A. (2004) *Future Girl: Young Women in the Twenty-First Century* (New York: Routledge).

Harris, A., Wyn, J. and Younes, S. (2007) 'Young People and Citizenship: An Everyday Perspective', *Youth Studies Australia*, 26(3): 19–27.

Harris, A., Wyn, J. and Younes, S. (2010). 'Beyond Apathetic or Activist Youth: "Ordinary" Young People and Contemporary Forms of Participation', *Young: Nordic Journal of Youth Research*, 18: 9–32.

Harris, M. (1983) *Cultural Anthropology* (New York: Harper & Row).

Harskamp, A. (2008) 'Existential Insecurity and New Religiosity: An Essay on Some Religion-Making Characteristics of Modernity', *Social Compass* 55(1): 9–19.

Hartmann, H. (1976) 'Capitalism, Patriarchy, and Job Segregation by Sex', *Signs*, 1(3): 137–170.

Hawkins, M. (1989) 'Market People, Mountain People. Identity in a South Kalimantan Transmigration Village', Unpublished PhD thesis, University of Sydney.

Hawkins, M. (2014) *Global Structures, Local Cultures* (Second Edition) (Melbourne: Oxford University Press).

Haylett C. (2003) 'Culture, Class and Urban Policy: Reconsidering Equality', *Antipode*, 35(1): 55–73.

Hebdige, D. (1979) *Subculture: The Meaning of Style* (London: Routledge).

Hebdige, D. (1993) 'A Report from the Western Front: Postmodernism and the 'Politics' of Style', in Jenks, C. (ed.) *Cultural Reproduction* (New York: Routledge), pp. 69–103.

Heelas, P., Woodhead, L. and Seel, B. (2005) *The Spiritual Revolution: Why Religion is Giving Way to Spirituality* (London: Blackwell Pub.).

Hetherington, K. (2003) 'Spatial Textures: Place, Touch, and Praesentia', *Environment and Planning A*, 35: 1933–1944.

Hobsbawm, E. (1983) *The Invention of Tradition* (Cambridge: Cambridge University Press).

Hobsbawm, E. J. (1996) 'Ethnicity and Nationalism in Europe Today', in Balakrishnan, G. (ed.) *Mapping the Nation* (London and New York: Verso), pp. 255–266.

Hobsbawm, E.J. and Ranger, T. (eds.). (1983) *The Invention of Tradition* (Cambridge: Cambridge University Press).

Hochschild, A. (1983) *The Managed Heart: The Commercialization of Human Feeling* (Berkeley: University of California Press).

Hodgetts, D., Stolte, O., Chamberlain, K., Radley, A., Nikora, L., Nabalarua, E. and Groot, S. (2008) 'A Trip to the Library: Homelessness and Social Inclusion', *Social & Cultural Geography*, 9: 933–953.

Hodkinson, P. (2012) 'Beyond Spectacular Specifics in the Study of Youth (sub)cultures', *Journal of Youth Studies*, 15(5): 557–572.

Holderness, B. (2006) 'Toward Bridging Digital Divides in Rural (South) Africa', in Buckingham, D. and Willett, R. (eds.) *Digital Generations: Children, Young People and New Media* (Hillsdale, NJ: Lawrence Erlbaum Associates).

Holloway, D. (2007) 'See Australia and Die: Shifting Discourses about Gray Nomads', *Tourism, Culture and Communication*, 7: 161–168.

Holt, M. and Griffin, C. (2003) 'Being Gay, Being Straight and Being Yourself: Local and Global Reflections on Identity, Authenticity and the Lesbian and Gay Scene', *European Journal of Cultural Studies*, 6: 404–425.

Hoshour, C. (1997) 'Resettlement and the Politicization of Ethnicity in Indonesia', *Bijdragen tot de Taal- Land- en Volkenkunde*, 4: 557–576.

Houlbrook, M. (2006) *Queer London: Perils and Pleasures in the Sexual Metropolis, 1918-1957* (Chicago, IL: University of Chicago Press).

http://www.oecdbetterlifeindex.org/topics/jobs/ (Accessed 18 June 2014).

http://www.oecdbetterlifeindex.org/topics/work-life-balance/ (Accessed 18 June 2014).

Hubbard, P. (2000) 'Desire/Disgust: Mapping the Moral Contours of Heterosexuality', *Progress in Human Geography*, 24(2): 191–217.

Hubbard, P. (2008) 'Here, There, Everywhere: The Ubiquitous Geographies of Heteronormativity', *Geography Compass*, 2(3): 640–658.

Hunt, L. (ed.). (1993) *The Invention of Pornography: Obscenity and the Origins of Modernity 1500–1800* (New York: Zone).

Huppatz, K. (2009) 'Reworking Bourdieu's "Capital": Feminine and Female Capitals in the Field of Paid Caring Work', *Sociology*, 43(1): 45–66.

Huppatz, K. (2012) *Gender Capital at Work: Intersections of Femininity, Masculinity, Class and Occupation* (Hampshire: Palgrave Macmillan).

ILGA. (2013) 'International Lesbian, Gay, Bisexual, Trans and Intersex Association Website' (Accessed 25 June 2013).

Illouz, E. (1997) *Consuming the Romantic Utopia* (Berkeley: University of California Press).

Illouz, E. (2007) *Cold Intimacies* (Oxford: Polity).

Inglis, F. (2010) *A Short History of Celebrity* (Princeton, NJ: Princeton University Press).

Jagose, A. (1996) *Queer Theory* (Carlton South: Melbourne University Press).

James, P. (1996) *Nation Formation: Towards a Theory of Abstract Community* (London and Thousand Oaks, CA: Sage).

Jenkins, H. (2006) *Convergence Culture: Where Old and Digital Media Collide* (New York: New York University Press).

Johnston, L. and Longhurst, R. (2010) *Space, Place and Sex: Geographies of Sexualities* (Plymouth: Rowman and Littlefield Publishers).

Jones, O. (2011) *Chavs: The Demonization of the Working Class* (London: Verso).

Jun, J. and Kyle, G.T. (2012) 'Gender Identity, Leisure Identity, and Leisure Participation', *Journal of Leisure Research*, 44(3): 353–378.

Kang, T. (2009) 'Homeland Re-Territorialised. Information', *Communication & Society*, 12: 326–343.

Karimi, F and Thompson, N. (2014) 'Uganda's President Museveni Signs Controversial Anti-Gay Bill into Law', *CNN*. http://edition.cnn.com/2014/02/24/world/africa/uganda-anti-gay-bill/ (Accessed 19 March 2014).

Kelly, D.M., Pomerantz, S. and Currie, D. (2005) 'Skater Girlhood and Emphasized Femininity: "You Can't Land an Ollie Properly in Heels"', *Gender and Education*, 17(3): 229–248.

Kelly, J. (2012) *Leisure* (Urbana, IL: Sagamore Publishing).

Kemp, M. (2012) *Christ to Coke: How Image Becomes Icon* (Oxford: Oxford University Press).

Kennedy, G., Dalgarno, B., Gray, K., Judd, T., Waycott,, J., Bennett, S., Maton, K., Krause, K., Bishop, A., Chang, R. and Churchward, A. (2007) 'The Net Generation Are Not Big Users of Web 2.0 Technologies: Preliminary Findings', ICT: Providing Choices for Learners and Learning, Proceedings ascilite Singapore 2007.

Kennedy, G., Judd, T., Churchward, A., Gray, K. and Krause, K. (2008) 'First Year Students' Experiences with Technology: Are they Really Digital Natives?', *Australasian Journal of Educational Technology*, 24(1): 108–122.

Kerr, C., Dunlop, J.T., Harbison, F.H. and Myers, C.A. (1960) *Industrialism and Industrial Man: The Problems of Labour and Management in Economic Growth* (Cambridge, MA: Harvard University Press).

Khazandec, O. (2014) 'Was This Australia's First Transgender Person?' *The Sydney Morning Herald*, 16 August 2014. http://m.smh.com.au/news-and-views/news-features/was-this-australias-first-transgender-person-20140815-3dqtt.html (Accessed 11 September 2014) (newspaper article).

King, R. (2012) 'Theories and Typologies of Migration: An Overview and a Primer', Willy Brandt Series of Working Papers in International Migration and Ethnic Relations 3/12 (Malmo: Malmo Institute for Studies of Migration, Diversity and Welfare).

Kinnvall, C. (2004) 'Globalization and Religious Nationalism: Self, Identity, and the Search for Ontological Security', *Political Psychology* 25(5): 741–767.

Kipling, R. (1929 [1899]) *The White Man's Burden: The United States and the Philippine Islands* (New York: Doubleday).

Kipnis, A. (2012) 'Constructing Commonality: Standardization and Modernization in Chinese Nation-Building', *The Journal of Asian Studies*, 71(3): August, 731–755.

Kleiber, D. (1999) *Leisure Experience and Human Development* (New York: Basic Books).

Knopp, L. (1998) 'Sexuality and Urban Space: Gay Male Identity Politics in the United States, the United Kingdom and Australia', in Fincher, R. and Jacobs, J. (eds.) *Cities of Difference* (London: Guildford).

Kohn, H. (1944) *The Idea of Nationalism: A Study of Its Meaning and Background* (New York: Macmillan).

Kymlicka, W. (2012) *Multiculturalism: Success, Failure and the Future* (Migration Policy Institute: www.migrationpolicy.org).

Lasch, C. (1982) *The Culture of Narcissism: American Life in an Age of Diminishing Expectations* (London: Abacus).

Lash, S. (1994) 'Reflexivity and its Doubles: Structure, Aesthetics, Community', in Beck, U., Giddens, A. and Lash, S. (eds.) *Reflexive Modernization: Politics, Tradition and Aesthetics in the Modern Social Order* (Cambridge: Polity Press).

Laurier, E., Whyte, A. and Buckner, K. (2002) 'Neighbouring as an Occasioned Activity', *Space and Culture*, 5: 346–367.

Lavater, J-C. (1885) *Essays on Physiognomy* (London: Ward, Lock & Bowden).

Lawler S. (2000) *Mothering the Self: Mothers, Daughters, Subjects* (London: Routledge).

Lawler, S. (2005) 'Disgusted Subjects: The Making of Middle-Class Identities', *The Sociological Review*, 53: 429–446.

Lehto, X.Y., Choi, S., Lin, Y. and Macdermid, S.M. (2009) 'Vacation and Family Functioning', *Annals of Tourism Research*, 36(3): 459–479.

Levine, M. (1979) 'Gay Ghetto', *Journal of Homosexuality*, 4: 363–377.

Levitt, P. and Jaworsky, Nadya B. (2007) 'Transnational Migration Studies: Past Developments and Future Trends', *Annual Review of Sociology*, 33: 129–156.

LGBT Resouce Center University of Southern California. 'Allies'. http://sait.usc.edu/lgbt/allies.aspx (Accessed 1 October 2013).

Lievrouw, L. and Livingstone, S. (eds.). (2006) *Handbook of New Media: Social Shaping and Social Consequences of ICTs* (London: Sage).

Lipovetsky, G. (1987) *L'empire de l'ephemere. La mode et son destin dans les societies modernes* (Paris: Gallimard Collection folio essais).

Lipovetsky, G. (1993) *L'ere du vide. Essais sur l'inividualisme contemporain* (Paris: Gallimard collection folio essais).

Lipovetsky, G. (1994) *The Empire of Fashion: Dressing Modern Democracy* (Princeton, NJ: Princeton University Press).

Little, J. (2003) 'Riding the Rural Love Train: Heterosexuality and the Rural Community', *Sociologia Ruralis*, 43(4): 401–417.

Livingstone, S. (2002) *Young People and Digital Media* (London: Sage).

Lorber, J. (2012) 'Feminisms and Their Contribution to Gender Equality', in *Her Gender Inequality* (Fifth Edition) (New York and Oxford: Oxford University Press), pp. 1–22.

Lyon, D. (1994) *Postmodernity* (Buckingham: Open University Press).

Lyon, D. (2013) *Jesus in Disneyland: Religion in Postmodern Times* (Cambridge: John Wiley & Sons).

Maclure, J. and Taylor, C. (2011) *Secularism and Freedom of Conscience* (Cambridge, MA: Harvard University Press).

Maddox, M. (2012) 'In the Goofy Parking Lot: Growth Churches as a Novel Religious Form for Late Capitalism', *Social Compass*, 59(2): 146–158.

Maddox, M. (2013) "Rise Up Warrior Princess Daughters": Is Evangelical Women's Submission a Mere Fairy Tale?' *Journal of Feminist Studies in Religion*, 29(1): 9–26.

Mai, N. and King, R. (2009) 'Love, Sexuality and Migration: Mapping the Issue(s)', *Mobilities*, 4(3): 295–307.

Mair, L. (1963) *New Nations* (London: Weidenfeld and Nicholson).

Manalansan, M.F. (1995) 'In the Shadows of Stonewall: Examining Gay Transnational Politics and the Diaporic Dilemma', *GLQ*, 2: 425–438.

Markus, A. (2014) 'Attitudes to Immigration and Cultural Diversity in Australia', *Journal of Sociology*, 50: 10–22.

Marsh, D., O'Toole, T. and Jones, S. (2007) *Young People and Politics in the UK: Apathy or Alienation?* (Hampshire: Palgrave Macmillan).

Martenius, I. (2014) 'The Swedish Emigration to America', http://www.comhem.se.

Martin, D.G. (2003) 'Enacting Neighbourhood', *Urban Geography*, 24: 361–385.

Massey, D., Arango, J., Hugo, G., Kouaouci, A., Pellegrino, A. and Edward, Taylor J. (2004) 'Theories of International Migration: A Review and Appraisal', in Mobasher, M. and Sadri, M. (eds.) *Migration, Globalization and Ethnic Relations. An Interdisciplinary Approach* (Prentice Hall, NJ: Pearson).

Matthews, A. (2008) 'Backpacking as a Contemporary Rite of Passage: Victor Turner and Youth Travel Practices', in St John, G. (ed.) *Victor Turner and Contemporary Cultural Performance* (New York and Oxford: Berghahn Books).

Matthews, A. (2009) 'Living Paradoxically: Understanding the Discourse of Authentic Freedom as it Emerges in the Travel Space', *Tourism Analysis*, 14(2): 165–174.

Matthews, A. (2014) 'Young Backpackers and the Rite of Passage of Travel: Examining the Transformative Effects of Liminality', in Lean, G., Staiff, R., Waterton, E. (eds.) *Travel and Transformation* (Surrey and Burlington: Ashgate).

May, J. (2000) 'Of Nomads and Vagrants: Single Homelessness and Narratives of Home as Place', *Environment and Planning D: Society and Space*, 18: 737–759.

McCabe, S. and Johnson, S. (2013) 'The Happiness Factor in Tourism: Subjective Well-Being and Social Tourism', *Annals of Tourism Research*, 41: 42–65.

McCracken, G. (1989) '"Homeyness": A Cultural Account of One Constellation of Consumer Goods and Meanings', in Hirschman, E. (ed.) *Interpretive Consumer Research* (Provo, UT: Association for Consumer Research).

McDowell, L. (1991) 'Life without Father and Ford: The New Gender Order of Post-Fordism', *Transactions, Institute of British Geographers* 16(4): 400–419.

McGuire, M.B. (1992) *Religion: the Social Context* (Third Edition) (Belmont, CA: Wadsworth).

McGuire, M.B. (1996) 'Religion and Healing the Mind/Body/Self', *Social Compass* 43(1): 101–116.

McGuirk, P. and Dowling, R. (2011) 'Governing Social Reproduction in Masterplanned Estates: Urban Politics and Everyday Life in Sydney', *Urban Studies*, 48: 2611–2628.

McKenzie, L. (2013) 'Fox-Trotting the Riot: Slow Rioting in Britain's Inner City', *Sociological Research Online*, 18(4): 10.

McKeown, A. (2004) 'Global Migration, 1846-1940', *Journal of World History*, 15(4): 155–189.

McLean, D.D. and Hurd, A.R. (2012) *Kraus' Recreation and Leisure in Modern Society* (Sudbury: Jones and Bartlett Learning).

Medicine, B. (1996) 'Gender', in Frederick, E. Hoxie (ed.) *Encyclopedia of North American Indians* (Boston, MA: Houghton Mifflin) http://go.galegroup.com.ezproxy.uws.edu.au/ps/i.do?id=GALE%7CA176911293&v=2.1&u=uwsydney&it=r&p=AONE&sw=w&asid=531fc4fae37c55b6f2ebf26c4bf5722d.

Meegan, R. and Mitchel, A. (2001) 'It's not Community Round Here, it's Neighbourhood': Neighbourhood Change and Cohesion in Urban Regeneration Policies', *Urban Studies*, 38: 2167–2194.

Milligan, L. (2013) 'Tecoma Residents Fight against having a Local McDonalds', *7.30 Report, ABC*, 18 September 2013.

Miranda, V. (2011) 'N° 116: Cooking, Caring and Volunteering: Unpaid Work around the World', *OECD Social, Employment and Migration Working Papers*, 20 September 2011. http://www.oecd.org/officialdocuments/publicdisplaydocumentpdf/?cote=DE LSA/ELSA/WD/SEM(2011)1&doclanguage=en (Accessed 18 July 2014).

Montagu, A. (1950) 'UNESCO 1950 Statement on Race', *Man*, 220: 138–139.

Morgan, L.H. (1976 [1877]) *Ancient Society* (New York: Gordon Press).

Mossberger, K. (2003) *Virtual Inequality: Beyond the Digital Divide* (Washington, DC: Georgetown University Press).

Muñoz, G. and Marín, M. (2006) 'Music is the Connection: Youth Cultures in Colombia', in Nilan, P. and Feixa, C. (eds.) *Global Youth?: Hybrid Identities, Plural Worlds* (New York: Routledge).

Nairn, T. (1968) 'The Three Dreams of Scottish Nationalism', *New Left Review*, 49: 3–18.

Nardi, P. (1998) 'The Globalisation of the Gay and Lesbian Socio-Political Movement: Some Observations about Europe with a Focus on Italy', Sociological Perspectives, 41(3): 567–586.

Nicholson, B. (2012) 'Abbott Slams Boatpeople as Un-Christian', *The Australian*, 10 July 2012. http://www.theaustralian.com.au/national-affairs/immigration/abbott-slams-boatpeople-as-un-christian/story-fn9hm1gu-1226422034305?nk=de47dadf3bd2ad2 eda7df22ed7c2e51c (Accessed 28 January 2015).

Nilan, P. and Feixa, C. (2006a) 'Introduction: Youth Hybridity and Plural Worlds', in Nilan, P. and Feixa, C. (eds.) *Global Youth?: Hybrid Identities, Plural Worlds* (New York: Routledge).

Nilan, P. and Feixa, C. (eds.). (2006b) *Global Youth?: Hybrid Identities, Plural Worlds* (New York: Routledge).

Noble, G. (2004) 'Accumulating being', *International Journal of Cultural Studies*, 7: 233–256.

Norris, P. (2002) *Democratic Phoenix: Reinventing Political Activism* (Cambridge: Cambridge University Press).

Oakley, A. (1972) *Sex, Gender and Society* (Aldershot: Gower).

Oakley, A. (1974) *The Sociology of Housework* (Oxford: Martin Robinson).

Office of the High Commissioner for Human Rights. (2014) 'UN Human Rights Chief Zeid Addresses the 27th Human Rights Council session', 10 September 2014. http://www .ohchr.org/EN/NewsEvents/Pages/UNHumanRightsChiefZeidaddressesthe27thHRC .aspx (Accessed 20 January 2014).

O'Dwyer, C. and Schwartz, Z.S. (2009) 'Return to (Illiberal) Diversity? Resisting Gay Rights in Poland and Latvia', in Prugl, E. and Thiel, M. (eds.) *Diversity in the European Union* (New York: Palgrave Macmillan).

Organisation for Economic Cooperation and Development (OECD). (2002) 'Women at Work: Where are They Now and How Are They Faring?' in OECD Employment Outlook, (OECD Publishing).

Organisation for Economic Cooperation and Development (OECD). (2012a) 'Gender Equality in Employment', in Closing the Gap: Act Now, OECD Publishing: http://www.keepeek.com/Digital-Asset-Management/oecd/social-issues-migration-health/closing-the-gender-gap/gender-equality-in-employment_9789264179370-5-en#page1 (Accessed 19 June 2014).

Organisation for Economic Cooperation and Development (OECD). (2012b) 'PISA in Focus', 14 March 2012 http://www.oecd.org/pisa/pisaproducts/pisainfocus/49829595.pdf (Accessed 1 July 2014).

Organisation for Economic Cooperation and Development (OECD). (2013a) 'Work-Life Balance', OECD Better Life Index.

Organisation for Economic Cooperation and Development (OECD). (2013b) 'Jobs', OECD Better Life Index.

Oswin, N. (2006) 'Decentring Queer Globalization: Diffusion and the "Global Gay"', *Environment and Planning D: Society and Space*, 24: 777–790.

Oswin, N. (2012) 'The Queer Time of Creative Urbanism: Family, Futurity, and Global City Singapore', *Environment and Planning A*, 44(7): 1624–1640.

Paisley, F. (2009) *Glamour in the Pacific: Cultural Internationalism and Race Politics in the Women's Pan-Pacific* (Honolulu: University of Hawaii Press).

Peirano, A. (2012) 'Google Wants the World to "Legalize Love"', dot429. http://dot429.com/articles/2012/07/06/google-wants-the-world-to-legalize-love (Accessed 26 June 2013).

Periasamy, M. (2007) '*Indian Migration into Malaya and Singapore during the British Period*', BiblioAsia (Singapore: National Library Board).

Pertierra, R. (2012) 'Diasporas, the Digital Media and the Globalized Homeland', in Fortunati, L., Pertierra, R. and Vincent, J. (eds.) *Migration, Diaspora, and Information Technology in Global Societies* (New York: Routledge).

Pfeuffer Kahn, R. (1995) *Bearing Meaning* (Chicago, IL: University of Illinois Press).

PFLAG. (2012) 'Straight for Equality', http://www.straightforequality.org (home page) (Accessed 1 October 2013).

Portes, A. (2003) 'Theoretical Convergencies and Empirical Evidence in the Study of Immigrant Transnationalism', *International Migration Review*, 37(Fall): 814–892.

Portes, A. (2004) 'Global Villagers: The Rise of Transnational Communities', in Mobasher, M. and Sadri, M. (eds.) *Migration, Globalization and Ethnic Relations. An Interdisciplinary Approach* (Prentice Hall, NJ: Pearson).

Possamai, A. (2009) *Sociology of Religion for Generations X and Y* (London: Equinox).

Possamai, A. and Possamai-Inesedy, A. (2007) 'The Baha'i Faith and Caodaism Migration, Change and De-Secularization (s) in Australia', *Journal of Sociology*, 43(3): 301–317.

Possamai-Inesedy, A. (2002) 'Beck's Risk Society and Giddens' Search for Ontological Security: A Comparative Analysis between the Anthroposophical Society and the Assemblies of God', *Australian Religion Studies Review*, 15(1): 44–56.

Prensky, M. (2001) 'Digital Natives, Digital Immigrants', *On the Horizon*, 9(5). http://www.marcprensky.com/writing/prensky%20-%20digital%20natives,%20digital%20immigrants%20-%20part1.pdf (Accessed 19 June 2011).

Probyn, E. (1996) *Outside Belongings* (London: Routledge).

Puar, J.K. (2002) 'Circuits of Queer Mobility: Tourism, Travel and Globalization', *GLQ*, 8(1–2): 101–137.

Putnam, R. (2000) *Bowling Alone. The Collapse and Revival of American Community* (New York: Simon & Schuster).

Reay, D. (1998) *Class Work: Mothers' Involvement in Children's Schooling* (London: University College Press).

Richards, L. (1990) *Nobody's Home: Dreams and Realities in a New Suburb* (Melbourne: Oxford University Press).

Roberts, K. (2011) *Class in Contemporary Britain* (London: Palgrave Macmillan).

Roberts, K. (2013) 'Youth and Leisure Experiences: Youth Cultures and Social Change in Britain since the Early Twentieth Century', in Elkington, S. and Gammon, S. (eds.) *Contemporary Perspectives in Leisure: Meanings, Motives and Lifelong Learning* (Hoboken, NJ: Taylor and Francis).

Robertson, R. (1992) *Globalization: Social Theory and Global Culture* (London: Sage).

Robertson, R. (1995) 'Glocalisation: Time-Space and Homogeneity-Heterogeneity', in Featherstone, M., Lash, S. and Robertson, R. (eds.) *Global Modernities* (London: Sage).

Robinson, C. (2011) *Beside One's Self: Homelessness Felt and Lived* (Syracuse, NY: Syracuse University Press).

Rodriguez-Garcia, D. (2010) 'Beyond Assimilation and Multiculturalism: A Critical Review of the Debate on Managing Diversity', *International Migration and Integration*, 11: 251–271.

Rojek, C. (2004) 'Postmodern Work and Leisure', in Haworth, J.T. and Veal, A.J. (eds.) *Work and Leisure* (London and New York: Routledge).

Roof, W.C. and McKinney, W. (1987) *American Mainline Religion: Its Changing Shape and Future* (New Brunswick: Rutgers University Press).

Rose, G. (2003) 'Family Photographs and Domestic Spacings: A Case Study', *Transactions of the Institute of British Geographers*, 1: 5–18.

Rostow, W.W. (1960) *The Stages of Economic Growth* (Cambridge: Cambridge University Press).

Rothenberg, T. (1995). '"And She Told Two Friends": Lesbians Creating Urban Social Space', in Bell, D. and Valentine, G. (eds.) *Mapping Desire: Geographies of Sexualities* (London and New York: Routledge).

Rozario, S. (2007) 'Outside the Moral Economy? Single Female Migrants and the Changing Bangladeshi Family', *The Australian Journal of Anthropology* 18(2): 154–171.

Runciman, W. (ed.). (1978) *Weber: Selections in Translation*, translated by E. Mathews (Cambridge: Cambridge University Press).

Salih, S. and Butler, J. (eds.). (2004) *The Judith Butler Reader* (Malden, Oxford and Victoria: Blackwell Publishing).

Saugeres, L. (2000) 'Of Tidy Gardens and Clean Houses: Housing Officers as Agents of Social Control', *Geoforum*, 31: 587–599.

Savage, M. (2000) *Class Analysis and Social Transformation* (Buckingham: Open University Press).

Savage, M., Devine, F., Cunningham, N., Taylor, M., Li, Y., Hjellbrekke, J., Le Roux, B., Friedman, S. and Miles, A. (2013) 'A New Model of Social Class? Findings from the BBC's Great British Class Survey Experiment', *Sociology*, 47(2): 219–250.

Sayer, A. (2002) 'What Are You Worth?: Why Class is an Embarrassing Subject', *Sociological Research Online*, 7(3).

SBNN. (2010) 'Straight But Not Narrow'. http://www.straightbutnotnarrow.org (home page), (Accessed 1 October 2013).

Schefold, R. (1998) 'The Domestication of Culture: Nation-Building and Ethnic Diversity in Indonesia', *Bijdragen tot de Taal- Land- en Volkenkunde* 154(2): 259–280.

Scott, J. (2009) *The Art of Not Being Governed: An Anarchist History of Upland Southeast Asia* (New Haven, CT: Yale University Press).

Seckinelgin, H. (2012) 'Global Civil Society as Shepherd: Global Sexualities and the Limits of Solidarity from a Distance', *Critical Social Policy*, 32: 536–555.

Sennett, R. (1976) *The Fall of Public Man* (Cambridge: Cambridge University Press).

Setiawan, N. (2009) 'Satu Abad Transmigrasi di Indonesia: Perjalanan Sejarah Pelaksanaan 1905-2005', http://www.pustaka.unpad.ac.id.

Sevilla-Sanz, A., Gimenez-Nadal, J.I. and Fernandez, C. (2010) 'Gender Roles and the Division of Unpaid Work in Spanish Households', *Feminist Economics*, 16(4): 137–184.

Shildrick, T., MacDonald, R., Webster, C. and Garthwaite, K. (2012) *Poverty and Insecurity: Life in Low-Pay, No-Pay Britain* (London: Policy Press).

Shils, E. (1957) 'Primordial, Personal, Sacred and Civil Ties', *British Journal of Sociology*, 8: 130–145.

Siddiqi, D.M. (2011) 'Sexuality, Rights and Personhood: Tensions in a Transnational World', *BMC International Health and Human Rights*, 11(Suppl 3): S5.

Siegel, J. (1969) *The Rope of God* (Berkeley: University of California Press).

Simmel, G. (1904) 'Fashion', in *The Sociology of Georg Simmel* (Chicago, IL: University of Chicago Press).

Skeggs, B. (1997) *Formations of Class and Gender: Becoming Respectable* (London: Sage).

Skeggs, B. (2004) *Class, Self, Culture* (London: Routledge).

Sluga, G. (2000) 'Female and National Self-Determination: A Gender Re-reading of the "Apogee of Nationalism"', *Nations and Nationalism* 6(4): 495–521.

Smith, A.D. (1991) *National Identity* (London: Penguin Books).

Smith, A.D. (1996) 'Nationalism and the Historians', in Balakrishnan, G. (ed.) *Mapping the Nation* (London and New York: Verso), pp. 175–197.

Smith, G. (2012) 'Sexuality, Space and Migration: South Asian Gay Men in Australia', *New Zealand Geographer*, 68(2): 92–100.

Snyder, R.C. (2012) 'What is Third Wave Feminism?' in Lorber, Judith (ed.) *Gender Inequality* (Fifth Edition) (New York and Oxford: Oxford University Press), pp. 307–313.

Spaaij, R. (2012) 'Beyond the Playing Field: Experiences of Sport, Social Capital, and Integration among Somalis in Australia', *Ethnic and Racial Studies*, 35(9): 1519–1538.

Stack, C. (1974) *All Our Kin*: Strategies for Survival in a Black Community (New York: Harper & Row).

Standing, G. (2011) *The Precariat: The New Dangerous Class* (London: Bloomsbury Academic).

Stark, R. (1999) 'Secularization, R.I.P', *Sociology of Religion*, 60(3): 249–273.

Stebbins, R.A. (2004) 'Serious Leisure, Volunteerism and Quality of Life', in Haworth, J.T. and Veal, A.J. (eds.) *Work and Leisure* (London and New York: Routledge).

Stone, J. (1995) 'Race, Ethnicity and the Weberian Legacy', *American Behavioural Scientist* 38(3): 391–417.

Strangleman, T. (2007) 'The Nostalgia for Permanence at Work? The End of Work and Its Commentators', *The Sociological Review*, 55(1): 81–103.

Strangleman, T. (2012) 'Work Identity in Crisis? Rethinking the Problem of Attachment and Loss at Work', *Sociology*, 46(3): 411–425.

Sullivan, N. (2003) *A Critical Introduction to Queer Theory* (Melbourne: Melbourne Publishing Group).

Swartz, D. (1997) *Culture and Power: The Sociology of Pierre Bourdieu* (Chicago, IL: University of Chicago Press).

Taga, F. (2005) 'East Asian Masculinities', in Kimmel, Michael, Hearn, Jeff and Connell, R.W. (eds.) *Handbook of Studies on Men and Masculinities* (Thousand Oaks, CA: Sage Publications). doi:10.4135/9781452233833.n5.

Tamney, J. (2002). *The Resilience of Conservative Religion. The Case of Popular Conservative Protestant Congregations* (New York and Cambridge: Cambridge University Press).

Tapscott, D. (1998) *Growing Up Digital: The Rise of the Net Generation* (New York: McGraw-Hill).

Telecommunications Union, I.T. (2013) *Measuring the Information Society* (Geneva: International Telecommunications Union).

The Australian. (2014) 'Scott Morrison Rejects UN Report on Refugee Treatment', *The Australian*, 30 November 2014. http://www.theaustralian.com.au/news/nation/scott-morrison-rejects-un-report-on-refugee-treatment/story-e6frg6nf-1227139642190 (Accessed 28 January 2014).

Third, A. and Richardson, I. (2009) *Analysing the Impacts of Social Networking for Young People Living with Chronic Illness, a Serious Condition or a Disability: An Evaluation of the Livewire Online Community* (Perth: Murdoch University).

Thompson, K. (2003) *'The Work' in His Emile Durkheim* (Oxfordshire: Taylor and Francis).

Tolia-Kelly, D.P. (2004) 'Materializing Post-Colonial Geographies: Examining the Textural Landscapes of Migration in the South Asian Home', *Geoforum*, 35: 675–688.

Tourism Australia. (2013a) 'Past Campaigns: No Leave, No Life'. http://www.tourism.australia.com/campaigns/no-leave-no-life.aspx (Accessed 6 June 2014).

Tourism Australia. (2013b) 'No Leave, No Life Research Findings'. http://www.tourism.australia.com/campaigns/no-leave-no-life/program-materials.aspx (Accessed 9 June 2014).

Trexler, R. (2002) 'Making the American Berdache: Choice or Constraint?', *Journal of Social History*, 35(3): 613–636.

Turkle, S. (1995) *Life on the Screen: Identity in the Age of the Internet* (London: Weidenfeld & Nicolson).

Turkle, S. (2011) *Alone Together : Why We Expect More from Technology and Less from Each Other* (New York: Basic Books).

Turner, V. (1982) *From Ritual to Theatre: The Human Seriousness of Play* (New York: PAJ Publications).

Tyler, I. (2008) 'Chav Mum Chav Scum: Class Disgust in Contemporary Britain', *Feminist Media Studies*, 8(1): 17–34.

Tyler, I. (2013) *Revolting Subjects: Social Abjection and Resistance in Neoliberal Britain* (London: Zed Books).

Tyler, I. and Bennett, B. (2010) 'Celebrity Chav: Fame, Femininity and Social Class', *European Journal of Cultural Studies*, 13(3): 375–393.

Ungerson, C. (1983) 'Why Do Women Care?' in Finch, J. and Groves, D. (eds.) *A Labour of Love: Women, Work and Caring* (London: Routledge and K Paul).

Urry, J. (2003) 'Social Networks, Travel and Talk', *British Journal of Sociology*, 54: 155–176.

Urry, J. (2007) *Mobilities* (Cambridge and England: Polity).

Vallas, S. (2012) *Work: A Critique* (Cambridge: Polity).

Valocchi, S. (2005) 'Not Yet Queer Enough: The Lessons of Queer Theory for the Sociology of Gender and Sexuality', *Gender and Society*, 19(6): 750–770.

Veal, A.J. (2004) 'Looking Back: Perspectives on the Leisure-Work Relationship', in Haworth, J.T. and Veal, A.J. (eds.) *Work and Leisure* (London and New York: Routledge).

Veal, A.J. (2011) 'The Leisure Society I: Myths and Misconceptions, 1960-1979', *World Leisure Journal*, 53(3): 206–227.

Veal, A.J. (2012) 'The Leisure Society II: The Era of Critique, 1980-2011', *World Leisure Journal*, 54(2): 99–140.

Veal, A.J., Darcy, S. and Lynch, R. (2013) *Australian Leisure* (Frenchs Forest: Pearson Australia).

Veblen, T. (1899) *A Theory of the Leisure Class* (New York: New American Library).

Verdery, K. (1996) 'Whither "Nation" and "Nationalism"?' in Balakrishnan, G. (ed.) *Mapping the Nation* (London and New York: Verso), pp. 226–234.

Vertovec, S. (2004) 'Migrant Transnationalism and Modes of Transformation', *The International Migration Review*, 38: 970–1001.

Waitt, G. (2005) 'Sexual Citizenship in Latvia: Geographies of the Latvian Closet', *Social and Cultural Geography*, 6(2): 161–181.

Waitt, G. and Gorman-Murray, A. (2011) '"It's About Time You Came Out": Sexualities, Mobility and Home', *Antipode*, 43(4): 1380–1403.

Waitt, G. and Markwell, K. (2006) *Gay Tourism: Culture and Consent* (New York: Haworth Press).

Waitt, G., Markwell, K. and Gorman-Murray, A. (2008) 'Challenging Heteronormativity in Tourism Studies – Locating Progress', *Progress in Human Geography*, 32(6): 781–800.

Wallerstein, I. (1974) *The Modern World-System: Capitalist Agriculture and the Origins of the European World Economy in the Sixteenth Century* (New York: Academic Press).

Wallerstein, I. (2004) *World Systems Analysis: An Introduction* (Durham and London: Duke University Press).

Wang, Gungwu (1985) 'Migration Patterns in History: Malaysia and the Region', *Journal of the Malaysian Branch of the Royal Asiatic Society*, 58(1): 43–57.

Warner, R.S. (1993) 'Work in Progress toward a New Paradigm for the Sociological Study of Religion in the United States', *American Journal of Sociology*, 98: 1044–1093.

Warner, R.S. and Wittner, J.G. (eds.). (1998) *Gatherings in Diaspora: Religious Communities and the New Immigration* (Philadelphia, PA: Temple University Press).

Wearing, B.M. (1996) Gender: The Pain and Pleasure of Difference (Melbourne: Longman).

Wearing, B.M. (1998) *Leisure and Feminist Theory* (London: Sage).

Weber, S. and Mitchell, C. (2008) 'Imaging, Keyboarding and Posting Identities: Young People and Digital media Technologies', in Buckingham, D. (ed.) *Youth, Identity and Digital Media* (Cambridge, MA: Massachusetts Institute of Technology).

Weeks, J. (1981) 'Discourse, Desire and Sexual Deviance: Some Problems in a History of Homosexuality', in Plummer, K. (ed.) *The Making of the Modern Homosexual* (London: Hutchinson and Co).

Welcome to Australia. (n.d.) http://www.welcometoaustralia.org.au/walktogether (Accessed 22 January 2014).

Welshman, J. (2006) *Underclass: A History of the Excluded 1880-2000* (Hambledon: Continuum).

West, C. and Zimmerman, D. (1987) 'Doing Gender', *Gender and Society*, 1(2): 125–151.

White, N.R. and White, P.B. (2004). 'Travel as Transition: Identity and Place', *Annals of Tourism Research*, 31(1): 200–218.

White, P.L. (2006) 'Globalisation and the Mythology of the "Nation-State"', in Hopkins, A.G. (ed.) *Global History: Interactions between the Universal and the Local* (Basingstoke: Palgrave Macmillan), pp. 257–284.

White, R. (1999) 'Introduction', in White, R. (ed.) *Australian Youth Subcultures: On the Margins and in the Mainstream* (Tasmania: Australian Clearinghouse for Youth Studies).

White, R. and Wyn, J. (2004) *Youth and Society: Exploring the Social Dynamics of Youth Experience* (Melbourne: Oxford University Press).

Wilding, R. (2012) 'Mediating Culture in Transnational Spaces: An Example of Young People from Refugee Backgrounds', *Continuum*, 26: 501–511.

Willett, G. (1997) 'The Darkest Decade: Homophobia in 1950s Australia', *Australian Historical Studies*, 27(109): 120–132.

Willett, G. (2000) *Living Out Loud: A History of Gay and Lesbian Activism in Australia* (Sydney: Allen and Unwin).

Williams, C. (1992) 'The Glass Escalator: Hidden Advantages for Men in the "Female" Professions', *Social Problems*, 39(3): 253–267.

Williams, J.P. (2007) 'Youth-Subcultural Studies: Sociological Traditions and Core Concepts', Sociology Compass, 1(2): 572–593.

Willis, P. (1977) *Learning to Labour: How Working Class Kids Get Working Class Jobs* (Hampshire: Saxon House).

Wimmer, A. and Glick Schiller, N. (2003) 'Methodological Nationalism, the Social Sciences, and the State of Migration: An Essay in Historical Epistemology', *International Migration Review*, 37: 576–610.

Wingfield, A. (2009) 'Racialising the Glass Escalator: Reconsidering Men's Experiences with Women's Work', *Gender & Society*, 23(1): 5–26.

Witz, A. (1992) *Professions and Patriarchy* (London and New York: Routledge).

Wotherspoon, G. (1991) City of the Plain: History of a Gay Sub-Culture (Sydney: Hale and Iremonger).

Wyn, J. and Woodman, D. (2006) 'Generation, Youth and Social Change in Australia', *Journal of Youth Studies*, 9(5): 495–514.

Yue, A. (2008) 'Same-Sex Migration in Australia: From Interdependency to Intimacy', *GLQ*, 14(2–3): 239–226.

Yue, A. (2012) 'Queer Asian Mobility and Homonational Modernity: Marriage Equality, Indian Students in Australia and Malaysian Transgender Refugees in the Media', *Global Media and Communication*, 8: 269–287.

Yuval-Davis, N. (2009) 'Women, Globalization and Contemporary Politics of Belonging', *Gender Technology and Development*, 13(1): 1–19.

Zangwill, I. (1901) 'The Melting Pot'. http://www.gutenberg.org/files/23893/23893-h/23893-h.htm (Accessed 15 April 2014).

Zelinsky, W. (1971) 'The Hypothesis of the Mobility Transition', *Geographical Review*, 61(2): 219–249.

Zuzanek, J. (2006) 'Leisure and Time', in Rojek, C., Shaw, S.M. and Veal, A.J. (eds.) *A Handbook of Leisure Studies* (Basingstoke: Palgrave Macmillan).

Index